THE BABYLONIAN CAPTIVITY

AND

DEUTERO-ISAIAH

HISTORY OF THE RELIGION OF ISRAEL

VOLUME IV

Yehezkel Kaufmann

HISTORY

OF THE RELIGION

OF ISRAEL

VOLUME IV

Chapters 1,2

UNION

OF AMERICAN HEBREW CONGREGATIONS

NEW YORK

THE

BABYLONIAN

CAPTIVITY

AND

DEUTERO-

ISAIAH

Yehezkel Kaufmann

THE PUBLICATION OF THIS BOOK

WAS MADE POSSIBLE THROUGH THE

GENEROSITY OF MR. WALTER ARTZT.

CONTENTS

TRANSLATOR'S PREFACE   ix

PREFACE   xiii

I The Babylonian Captivity   3

II Deutero-Isaiah   61
   1. The Political Background   62
   2. Composition of the Book   66
   3. Censure and Vision   94

APPENDIX I
The Literary Style of Deutero-Isaiah   193

APPENDIX II
Missionary Activity Among the Gentiles   199

BIBLIOGRAPHICAL ABBREVIATIONS   204

BIBLIOGRAPHY   205

NOTES   209

TRANSLATOR'S PREFACE

THE PRESENT VOLUME comprises Chapter I (The Babylonian Captivity), Chapter II (Deutero-Isaiah), Appendix I (Literary Style of Deutero-Isaiah), and Appendix II (Missionary Activity Among the Gentiles) of Volume IV, Book I, of the four-volume *History of the Religion of Israel* by Yehezkel Kaufmann ([Hebrew] Tel Aviv: Bialik Institute-Dvir, 1937–1956). The publication, *The Religion of Israel, from Its Beginnings to the Babylonian Exile*, University of Chicago Press, 1960, is an abridged translation by Moshe Greenberg of the first three volumes of the Hebrew original.

In the present volume, all cross references to the original four-volume work (including the chapters here translated) are to the original Hebrew edition. Quotations from Scripture and chapter and verse citations are according to the Jewish Publication Society translation[1] (1916), 1965 edition, with a small number of changes and also in a few instances alternative English wording which, in the translator's judgment, were required for clarification. Quotations and citation references from the Apocrypha and the books of the New Testament are according to the American Translation of (Smith and) Goodspeed (*The Complete Bible*, University of Chicago Press, 1939). Translations of talmudic and rabbinic writings are, with a few exceptions, according to the various Soncino (English) editions; pseudepigrapha, etc., for the most part, as in R. H. Charles.[2]

The present bibliography does not coincide with that given in Vol. IV, pp. 1–7 of the original (which is relevant to the whole of Vol. IV); it includes only those books referred to in the present volume. Titles of works in Hebrew are cited variously: (1) in English translation, if the book has been translated, or if it is generally known by its translated title; or (2) in transliteration by a loose system of sound-approachment (*e.g.*, Klausner, *Historia*). Authors' names (Hebrew) are transliterated, as generally customary. Talmudic tractates, midrashic and rabbinic commentaries, as well as classical writings (Josephus, Virgil, Tacitus, etc.), are not listed in the bibliography. For most of the rabbinic literature the reader is referred to Hermann L. Strack, *Introduction to the Talmud and Midrash*, New York, 1931.

The list of abbreviations is not identical with that of page 8 in the original. Books of the Bible, the Apocrypha, rabbinic sources, etc., are abbreviated according to Webster's *New Twentieth Century Dictionary*, unabridged, second ed., 1966, and Taintor and Monro's *The Secretary's Handbook: A Manual of Correct Usage*, The Macmillan Co., 1934. The letter "f." indicates usually, but not always, the single following page or verse.

The translator regrets the absence of an index and of a list of (scriptural) passages cited. He hopes that these will be provided when the translation of the whole of Vol. IV shall be published.

The translator is heavily indebted to the librarians of the Hebrew Union College–Jewish Institute of Religion, both Cincinnati and New York, and the Jewish Educational Association, Indianapolis; and especially to Miss Thelma Hodges and other members of the staff of the library of the Christian Theological Seminary, Indianapolis; and for very helpful suggestions and detailed critical reviews to many scholars, including, in particular, Rabbi Jacob Bemporad, Union of American Hebrew Congregations; Dr. Samuel Greengus and Dr. Matitiahu Tsevat, Hebrew Union College; Dr. Menahem Haran and Dr. Haiim M. I. Gevaryahu, Jerusalem; and Mr. Max M. Furer, Jewish Educational Association, Indianapolis.

Finally, and certainly far from least, the translator gratefully acknowledges the assistance and encouragement of

Madelyn S. (Mrs. Joseph Russell) Brown, without whose painstaking, expert, and ever cheerful aid this volume would never have come into being.

It goes without saying that only the translator, and none of the foregoing, is responsible for the errors and inadequacies of the present volume.

C. W. Efroymson

Carmel, Indiana, 1968

PREFACE

THE PERIOD of the second Temple is an age of most remarkable events in the history of Israel. The catastrophe destroyed the natural national base of the life of the nation and of its cultural activity. The nation was now dispersed in foreign lands and began to assimilate into the gentile cultures. And yet, we observe that about fifty years after the catastrophe a significant portion of the Babylonian diaspora returned to Judah and repossessed Jerusalem and its environs. Those who returned to Zion lived and labored in difficult conditions. But they endured poverty and stress in love and faith. They built the Temple and later, also, the city. The diaspora supported the returnees. Its heart also was in Jerusalem; and Jerusalem became the focus of the diaspora.

Further, after the catastrophe, though scattered among the gentiles and dwelling in the midst of pagan culture, the nation purged itself of idolatry finally and completely. Israel became a people zealous for God, the servant of the Lord. Moreover, precisely following the catastrophe, the religion of Israel emerged from its national matrix house and began to function as a universal historical force. There began the struggle of Judaism against the idolatry of the nations. A people in exile was crystallized, assimilated or half-assimilated, from the cultural point of view, but cleaving to its faith; living among strangers, but anticipating the ingathering of the exiles. Most remarkable is the fact that the Jews, scattered and assimilating, continued strangers to the paganism of their surroundings, even as they had been while still in their homeland. During this period, in the days of Ezra and Nehemiah, the Torah book was compiled and completed and made the book of life of the nation. Israel became the people of the book. A new way of life evolved, the way of Torah and the commandments. A fundamental change occurred in the oral tradition of earlier times. It became the oral law. The sacred literature was reduced in this period to a set of books of fixed content and number. At this time of the law and commandments and of the fear of heaven, the holy spirit departed from Israel and prophecy ceased. But later a new kind of prophecy appeared. At the close of the period Jewry was a world replete with new concepts, which developed partly from within and partly under the specific influence of the alien civilization. Jewry was a world in ferment; and its influence was great among many peoples.

Scholars regard the change in the history of Israel after the destruction as a transition from earlier idolatry to monotheism. It is the general opinion that the Jewish nation accepted monotheism only in the postexilic period. This opinion, it seems to me, is wholly in error. The history of the second Temple can be understood only as the continuation of the history of a people which was monotheistic from its beginning. The history of the Babylonian exile and of the Persian period, which herewith is handed over to the reader, is written from this point of view.

The seventh book of this series appeared in the year 5708 (1948). Thus the preparation of this eighth book occupied considerable time. This was not only because it includes subjects of unequaled difficulty and obscurity, such as the prophecies of the Second Isaiah and the visions of Zechariah, but also because of the extreme difficulty of historical research into this period. The sources are few and fragmentary. Extreme and exaggerated criticism wreaked havoc on the sources. Literally nothing has been left untouched. Also, there are periods for which we have no direct sources. All this resulted in difficulties and delay.

I dealt with much of the subject matter of this book in lectures at the Hebrew University in Jerusalem, and many matters became clear to me in seminars. I came to understand the truth of the words of that sage who said, "Much have I learned from my teachers, but from my students more than from all of them."

Y. K.

Jerusalem, Tamuz, 5716 (1956)

THE BABYLONIAN CAPTIVITY

AND

DEUTERO-ISAIAH

I

The Babylonian Captivity

THE half-century from the fall of Jerusalem (586) to the fall of the Chaldean kingdom (538) was a period of severe crisis, of far-reaching change and fateful decision in the life of the nation Israel. The prophet of destruction envisioned the house of Israel in exile as dried bones scattered in the valley of the slain. But he envisioned also rebirth for the dried bones (Ezek. 37). The fateful question was: would the vision be realized? would the dry bones be reborn? and whence would come the breath of life?

The diaspora of Israel

Even in that early period Israel was scattered and separated into all lands. The dispersion dated from the time of the Assyrian kings, Tiglath-pileser and Sargon, who exiled the ten tribes. According to II Kings 17:6, the king of Assyria settled the exiles of Samaria (722) in Halah, Habor, on the river Gozan, and in the cities of the Medes. This diaspora maintained itself into Jeremiah's time. Jeremiah turned toward it with his call for return (3:11–15) and proclaimed for it the good news of redemption (3:14–18; 31:1–19, 27, 31; 33:7, 14, 24–26). Ezekiel also refers to this diaspora. He

3

prophesied the ingathering of the exiles of Ephraim and Judah and their unification into one kingdom in the time to come (37:15–28). Although we have no certain reports of the fate of these exiles, we may surmise that they were for the most part absorbed into the diaspora of Judah, and that Babylonian Jewry, with its great numbers in the days of the second Temple and the talmudic period, was descended from this combined diaspora.

The Egyptian diaspora, which existed as early as the time of Zedekiah, is mentioned in Jer. 24:8. The story of the flight of the "remnant of the people" from Judah to Egypt after the murder of Gedaliah is told in Jer. 41–44. We read in Jer. 44:1 that there were Jewish settlements in Migdol, Tahpanhes, Noph, and the land of Pathros, in upper Egypt, some of them dating back, without question, to the time before the "remnant of Judah" came down to Egypt. This is confirmed in the Elephantine papyri. In the letter of Yedoniah and his associates to Bagoas (Bigvai), the governor of Judah, the Jewish temple in Elephantine is said to have been constructed in the period of the Egyptian kings, before the conquest, in 525, by Cambyses.[1]

There were Jewish refugees also in Moab, in the land of Ammon, and in Edom (Jer. 40:11–12); and certainly they did not all return in the days of Gedaliah. Ishmael ben Nethaniah and his followers took refuge in the land of Ammon (ibid., 41:15). Also, in the land of Israel itself, the Jews were scattered among the gentiles in those areas which had been occupied by the Cuthites and the Edomites. Obadiah, v. 20, mentions Jewish exiles in Sepharad in Asia Minor. In the days of Deutero-Isaiah, the Jews were dispersed to the four winds of heaven (Isa. 43:5–6), to the north, to the west, to the "land of Sinim" (49:12), and to the far-off isles (60:9; 66:19–20). Zechariah speaks of the scattering of Israel to the four winds of heaven (Zech. 2:1–4, 10). Israel is dispersed in the north, the east, and the west (2:11; 8:7); it dwells among all the nations (7:14). According to Esther 3:8, the Jews were dispersed in the days of Ahasuerus in all the provinces of the Persian empire.

But the most important diaspora, the center, was the Babylonian; and the exiles from Judah and Jerusalem were its nucleus. These exiles were transported to Babylonia when Jerusalem was conquered in the time of Jehoiachin, in the year 586, as told in II Kings 24:12–16; 25:11. The number of exiles is estimated at about forty thousand. Among them were Jehoiachin and his household, the princes, the aristocracy, the military leadership, the craftsmen and smiths, the cream of the nation. From Jer. 52:28–30, it follows that the Chaldeans at various times sent other groups of exiles from Judah and Jerusalem to Babylon. Further, it is to be surmised that after the land was pacified large numbers emigrated from the ruined land to Babylon for family and economic reasons. Jehoiachin, even after he was transported to Babylon, was looked upon as the king of Judah. After the execution of the sons of Zedekiah, Jehoiachin and his sons were the symbol of the monarchy in the eyes of the people, and on them rested the hope of the renewal of the kingdom of the house of David. Thus, the king and the princes and the propertied and learned classes of the Jewish nation were in Babylon. This captivity was the heart of the nation, whence would come the movement of the return to Zion and the building of the Temple (see below Chapter III).

Among the exiles, there were various categories. There were captives, those who had taken active part in revolt and war, and who were sent into exile in chains and imprisoned. There were those who had been "torn away," those whom the kings of Assyria and Babylon transported ("plucked off") from the homeland in order to weaken and end the strength of the rebellious nation. There were refugees, men who fled their country because of the terrors of war. There were emigrants, men who departed for reasons of family or material well-being. We must distinguish these various categories in order to understand the sources which bear on conditions in the diaspora.

5

Social and economic conditions

The social and economic situation of the Babylonian diaspora was very favorable, a fact for which there is clear and irrefutable evidence in Scripture.

There are, however, scholars who deny this. They argue that the exiles suffered greatly at the hands of their captors, that they were put to hard labor and burdened with heavy taxes, that many were sold into slavery, some imprisoned, and that others lived in dire poverty.[2] But the proofs of these scholars are imagined, and their arguments depend on confusions and failures to discriminate. Obviously, the exile was a matter of compulsion and subjugation both for the community and for the individual. The uprooting of masses of people and their transport abroad entailed political-national ruin, and much physical and mental suffering. But our problem is not the character of the banishment. We are concerned with the situation of the exiles in the land of their exile after they had drained this cup of affliction.

There are many references in Scripture to the torments of the destruction and the captivity; but this is not decisive with respect to our problem. Even if it be assumed that all the prominent exiles were transported in chains,[3] this is still only a temporary suffering, and irrelevant to the condition of the diaspora. Also, Ps. 137 is a description only of the torment of the caravan of exiles on the way to the land of exile. Lamentations reflects the sufferings of Jerusalem in the hour of destruction, and not the situation of the diaspora. From Lamentations, including the verses which mention forced labor (1:1; 5:5)[4] we learn nothing of the life of the exiles in Babylon. Isa. 47:6 and 51:23 are also descriptive of the hour of the catastrophe. In Deut. 28 there is a visionary description of the stress of the exile, but it has nothing to do with the real exile.

6

Jer. 5:19; 28:14[5] are general expressions symbolic of political-national subjugation. There is no doubt that many of the captives and exiles were sold into slavery;[6] but this fact also is not decisive with respect to the state of affairs in the diaspora. There were also slaves who were of the sovereign peoples. From Neh. 5:8 we learn that the diaspora was sufficiently well-off to be able to redeem the slaves. Isa. 42:22–25 describes explicitly the terrors of the destruction. The people, imprisoned in the prison-houses of v. 22,[7] are the captives who had rebelled, such as Jehoiachin and his followers. Those who were plucked up, who were the majority of the exiles, and also those who voluntarily emigrated, were not imprisoned. Jer. 51:34–35[8] describes the plundering of Jerusalem in the hour of conquest, in Jehoiachin's time, which is no description of the diaspora.

We learn from Isa. 58:10 that there was poverty among the exiles.[9] But what does this prove? The exiles were forced to serve the king and were saddled with heavy taxes.[10] But enforced service and taxation were not peculiar to the captivity. These were obligations of all the provinces and of all their inhabitants.[11] There is no reference to discrimination against the deportees, either generally in the law or specifically with respect to forced labor and taxation.[12] The kings of Assyria and Babylon sought to assimilate the transportees, and to cause them to strike roots in their new homeland, which purpose inhibited discrimination against them. It was the custom of the kings of Assyria to require the exiles from various lands to participate in the construction of new cities.[13] But these were settlements destined for the exiles themselves. Such labor is, in fact, the portion of new settlers everywhere.

And against this there is clear proof that the situation of the exiles was favorable. Convincing evidence is found in the first paragraph of the "letter" which Jeremiah sent to the Babylonian diaspora in the days of Zedekiah (Jer. 29:1–7). In this letter Jeremiah, in the name of the Lord, orders the exiles to build houses, plant gardens, take wives and beget sons, and also to seek the peace of Babylon, for in the peace thereof they would find peace. The presupposition of the epistle is that the exiles can flourish in the foreign land, and that this depends only on their will.

Additional conclusive proof is contained in the account in Ezra 1–2 of the first aliyah, some sixty years after the epistle of Jeremiah. The diaspora gave support to the returnees to Zion with silver, with gold, with goods, and with cattle (Ezra 1:4–6). The returnees brought with them 7,337 menservants and maidservants, 200 singers, male and female, 392 temple slaves, and horses, mules, camels, and asses in great numbers. Heads of the fathers' houses and the people contributed a large sum for the building of the Temple (Ezra 2:68–69; Neh. 7: 70–72). The immigrants had retained their tribal and social structure. They were organized according to tribes and patriarchal families, or into urban units according to origin in the towns of Judah. They included princes, commoners, and slaves. They even brought genealogical registers with them (Ezra 2:59–63). All this is evidence of economic well-being, retention of rights, and the maintenance of a certain degree of autonomy. These two documents, one from the beginning and the other from the end of the Babylonian exile, together are convincing proof. And everything we know of the Babylonian exile confirms this evidence.

In the book of Ezekiel there is no reference to the suffering of the exile, even though Ezekiel is influenced by Lev. 26 and looks upon the exile, ideologically, as a chapter of afflictions and terrors. There is no mention of attacks or persecutions. Ezekiel possesses a home spacious enough to accommodate the gathering of the elders (Ezek. 8:1). The captives at Tel-abib sit in the doorways of their homes, discuss the words of the prophet, and come "as the people cometh" to sit before Ezekiel (33:30–31).

Ezekiel, it seems, did no manual labor. He had time to perform dramatic acts lasting many days (4:1–5:4) and the people come to observe his acts and to inquire their meaning (12:1–20; 24:15–24).

This diaspora is a social-national unit, with the elders at its head, as in the homeland. It leads its own life, its thought centered in Jerusalem and what happens there. Captivity did not transform it into a mass of slaves, oppressed and dispersed, the debris of a nation. Jeremiah also turned to the captivity as an organized national body, led by elders, priests, and prophets (Jer. 29:1). The exiles negotiated with Jerusalem. They concerned themselves with the politics of the kingdom of Judah; and they dared to send "letters" of dangerous political import to Jerusalem. They carried on negotiations with emissaries of the province whence they were exiled as rebels or as associated in rebellion (*ibid.*, 29:3, 20–32). This indicates a considerable degree of autonomous organization.

That there were Jews who were learned in the wisdom of Babylonia, serving in the royal court and attaining high rank, is apparent from the stories of the book of Daniel (Dan. 1:1–21; 2:48–49; 3:12; 5:29). From cuneiform writings we know that some of the important officials of the kingdom of Assyria were Israelites.[14] Babylonia followed the example of Assyria in its manner of dealing with the subjugated peoples; and it is not to be assumed that the condition of the exiles in Babylonia was worse than the condition of those in Assyria. Also, the release of Jehoiachin by Evil-merodach (II Kings 25:27–30) indicates Jewish influence in the royal court.

The economic well-being of the diaspora is reflected in the documents of the house of Murashu in the time of Artaxerxes I and Darius II (464–405).[15] The high rank of Ezra and Nehemiah and the success of their undertakings reflect the social and political importance of the diaspora. This is no new phenomenon of the Persian period; rather, it is the continuation of what had occurred in the days of the Assyrian and Babylonian monarchs. The assumption that there were persecutions of the Jews in the time of Nabonidus[16] is without any support.

Before antisemitism

Thus, in the first half-century after the destruction, the Jewish people were already dispersed, scattered in many lands. And yet they were still not in an "exilic" situation. That "exile," the nature of which was to be known later on, did not yet exist. Jewry was not yet recognized as a politico-religious community of unique character, destined to a unique historical role. The nation had been rooted up from its soil, but it was not yet in the situation of exilic, permanent alienation. Only in the course of generations could the alienation of the exile be experienced as an active agent.

The Jewish diaspora in that early period seemed, from without, to be similar to that of other uprooted peoples. There was no special Jewish legislation, no ghetto, and no religious persecutions or interdictions. There was not then any crystallized, active "antisemitism." To be sure, antisemitism began to consolidate about a century after the destruction. Haman, accuser of the Jews, comes forward to say, "There is a certain people scattered abroad and dispersed among the peoples . . . and their laws are diverse from those of every people" (Esther 3:8). This situation of dispersal and separation had, in fact, existed from the beginning of the diaspora. We know that the Jews of the diaspora separated themselves from the nations, and did not worship their gods. On the contrary, they were scornful of idolatry; they hated and despised it. This separation undoubtedly caused surprise and hatred. The natural reaction to rejection of idolatry was recrimination and attack. Group antisemitism surely lurked even at the beginning of the diaspora. Between Jewry and the pagan world there was opposition and suppressed warfare, a situation reflected in the prophecies of the Second Isaiah, as we shall observe shortly. And yet there was no active antisemitism, and certainly no official political antisemitism.

The subsequent history of the diaspora teaches that empires, kingdoms which include many nations, were more favorable to Jewry than were national monarchies. The protagonist of the hatred of Israel was the nation; whereas the imperial regime served as a natural barrier against the force of this hatred. The diaspora leaned on the imperial power and sought to fortify itself in the international climate of empire. This also was a cause, no doubt, of the relatively slow development of antisemitism.

Assyria, Babylonia, and Persia were great empires, containing and restraining many nationalities. The conquered peoples were uprooted and moved from one province to another. In these empires no decisive value was attached to the feelings of the peoples and their wants. All the peoples were servants of one ruler. The sentiment of the national homeland was canceled by force of the political sovereignty. In this "international" atmosphere of general servitude, the diaspora was able to live peacefully under the protection of the monarch. The Jews were "strangers" in the provinces of their dispersion; but in the empire they were not strangers. They were subjects of the monarch, even as all other citizens. Thus the rise of antisemitism was inhibited.

In the period of the Babylonian exile antisemitism was still in its infancy. The terrors of the exile—banishment, persecution, pogroms—had not yet begun. The threats of Lev. 26 and Deut. 28, and also those of Jeremiah and Ezekiel, were merely visionary phrases. The land of the enemy did not "devour" the Jews. They found rest in the land of the gentiles. Land was given them to cultivate and to eat its produce. There was no change in their economic-social way of life. They continued in the diaspora an agricultural people; and for the most part, they derived their keep from the soil.

From the Murashu documents we learn that they began also to busy themselves with trade. But the opinion that the Jews in Babylonia became a nation of traders is superficial. Most of those who returned to Zion were husbandmen, and even the Levites among them were men of the field (Neh. 13:10). Even in the postexilic period, the Jews continued to be a predominantly agricultural people, and the later Babylonian diaspora was also for the most part agricultural. Moreover, the movement of some Jews of the Babylonian diaspora from agriculture or the crafts to trade was not because of any external pressure. Rather, it was a natural development, and of the nature of social advancement.

All occupations were open to the Jews of the diaspora. It was possible to take root in the land and merge with its inhabitants. There was no political, social, or economic pressure which forced them to remain apart; no "Jewish question," with all that that implies. There was no exilic pressure calculated to unite and consolidate them and to engender among them the longing to flee the lands of the gentiles. They could have gone the way of all the other uprooted nations.

Assimilation. The crucial question

In order to understand the crisis which rocked the diaspora, we must bear this aspect of the diaspora in mind. The crisis was severe precisely because the situation was favorable. The exiles were beginning to merge into the life of the country of their captivity and into its culture. Political, economic, and social influences worked in the direction of assimilation and national disintegration. On the opposite side were the spiritual and cultural factors. The crisis was of the spirit, in the soul of the nation. The trial was severe. We know the outcome: the diaspora did not go the way of the other uprooted peoples. But what was it which determined that outcome?

There is little information concerning the events of those fifty to sixty years of profound agitation and fateful decision. We know from Jeremiah and Ezekiel that the exiles of Jehoiachin did not believe that Jerusalem and its Temple would be destroyed, and that they thought of the exile as a passing phase. They were in Babylon, but they yearned for Jerusalem; and they thought that the Lord would shortly bring them up from Babylon. They did not want to build houses and plant gardens and take wives, and they thought it a favorable omen that the Lord raised up prophets for them in Babylon (Jer. 29:15). Their prophets predicted that their exile would not be long. But their hope was disappointed. The catastrophe came, and it stirred them to the depths. It was the end of their world. We learn from Jer. 44:14 (*cf.* 42:18) that even after the destruction and after the murder of Gedaliah, the exiles of Egypt still believed in early redemption; and certainly a similar belief smoldered among the exiles of Babylon.

Jeremiah and Ezekiel fought the belief in an early redemption, which was to take place before the termini which they fixed for it. Depression and despair increased. The exiles felt themselves "pined away" in their transgressions; they were taken aback, and they inquired, "how then can we live?" (Ezek. 33:10). They said, "Our bones are dried up, and our hope is lost; we are clean cut off" (*ibid.*, 37:11).

We observe the masses of the Egyptian captivity for the last time in a nationwide convocation somewhere in Egypt. Then they disappear in the black obscurity of the anger and terrible threats of Jeremiah (ch. 44). We hear the final cry of despair of the exiles of Babylon in Ezekiel's vision of the dried bones (Ezek. 37). Thence for about a half-century the diaspora is swallowed up, as it were, in thick darkness. The lone historical report concerning it which reaches us is the brief account at the end of the book of Kings of the freeing of Jehoiachin in the year 562. During the period of about fifty years the diaspora is without "history." The nation Israel descends, as it were, from the stage of history. The prophets of early redemption are stilled. The prophets of destruction had completed their prophecies. From Ezekiel to the Second Isaiah the diaspora had no prophet. No new prophet prophe-

13

sied to the diaspora or concerning it, and no chronicler recorded its doings. Darkness and silence closed in on "the valley of bones."

But if the national history of the diaspora came to an end, so to speak, everyday life went on. Even as their ultimate hopes proved to be illusions, the exiles set about to build and to establish themselves in the land of their captivity. They entered into the economic life of the country; they came in contact with its inhabitants; and Babylon's high civilization began to exert its influence. The leaders of the people, those who represented it before the government, Jews who were attached to the court, officials and merchants, were particularly susceptible to the influence of the alien culture. The richness and brilliance of the Babylonian material environment dazzled the eye. There began the natural and inevitable process of cultural and national assimilation. In the sixty years of the captivity of Jehoiachin and the fifty of the captivity of Zedekiah, a new generation grew up in Babylon. These were men who did not know the national homeland, men who had not heard the song of the Lord on the sacred soil, who had never seen Zion and its Temple. They had grown up and spent most of their years in a land which was appointed to be a new homeland to them; and among them there appeared that process which is the beginning of every assimilation: the change of language. Aramaic began to supplant Hebrew. Great numbers forgot their language or became bilingual, using the language of Judah and a foreign tongue. This was the hallmark of the diaspora and the ghetto, a foreign language or bilingualism. With the foreign language there came also the custom of non-Jewish names.

This process of national assimilation went on during the years of historical silence which enveloped the diaspora. The fateful question was whether the hour had indeed come when the people of Israel would depart the stage of history. Would the assimilatory forces sever the life roots of the nation?

Would the pagan civilization swallow it up? On the surface assimilation prevailed. But what was happening in the recesses of the soul of the nation? Was this silence the final stillness of the valley of dried bones, or only a temporary silence? "Watchman, what of the night? Watchman, what of the night?"

Dawn of a new era

And then, after fifty years, a voice tore through the silence saying, "Comfort ye, comfort ye My people, Saith your God." The voice is the voice of the nameless prophet of the captivity, the Second Isaiah. Once more, the Lord had raised up a prophet in the diaspora. This was a man of powerful emotions, and it is to be assumed that he was of the younger generation, the only prophet born in the diaspora and who did not know the land of Israel. His was the voice of the second and third generation born on foreign soil; for which reason his message is so significant. It is witness that the Jewish diaspora, assimilating and in alien environment, was able to produce its own particular climate of national-religious life. It was able in alien environment to raise sons who were faithful to its God and to implant within them a vibrant love for Zion, the holy city. The gospel of this prophet was the good news of rebirth, wherewith Israel was to ascend once more the stage of history. The people Israel lives! It had not been swallowed up by paganism. It had not forgotten its God; it was replete with the flame of faith, and prepared to confront paganism anew on foreign soil, to do battle for the Lord. It had been defeated. Yet it took pride in the awareness of its having been chosen, confident of its future. In the years of silence decision had come in the depths of the soul of the nation. To this decision the prophet of the new generation gives enthusiastic and sublime expression.

15

This good news marks the beginning of a new era in the history of Israel and, also, as would become apparent in the course of time, in the history of man.

The end of idolatry

The half-century of captivity was a period of apprehension and dejection, of decay and the drying up of bones, of alienation and assimilation, and change of language, of unspoken anticipation and tangled hopes. And yet during these years there occurred the great miracle; there came an end to the sin of idolatry. The tendency to idolatry died in Israel.

The Babylonian captivity is the great watershed in Israel's history, separating the age of idolatry from that of no idolatry. It was the hour when idolatry was buried. The historical books speak repeatedly of the putting away of strange gods and of the purging of idolatry from Israel. This time the strange gods are removed forever and buried finally. The admonitions concerning idolatry, so frequent in all the books of the Bible to the Second Isaiah, come to an end. We still hear in the prophecies of Isaiah II the final blasts of this reproof, and thereafter no more. There can be no question but that the nation Israel remained faithful to its God. Verily, it repented for its sin of idolatry, and its repentance was "eschatological," final and absolute. Individuals, of course, drifted off and were absorbed into paganism. But the nation was faithful. There is no basis for the opinion that the masses were absorbed into the pagan culture, and that only a "small Jewish community" kept faith and gathered around the prophets.[17] This opinion reflects the Christian theological tendency to picture monotheistic Jewry as a congregation. But those who returned to Zion were a nation, farmers, artisans, priests, functionaries, and servants —a people. The returnees were a great multitude. Large numbers of the faithful also remained in the diaspora, but their hopes were with the returnees. Nor was the sin of idolatry to be found among the returnees. The royal family, which in earlier times had sinned so often and caused the people to sin, now returned in repentance; and likewise the priests, who previously had opposed the prophets. The instance of the Nethinim, who were a unique non-Israelite racial group, is evidence of the scope of the movement of religious return. The Nethinim were a serving class, temple slaves. In Babylon they were slaves of a Temple which had been burnt, in a city which had been destroyed. Obviously, they might then have attained freedom. In Babylon there were no masters; and yet they also returned as part of the nation to Zion. Better in their eyes servitude in the Temple of the Lord than freedom on unclean soil.

This is the great miracle: out of the ashes of the destruction there emerged a people zealous in the service of a zealous God! This nation dwelt on foreign soil, cast out in anger from before the presence of God, conquered and in chains. And from the midst of the triumphant, arrogant pagan civilization, this people repented with whole heart and soul, and entered into a covenant of truth and eternal faith with its God.

What is the explanation of this miraculous event?

The prevalent explanation

The accepted opinion among biblical critics is that the change which took place in the Babylonian diaspora was the triumph of prophetic monotheism over the popular religion of Israel. The significance of the turning from idolatry is thought of as the abandonment of the pagan syncretistic YHWH religion, and its replacement by the monotheism of the prophets. In Babylon the prophetic monotheistic concept of YHWH as the God of the universe drove out the popular polytheistic concept of YHWH, a national god, one among many. Back of this opinion is the assumption that the YHWH of popular Israelite faith was a territorial national deity, not the one God of the entire universe. He was "the god of the land of Canaan," with sovereignty restricted to Israel and its land. He was the Israelite-Canaanite god, YHWH—Baal, indissolubly linked to his territory. The gods of the gentiles ruled in other lands; and in them there was no room for the worship of YHWH. This implies an essential bond between the god and his territory, an idolatrous concept which gave rise to the popular belief of the period prior to the catastrophe that YHWH would defend Zion and its Temple. Thus, with the destruction of Zion, the god was driven, as it were, from his dwelling place on earth. According to this interpretation, the quarrel between the nationalistic zealots, who rebelled against Babylon and expected salvation by YHWH, and the prophets of the destruction was a dispute between an idolatrous faith in a national god and monotheistic faith in a universal God, who is bound to no people or land and to no sanctuary or cult. The critics regard the prophecy of destruction as the negation of the essentially idolatrous nationalistic limitation. In the idea of the national catastrophe, monotheism attained, as it were, the stage of universalism; and the aspiration toward universalism is expressed in the prophecy of destruction. In fact, only after the destruction did monotheism, in the prophecies of the Second Isaiah, become really universal. The catastrophe precipitated and consolidated monotheism; it was the victory of prophecy and its doctrine over the popular religion, the victory of the God of prophecy over the popular god. Thereupon idolatry ceased in Israel. The abandonment of idolatry was not merely the forsaking of foreign gods, but primarily the abandonment of an idolatrous syncretistic concept of YHWH himself.

According to this view, the turning from idolatry was the result of the influence of the prophets. The world of the popular religion collapsed when the catastrophe occurred, and prophecy, in particular the prophecy of destruction, was the only lifebelt. Prophecy alone could explain what had happened from within the YHWH faith. The essence of the national crisis following the catastrophe was the collapse of the foundation of the popular YHWH religion. In the semitic world, and in the pagan world generally, the belief prevailed that the victory of a nation was the victory of its god, and its defeat the ruin of its god. If the nation was conquered, its god was conquered. This was also the view of the folk-religion of Israel. Babylon had destroyed Jerusalem, and Babylon's gods had triumphed. Babylon's triumph was the victory of Marduk over YHWH. It followed that, since Israel was now subject to Babylon, Israel ought to worship Babylon's gods. The prophets opposed this state of mind. Their primary objective after the catastrophe was theodicy, to justify God. They sought to expunge from the heart of the people the idolatrous thought that Marduk had overcome YHWH. The destruction was not Marduk's doing; rather it was of the finger of YHWH himself. Babylon was the rod of the anger of YHWH, appointed by YHWH to punish Israel for its sin. For YHWH is the universal God, the ruler of all kingdoms. Only this doctrine could save the honor of the Lord and faith in Him.[18]

Why, after the catastrophe, did the nation accept this doctrine? It was because the destruction caused a change in the attitude toward prophecy. Prior to the destruction the people trusted the prophets of salvation and rejected the prophets of doom, judging these to be false prophets. The catastrophe confirmed the words of the prophets of destruction so that, in the eyes of the people, they became true prophets. That their prophecies had come to pass was decisive. The event of their prophecies was in the eyes of the people a true sign and conclusive proof of the truth of their teaching. Therefore the prophets were now able to achieve what they could not achieve prior to the destruction. It helped also that the nation was removed from the soil of Canaan, where it was closely tied in with the syncretistic religion of Baal–YHWH. The god of popular faith was destroyed by fire along with the Temple. Furthermore, on foreign soil the people could not maintain their old syncretistic faith. The popular YHWH was the god of the land of Canaan, who could not be worshiped on foreign soil. In Babylonia the exiles could serve only the Babylonian gods or the universal God of the prophets. Therefore the old syncretistic YHWH religion was ended.[19]

Critique: pagan universalism

But the foregoing view is wholly in error. Rooted as it is in Christian theological preoccupation and the tendency to view the national catastrophe of Israel as the decisive factor in its religious development, it completely distorts the history of Israel.

In the first place, the underlying assumption that in the pagan world it was accepted doctrine that the victory of a nation was the victory of its god is incorrect. Further, the opinion that a pagan people which had been conquered and exiled could not worship its gods in foreign lands and was forced to abandon them is also incorrect. In fact, two different views were widespread among pagan peoples: one, that the downfall of the nation was the ruin of its gods; and two, that the national god had summoned the enemy against his nation and given it victory because he was wroth with his nation.

The belief that the enemy acted as the rod of God's anger was not peculiar to Israel's prophecy; rather, it was common property of the pagan world. A victorious people was inclined to boast of its victory over the gods of the conquered nation, although there were exceptions also to this. But the conquered nation was likely to view the enemy as the rod of the wrath of its gods. In the ninth century, Mesha, king of Moab, in the inscriptions describing the victories of Omri over Moab, explains them with the words, "For Chemosh was angry with his land" (line 5). Esarhaddon explains the destruction of Babylon by Sennacherib in that Marduk was angry and himself destroyed his city. Likewise, Nabonidus explains this destruction as due to the anger of Marduk. Marduk was wroth, and dwelt twenty-one years in Assyria, and only when the time was fulfilled did he remember Esagila and Babylon.

Nabonidus explains the history of the temple of Sin in Haran similarly. The army of the Medes destroyed the temple because of the wrath of the gods. The wrath continued fifty-four years, and when the allotted number of years was fulfilled, Marduk strengthened Nabonidus' hand to restore the temple. Cyrus did not consider the conquest of Babylon a triumph over Marduk, but as the work of Marduk himself. Marduk was wroth with Nabonidus, king of Babylon, because of his many transgressions. Thereupon he chose Cyrus, crowned him, stood by him, and delivered Babylon, his city, into Cyrus' power.[20]

Also, pagan nations which were conquered and sent into exile did not abandon their gods. Instead, they carried their gods with them into exile. Rib Addi, king of Gebal, entreated Pharaoh Akhenaton, if he could not dispatch military aid, at least to send ships to bring him and his gods alive to Egypt. Marduk-Baladan, fleeing before Sennacherib, carried the gods with him aboard ship.[21] Aeneas, in flight from Troy after its fall, brought the gods with him to Latium.[22] Pagan nations clung to their gods even after they were despoiled by their enemies. The king of Arabia besought Esarhaddon to return the gods which his father, Sennacherib, had taken from the Arabs. Esarhaddon repaired them, engraved on them the word "Assyria" and his name, and returned them.[23]

Among the Romans, it was customary before a battle to summon the enemy's gods to abandon their station and come over to them. This evocative ritual, formerly known as a Roman ritual, was in fact a very ancient practice. A Hittite text, found in Boghazkoy, describes evocative rituals whereby a sorcerer can induce gods of the fields, mountains, streams, the sea, springs, fire, the heaven and earth to cross over from the enemy territory to the Hittite land.[24]

In Scripture, also, there are passages which bear witness to beliefs of this nature. Rab-shakeh, envoy of Sennacherib, combined the two points of view. On the one hand, he proclaimed that YHWH could not deliver Jerusalem from the power of the king of Assyria (II Kings 18:30–35). At the same time, he argued that he had been sent by YHWH himself to destroy the land (*ibid.*, 22, 25). Certainly the second argument conformed to pagan thought. The exiled Samaritans carried their gods with them to the land of Israel and worshiped them there (II Kings 17:29–33). But they also worshiped YHWH, who had been, according to their ideas, conquered, as it were, by the Assyrians (*ibid.*, 25–41).[25] Jeremiah prophesied to Chemosh and Malcam that they will go into exile with their priests and princes (Jer. 48:7; 49:3). The Second Isaiah prophesied to Bel and Nebo that, laden on beasts of burden, they would go into captivity with their worshipers (Isa. 46:1–2).

Thus, the argument that the prophetic explanation of the destruction was possible only on the basis of monotheism, and that its acceptance implied the abandonment of idolatry is invalid. In fact, a pagan people also would have been prepared to explain the catastrophe as the act of YHWH himself, such explanation being not incompatible with idolatry. It was by no means necessary to accept prophetic monotheism in order to save the honor of the national god. Likewise, it is evident that the catastrophe and the exile could not of themselves have put an end to the old syncretistic cult. It certainly was possible, also according to the pagan ideas, to worship YHWH on foreign soil. According to II Kings 17, the Samaritan cult, which combined worship of "conquered" gods on foreign soil with worship of a "conquered" god in his own territory, was strikingly syncretistic.

The exiles, therefore, did not have to choose between the YHWH of the prophets and Marduk. To the contrary, there was then the possibility of a new syncretism: YHWH with Marduk and the other Babylonian gods. Among the Elephantine Jews there is no indication of prophetic influence. But they even built a temple to YHWH on foreign soil. The Babylonian captivity could have done the same without any recourse to prophetic doctrine.

Prophets and the nation

Also, there is no basis for the opinion that the catastrophe justified the prophets of destruction and was regarded by the people as proof of the truth of monotheism. The catastrophe could be clear proof only to those who were already believers in the one God, and not to a pagan people. It could not convince those who believed in the gods of the nations that these gods were not gods. It did not signify the ruin of the god of the conquered nation; and it was no sign that the gods of victorious Babylon were not gods.

It is to be observed that not only the prophets of doom, but also the soothsayers and diviners of Nebuchadnezzar, prophesied the destruction of Jerusalem. In antiquity nothing was undertaken without inquiring of the gods. The rulers of Assyria and Babylon regularly report oracles and dreams whereby the gods foretold their victories. Nebuchadnezzar did not attack Jerusalem without inquiring of the gods and without receiving an oracle predicting victory. An inquiry of this kind is described in Ezek. 21:26–27, and the description, though visionary, is true to history. The destruction, therefore, justified both the prophets of destruction and Nebuchadnezzar's diviners. But it was no basis for choosing between idolatry and monotheism. According to pagan ideas, the prophets of destruction expressed the decree of the "gods." Such an opinion is reflected in the relationship of Nebuchadnezzar and Nebuzaradan to Jeremiah. It would have been natural also to an idolatrous Jewish nation.

The fact is that the problem of the decree of destruction was at that time after all only of historical and theological interest. Much more pressing for the nation were the immediate problems of the day and the morrow. Events had confirmed the prophets only insofar as they had dealt with the same events as the Babylonian soothsayers, that is, the national catastrophe. For the rest, the prophecies were still unfulfilled. The prophets had foretold terrors for the exiles, and there were no terrors. They had foretold a glorious redemption, and it gradually became clear that the redemption had not come. The faithful believed. But how would a pagan people view these things? It was possible to justify the fall of Jerusalem, as we have seen, according to pagan ideas and without abandoning the cult of YHWH. Marduk, however, needed no "theodicy." His cities and his temples were intact. In this situation, could the fulfillment of the prophecy of destruction turn the heart of an idolatrous nation?

The popular monotheistic interpretation of the catastrophe

If, then, the crisis of the destruction brought the nation to repentance, and if the people believed the words of the prophets, including those which were still unfulfilled, this could have been only because the faith of Israel was monotheism before the destruction. Monotheism was in no wise a subject of factional dispute. It was the faith of a whole people, of all factions. The crisis was not a matter of deciding between a nationalistic-pagan god and the one universal God. From the days of Moses the one universal God was the God of the whole nation. The opinion that the political struggle in Israel in the time of Jehoiachin and Zedekiah was a contest between paganism and monotheism is an invention of Christian theologians and, in fact, a falsification. Hananiah ben Azzur was the political rival of Jeremiah (Jer. 28); but their opposition was not with respect to faith in God. The patriotic party of Zedekiah's reign believed in the victory of Jerusalem. But so did Isaiah. In fact, it was monotheism which was the basis of such belief. This was also the belief of the Zealots of the final days of the second Temple. The desperate struggle of a handful of men against a mighty world empire which closed in on them from all sides can indeed be understood only on the basis of belief in one God. The Chaldean struggle set the pattern for the Roman war. The two wars resulted from the same state of mind.

Moreover, there is no indication that after the destruction of Jerusalem the exiles concerned themselves with the problem of why Marduk had triumphed over YHWH, or that the prophets undertook to salvage the reputation of YHWH among the people and to expunge the thought that YHWH had, as it were, succumbed. From start to finish, the defeat of YHWH and the struggle of the prophets against that idea is a baseless fabrication of the biblical criticism. Also among pagans there were, as we have observed, two possible answers to the question: whence did the evil decree go forth? Indeed, there is no evidence that Nebuchadnezzar interpreted the destruction of Jerusalem as a victory over Israel's God. His relationship to Jeremiah (Jer. 39:11–14; 40:1–6) indicates the contrary. Scripture attributes no such opinion to him, nor is he charged with blasphemy. The point of view of the triumphant Chaldeans is stated clearly in Nebuzaradan's statement to Jeremiah, "The Lord thy God pronounced this evil upon this place; and the Lord hath brought it, and done according as He spoke; because ye have sinned against the Lord," etc. (*ibid.*, 40:2–3). Even if these words betray the style of a Jewish scribe, they accord nonetheless with essentially pagan concepts. We know that the Romans who destroyed the second Temple did not interpret their victory as a victory over God. Tacitus, in typical pagan fashion, reports the omens which, according to Jewish sources, were seen in the Temple prior to its destruction.[26] "The gates of the Temple opened suddenly, and a super-human voice was heard: 'The gods go forth!' And a great sound of the outrushing was also heard."[27] The "gods," therefore, deserted the Temple, and for that reason the Romans were able to destroy it.

In any event, there is no indication of any ambiguous answer along pagan lines to the problem of the destruction which might have been widely held among the Jewish exiles in Babylon. Prior to the catastrophe there was a question whether God would, or would not, destroy Jerusalem. But after the catastrophe all were agreed that it was God who had wrought the destruction. The prophets had no need to argue this opinion. The assumption, therefore, that the acceptance of this idea was the basis of the triumph of the belief in one God is certainly unfounded.

Ezekiel castigated Israel, stating that by its sins it brought on the catastrophe; and that it had profaned God's name among the nations (36:20–23); wherefrom we learn that the nations did indeed express the opinion that Israel's God was unable to rescue His people. There is no doubt that this was a reaction to the exiles' scorn of the gods. But Ezekiel does not say that the exiles themselves profaned the name of God by such utterances. The elders of Israel who sat before Ezekiel (20:1) did not argue that the gods of the gentiles had triumphed, and that the catastrophe was their work. In the extremity of their despair they say, "We will be as the nations, as the families of the countries, to serve wood and stone" (32). They also are certain that the gods of the nations are wood and stone. It is no pagan belief which they express, but the depth of despair and spiritual nihilism. The people cry out to the prophet, "Our transgressions and our sins are upon us, and we pine away in them; how then can we live?" (33:10). Likewise the old women, survivors of the generation of Manasseh, who contend with Jeremiah concerning the worship of the queen of heaven (Jer. 44) do not say that God could not have saved Jerusalem; or that the gods of Babylon had triumphed over Him. The triumphant gods of Babylon are not mentioned in the entire chapter. The worship of the queen of heaven is not for these women, as it is for Jeremiah, the worship of a foreign goddess. They argue that the incense and the libation to the queen of heaven are a custom of their fathers, and that those observances had secured their well-being. They see in the cessation of those rites the cause of the catastrophe. But even they do not say that the queen of heaven herself brought on the destruction. We must assume that they believed that God had punished the nation because of its disrespect for the queen of heaven. That self-same assembly vows in the name of YHWH, and Jeremiah's most terrible threat is that God's name will no more be named in their mouths (*ibid.*, 26).[28]

Also, Deutero-Isaiah does not refer to the belief that YHWH had been conquered, or argue against such an idea in any fashion. In his polemic against idolatry he stresses God's unwillingness to share His glory and His praise with graven images (42:8; 48:11). But these verses deal with the victories of Cyrus, whom the prophet views as the finger of God. Deutero-Isaiah argues that YHWH had revealed coming events to Israel in advance in order that it should not be said, "Mine idol hath done them, and . . . my molten image, hath commanded them" (48:5). But here he is concerned with ignorant fetishism, and not with the problem of Jerusalem's destruction. The idea that Marduk had triumphed is completely foreign to his thought. He is not concerned with any belief in the "wisdom and omnipotence" of the "imposing gods of Babylon."[29] He knows only the idols of Babylon.

Thus, the monotheistic interpretation of the catastrophe was the popular explanation and no new prophetic doctrine. A dualistic interpretation along pagan lines was utterly foreign to the nation. Nor is there any basis for the assumption that the catastrophe caused men to think that YHWH had been conquered and ought now to be abandoned in favor of the gods of the conquering nation. Groundless also is the assumption that it was the spiritual distress of their situation which moved the exiles to acceptance of the prophetic teachings. Certainly the catastrophe caused profound distress. But there had been many earlier events which might have given rise to the idea that the gods of the nations had conquered the God of Israel.

The need of a theodicy was ancient indeed, no new birth of this day. The history of Israel after Solomon is one long decline. Aram had long since caused Israel to be "like the dust in threshing." The success of Jeroboam ben Joash was but an episode. Assyria had destroyed the kingdom of Ephraim. Ephraim "bemoaned himself" and pondered his fate (Jer. 31:18). Assyria also humiliated and subjugated Judah; and Rab-shakeh had argued that YHWH was unable to save His city. In Manasseh's reign the kings of Assyria were in fact the rulers of Jerusalem. Nebuchadnezzar conquered Jerusalem during the reign of Jehoiachin and plundered the Temple. Was not this conquest calculated to cause consternation and confusion no less than the final catastrophe which was to follow? Was it not, from a pagan point of view, the victory of Marduk over YHWH? The city was not yet destroyed, but Nebuchadnezzar and his gods held sway in it. Ezekiel was not the first to decry the desecration of God's name. Micah had already done so (Mic. 7:10). The problem of the honor of the Lord had arisen, therefore, with all its difficulty long before the destruction. The answer had been given by Amos and Hosea and Isaiah and other prophets. Indeed, the answer had been given in Israel's earliest historical writings, before the period of classical prophecy.

The final catastrophe came in the year 587. But the idea of the destruction, together with the monotheistic explanation, had hovered in the intellectual atmosphere of the nation for many generations. Micah expressed it (3:12), and it is dominant in the two great invective passages of the Pentateuch, Lev. 26 and Deut. 28. Both were composed before the Babylonian exile, and without knowledge of what the exile was really like, and the prophets of doom were influenced by these early warnings.

The opinion that it was the prophets who formulated the monotheistic explanation of the catastrophe is based on the assumption of the school of Wellhausen that prophecy preceded the Law, which assumption is specious. The priestly-popular religion which is crystallized in the Pentateuch preceded classical prophecy. The nation did, indeed, come to terms with the fact of the catastrophe; and it justified the decree against itself. But that was not due to the influence of the prophets, or because the nation accepted the God of the prophets, etc. Rather, it was because the people remained faithful to the ancient monotheistic belief.

Proof of this fact is the dominance, both in the life and the literature of the period, of the popular-priestly view that the cause of the catastrophe was the sin of idolatry, and also the absence of any mention of the prophetic view that moral evil was the cause of the catastrophe. The pentateuchal, as opposed to prophetic, view prevails in the book of Kings, which was completed during the Babylonian captivity. The "repentance" of the age was cultic. The deeds which are described in Ezra and Nehemiah are centered in the Torah and its commandments. The tendency to exaggerate the importance of the influence of the prophets is one of the basic errors of the biblical criticism, with which we shall be concerned in the following.

The cultic return

It follows from the foregoing that the revolution in the life of the nation which occurred during the Babylonian exile was not a change in its religious world outlook, not a transition from polytheism to monotheism. Rather, it was a firm determination to end pagan cultic practices. Monotheism was the birthright of the nation from its inception; and idolatry had long since been forgotten. Even the paganism of Babylon seemed to be only stupid belief in idols. The catastrophe was viewed as proof, not of the greatness and might of the gods of Babylon, but of the fierce wrath of the Lord God, which came upon the nation because of the sin of idolatry. Was there hope, then, of allaying that wrath? How was God to be appeased? This was the problem, and the nation was "pined away" beneath the burden of the wrath. The question was not, "What hope is there for this nation together with its God?"[30] Such a problem is an invention of modern critics. The crisis was of Israel, not of Israel's God. The wrath gave rise to a mood of repentance and soul-searching and of seeking for God, a mood in fact which was not new. The reforms of Hezekiah and Josiah were the products of similar moods. But now the agitation went deeper. The destruction was especially perplexing because the nation, ever since the time of Josiah, had believed that it was reconciled to God. The Temple had been purified, the high places removed, the false priests killed, the covenant based on God's Law concluded. To be sure, the nation had not been cleansed completely of pagan cultic sin. There did remain vestiges of idolatry: women baking cakes for the queen of heaven and, now and again, idols and teraphim. The nation had tolerated such things. But there was no public recognized idolatry, and the nation was confident that God would shortly make His face to shine upon it. Then came the catastrophe. YHWH destroyed His city, set fire to His Temple, and brought low the throne of David. He executed vengeance on His people. The repentance of Josiah's reign had not sufficed; a new purification was required. With this insight came the turn. But the turn was not acceptance of monotheism. Rather it was the determination to draw the extreme cultic implications of monotheism. Idolatry must be totally expunged from Israel. If Israel tolerated even the vestiges of idolatry it could not be God's people. In this mood was born the zealous nation of the days of the second Temple.

The acid test

This crisis and the cultic answer were not, however, the decisive events. This crisis was of the spirit, psychological, subjective, in the realm of consciousness. It was an agonizing reappraisal, and from it the nation drew practical conclusions.

But during that same period the nation passed through another crisis, which, although interlaced with the spiritual crisis, was in fact an objective trial in history. It was not a matter of which belief or law the nation would accept, whether its faith would continue to be idolatrous, or whether it would turn from idolatry to prophetic monotheism. Indeed, as stated above, no such problem existed. The nation had been monotheistic from of old.

The fateful question was: what is the strength in history of monotheism? Is there in the nation the strength to adhere to monotheism when it lives in exile? The religion of Israel, though indeed essentially universalistic, was in its historical formulation of the nation Israel. It had been revealed in the life of Israel, and within the forms of the nation's culture. The annals of the nation Israel were its chronicles. The land of Israel was the locus and the nation Israel the historical arena of revelation. The land of Israel was holy. The ordinances and festivals of monotheistic faith, the altars and priests and prophets had been in Israel and only in Israel. The life of Israel on its soil was the natural habitat of this faith. Until the destruction, it had endured, not by reason of its innate universalism, but naturally as a national religion, as the historic religion of one among the nations. Like the religions of Egypt, Canaan, Moab, Ammon, Edom, etc., it was the religion of a people and a land, existing naturally just as the national culture of Israel, the language, literature, political state, etc. This natural existence was ended by the catastrophe. The catastrophe uprooted it from its soil, and scattered its people. The national culture, wherein it had been rooted in the period of its historic development, was gone. The exiled Jewish nation was unable now to carry on its own national culture in a natural manner, and the faith of Israel could not continue as a natural, national-territorial religion. The problem was: what strength would there be in the religion of Israel after the destruction of its historical base? Would it suffer the fate of other national religions?

Pagan national religions did not perish in those days because their gods were thought to have been conquered, or because they could not be worshiped in foreign lands. It was the assimilation of the peoples who worshiped them which determined their fates. Exiled peoples continued for a while to worship their gods in foreign parts. But in the course of time they were absorbed into the alien culture, and cultural assimilation entailed religious absorption. New gods replaced the old; and the latter were pushed into remote corners, to be covered in time with dust. The second or third generation forgot them and they became shades, merely names. The question was: would Israel go this way?

Ezekiel warned the exiles of Judah that the Lord would rule over them "with a mighty hand . . . and with fury poured out" (20:33). But the fury was not poured out. The exiles could have gone the way of other nations. The gateway to the pagan society was open before them. Strong conviction and boundless love and determination to sanctify the name of God were requisite if pagan culture and its spell were to be fended off; an idealism pervading the whole people. Two millenia of diaspora are witness to the strength which is required to maintain national-religious separateness in alien surroundings.

Such was the decisive test of history.

The iron law of the diaspora

However, by the end of the Babylonian exile, it was clear that Israel and its religion had stood the test. The religion of Israel had begun to reveal its potency as a national and universal force, capable of sustaining the people Israel as a distinct entity in foreign lands. Though torn from its native environment, Israel's religion lived on with unabated vitality. The exiles adapted themselves to the pagan culture, but they rejected its idolatry. After fifty years of exile they were ready to return to the homeland, which was a phenomenon without parallel in world history. Thus was proven the uniqueness of the nation Israel: pagan culture could not accomplish its extinction.

In remaining apart from their alien surroundings, the exiles revealed the working of that historical force which was to determine the fate of Jewry through all the generations of exile.

The spread of Judaism, Christianity, and Islam have since laid bare the mystery of that force which subsequent history was to reveal. In the course of fifteen hundred years, the nations among whom the Jews were dispersed forsook their pagan beliefs and accepted monotheism. The direction of religious change was always from idolatry to monotheism, never the reverse. No people has turned from monotheism back to idolatry. In this historic fact is expressed an historic law of development. The operation of this law was revealed in Israel after the destruction. Israel had passed from idolatry to monotheism in antiquity, and Israel could not travel the reverse route, from monotheism to idolatry. Monotheism determined the separation of Israel from the pagan world by the high wall of religious faith; the separation could not be negated even by the destruction. The exiles adopted the pagan culture, but they could not descend to the level of idolatry. Religious disparity insulated the diaspora from its pagan surroundings despite its cultural assimilation.

Thus, it was their monotheistic faith which stood in the way of complete assimilation. Life in the diaspora could destroy the national culture and make the exiles participants in its economic life and culture. But there was one thing it could not do. It could not bring them to sincere acceptance of pagan faith. Therein they differed from all other exiled communities. Other deported peoples accepted foreign gods and believed in them. After a while the old national gods were supplanted by the new gods and forgotten.

But with the Jews it was different. National acculturation could not bring them to acceptance of the religion of their foreign environment. In this historical fact of Jewish existence in that period there appears the working of that force which was to determine the fate of the Jews in future generations. The Jews were unable honestly to accept the religions of their environment: conversion could be only apostasy, that is, without conviction, for the sake of material advantage. This is the iron law of the diaspora.

A striking example of this is the statement of the elders of Israel to Ezekiel: "We will be as the nations, as the families of the countries, to serve wood and stone" (20:32). Idolatry for the Jews could be nothing other than worship of no-gods, gods of wood and stone. The elders of Israel were not stating what they really wanted to do. The idea which they expressed was dreadful, a bitter, despairing complaint uttered before the prophet of the Lord. Individuals might "serve wood and stone"; they might apostasize for material advantage. But the nation could not accept a religion of wood and stone. Religion stood as a rock in the way of cultural assimilation and determined the uniqueness of the nation Israel.

Such was the meaning of Ezekiel's "mighty hand." The law of religious development operated with objective necessity.

Awareness of religious supremacy

Obviously, however, the nation did not think of its separateness as ineluctable. In its view, its religious uniqueness was, rather, a matter of choice, the consequence of ardent faith. True, the exiles were faced with God's wrath in all its severity. They were oppressed by the dreadful catastrophe, and they were often near to despair and hopelessness. If God had taken everything from them and delivered them into the hands of the nations, was there, indeed, any hope of being reconciled to Him? Was the covenant still valid? Were they still His chosen people? But withal, the terror of the destruction could not root out the consciousness of election and uniqueness. They knew that, from the point of view of religion, they were superior to the pagan world. This superiority was an established fact, a firm rock which the catastrophe could not dislodge. They alone of all the peoples of the earth knew God and swore by His name. God had taken everything from them: land, freedom, the kingdom, their holy city, and their Temple. But one thing He had not taken: the awareness of the living God, of His holy spirit, His Law, His prophets. The loving kindness, the grace of God, of His name and His word, was their treasure, an inheritance given only to them. And this grace they could not and would not relinquish. This grace accompanied them into the exile and remained with them in their defilement. They were not as the gentiles, as the families of the earth: wood and stone they would not serve. They were God's people and, therein, different from all other peoples on the face of the earth. Therefore they did not abandon hope.

This decision, which took place in the very depths of the soul of the nation, was the essential event of the epoch. In comparison with it, the cultic reform, which implied the removal of the remnants of fetishistic idolatry, was of secondary importance.

The new covenant

Thus Israel, while in exile, entered into a new covenant with its God. The first covenant was of the day of deliverance from Egypt and in anticipation of a land of milk and honey. This covenant was of a day when the nation was in exile, in bondage; a time, moreover, when milk and honey were the promise of paganism. This covenant was concluded in profound faith, for the sake of God's name. There were no terrors of the exile and no decrees of pharaoh. The nation yearned for the holy land, the land of the grace of its youth, and therein the bond between Israel and its God achieved new exaltation. In foreign parts and amidst the wrath of the destruction, Israel prepared to do battle with paganism in its own lands. Israel prepared itself for the sanctification of the Name. The destruction had divested it of all national material goods. But it was specifically the catastrophe which demonstrated that Israel's supreme treasure was its belief in God; that this belief was independent of any material well-being, and that for its faith Israel would make any sacrifice. After the half-century of exile, it was obvious that—beyond the politico-national warfare of Israel with its foes—there loomed another struggle, that of the religion of Israel against idolatry. Idolatry had triumphed in the political arena. With iron fist it had destroyed the cities of Israel and exiled its sons. But in the warfare of the spirit it had not triumphed. The conquered nation was destined in the course of time to triumph over idolatry, to destroy paganism and to pull down its altars. The basis for this future struggle was laid during the Babylonian exile. Israel made its peace with the catastrophe. In the face of calamity on every front, the nation held to its faith in God. The problem of faith was detached from the problem of Israel's politico-national welfare. The Lord, He is God, even though His nation is conquered and reduced to servitude. In exile and under the yoke of the gentiles, Israel does yet proclaim the name of the Lord.

History demonstrates that Israel, conquered and in exile, was destined to do battle with the paganism of the nations. The throne of David was not restored. The nation had to come to terms with the catastrophe in order to fulfill this, its historic role. And in the acceptance of its fate, there was born a new Israel, an Israel unconditionally faithful, and itself justifying the fateful decree, an Israel doing battle for the Lord, Israel the servant of the Lord.

In this spirit with which Israel was filled, the prophecy of the Second Isaiah was born. Its spiritual fortitude was the source of everything which developed in that period.

Within the pagan world

The exile was without history, a period of no "events" in the life of the exiles. And yet it was a period of development, of inner strengthening, of self-appraisal, and of the creation of new life patterns.

That the Jewish diaspora remained in the midst of the alien society a world to itself, closed, sealed off, monotheistic in the midst of a pagan civilization which differed from it completely, is astonishing, indeed, almost incredible. The Babylonian exiles lived within the pagan culture, and yet they knew nothing of paganism, that is, of the world of pagan mythology. For Ezekiel and Deutero-Isaiah, just as for the other biblical authors, idolatry was merely fetishism. There is no indication of awareness of the character of pagan mythology. To the elders of Israel, idolatry was as worship of "wood and stone." Life in the pagan environment did not, therefore, bring them closer to pagan beliefs, which indicates how shallow and unimportant was the influence of paganism on Israel in general and on the exiles in particular.

It is, however, to be assumed that in the diaspora, for all the mood of repentance, paganism did exert its influence in certain circles. But the conclusion, drawn by biblical critics from the recriminations of Isa. 57:3–13; 65:3–5, 11; 66:17, that in that period the popular faith was syncretistic and idolatrous, is incorrect. Isa. 57 is, as we shall shortly observe, a reproof referring generally to the past. Other passages concern household rites and dark practices connected with the eating of detestable things. These were various magical rites adopted by some of the people under the influence of the pagan environment. The fact, however, that neither Ezekiel nor Deutero-Isaiah accuses the people of participation in the public worship of Babylon is decisive and instructive. The idolatry of the exiles was domestic and private, like that of the women of Jerusalem who made "cakes" for the queen of heaven and baked them on sticks which the children had gathered (Jer. 7:18). There is no statement that the exiles sacrificed in the temples of Babylon, or that they participated in the great splendid festivals, or in the solemn processions of the gods; and certainly there is no indication that the exiles built Babylonian temples in their settlements, or that there were priests among them who served Bablonian deities, or that they studied the "law" of the gods of Babylon. Similarly, they are not chided for seeking oracles from Babylonian gods or from Babylonian diviners or magicians. Ezekiel mentions certain magical practices of women who prophesy and sew cushions (13:17–23). But these are Israelite sorceresses. There were sorcerers, male and female, in Israel and among other monotheistic peoples in every generation, indeed even to this day. But there is no record of any resort to the public magic of the heathen temples. The elders of Israel who had "set up their idols in their mind," and who said that Israel was to be as the "families of the countries, to serve wood and stone," came to "inquire" of YHWH! (Ezek. 14: 1–3; 20:1–3, 32).

Cessation of the cult

However, the most characteristic occurrence of the Jewish diaspora, and that which symbolizes its special situation, was the cessation of sacrificial cultic practices. Not only did the exiles not participate in the Babylonian temple rituals, but they also, while in exile, did not institute any temple cult of YHWH, that is, any of the sacrificial rites which in that period were thought of as the sole means of worship. The exiles had no temples and no altars. They offered no sacrifices and dedicated no food. They lived without cult. The worship of the Lord was bound to the holy land and, according to Deuteronomy, to Jerusalem and its Temple. Accordingly, the exiles could not serve God on "unclean land." They thought it dreadful even to "sing the Lord's song in a foreign land" (Ps. 137:4).[31] This diaspora, living without cultic practices, was something completely without precedent. There had never been a community which proclaimed a god and yet did not "serve" him; which believed in a god who had abolished his cult; a religious community which "served" no god. There is no doubt that this puzzled and amazed the pagan world. In this fact the contrast between this nation and the gentile nations was highlighted.

Some critics view the cessation of the cult in the diaspora as an indication of national exclusiveness, of the concept of YHWH as a national god in the spirit of popular polytheism, a god linked indissolubly to his soil, and who cannot be worshiped in territory ruled by other gods. Such a view, however, is superficial. We have already pointed out that the pagan faiths did not think that their gods were linked indissolubly to their lands. Although the gods were national and territorial, they could be worshiped abroad. Gods passed from one people to another and were established in foreign pantheons. Exiles were wont to carry their gods with them. Pagan transportees generally did as the Cuthites in the land of Israel.

The religious beliefs and practices of the remote Jewish colony of Elephantine were by no means typical of the popular Israelite religion. Israelite religious customs had been forgotten, and pagan influence is evident. A temple was built to YHWH on foreign soil, and pagan practices were followed. But the diaspora generally, while retaining the popular faith in the cult, did not build temples. The cessation of the national temple cult is a phenomenon peculiar to the Jewish diaspora, marking it off from every heathen diaspora. This phenomenon complements another, the abstention of the exiles from participation in the local pagan cult. Pagan exiles were wont to worship their gods and also the local gods. The Jewish exiles lived without cultic worship. The source of this surprising fact is the popular monotheism of Israel.

The national-territorial restriction of Israel's sacrificial cult is a manifestation of Israel's monotheism, and has no connection with nationalistic polytheism, or with the idea of a territorial deity. This restriction is rooted in the idea of election: the universal God chose one people, gave His law to it; and sanctified one land as the place of His service. He selected one city, Jerusalem, in the holy land and endowed it with peculiar sanctity. In Deuteronomy there is the additional step: within the holy city God chose one "place"; and there only was sacrifice permitted. The land of the gentiles was "unclean." The belief in God's unity is expressed in this idea of the unity of sanctity. The land of the gentiles is unclean because the nations worship no-gods. The territorial restriction reflects the historical fact that God was known only to Israel. This thought is dominant in the Pentateuch, in the deuteronomic, and also in the Priestly Code, both of which are absolutely monotheistic. The prophets envisioned the turning of all nations to the God of Israel. But in their writings, also, the idea of the sanctity of Israel and its land and city is predominant. And if the exiles felt themselves in an unclean land, and refrained from erecting altars to God, that was simply the expression of monotheistic faith, as it had crystallized in the ancient biblical literature and, above all, in the Pentateuch.

A new cult

It was in the nature of things, however, that this negative expression of their devotion could not satisfy the religious needs of the exiles. The religious emotion demanded positive expression. Monotheism in its historical development had been tied to the idea of election, and had developed a national-territorial cultic pattern. Yet it was essentially universalistic. Its God was lord of the whole earth, attentive to the cry of every living creature; and to Him men prayed in every land. Thus there emerged two aspirations: one, to create a new mode of worship or, rather, a substitute of universal quality which could be carried out in all lands; and two, for the restoration of the prescribed cult in the holy land.

In that period, the synagogue service, a non-sacrificial worship, began to develop. This new and original creation, without precedent in the pagan world, was comprised of prayer, confession, and fasting. The holidays were detached from sacrifice, and included in this new cult. In Zech. 7:3, 5; 8:19, we find that the exiles observed four fasts which were connected with the events of the destruction: that of the fourth month on the ninth of Tamuz, the date of the fall of Jerusalem (Jer. 52:6–7); that of the fifth month, the ninth of Ab, when the Temple was burned (*ibid.*, 12–13); that of the seventh month, on the day when Gedaliah ben Ahikam was murdered (*ibid.*, 41:1–2); and that of the tenth month, on the tenth of Tebeth, the date of the beginning of the siege of Jerusalem (*ibid.*, 52:4).[32] On fast days the people would weep and mourn (Zech. 7:3, 5). They would bow their heads and spread sackcloth and ashes (Isa. 58:5; Esther 4:3); and confess and pray for deliverance. Isa. 63:7–64:11 is an example of prayer-confession in the manner of the period. (See also Ezra 9:6–10; Neh. 1:4–11; 9:1–37.) According to Dan. 6:11, Daniel prayed three times daily, kneeling, with windows open toward Jerusalem. This is the earliest reference to the custom of praying three times daily and of facing toward Jerusalem. It is certainly possible that these customs developed during the Babylonian captivity. We may guess that people would assemble for prayer and fasting in one place—a house of assembly (synagogue) or house of prayer. The expression, house of prayer, is to be found in Isa. 56:7. In Esther 4:16, there is indication of a synagogue.

We do not know how the holidays were observed in the diaspora. We may suppose that the exiles tried to find rites which were reminiscent of the holiday observances of the land of Israel. The sabbath took on particular significance. In fact, its observance had been detached from the temple service when the high places were removed in the reign of Josiah. Of all the holy days the sabbath was, therefore, best adapted to the new order of worship; and its observance now took on new forms. In the Pentateuch it is a day of relaxation and rest. Jeremiah also refers to it only as a day of rest (17:21–27). The prescribed ritual for the sabbath was the additional sacrifice, which was offered in the Temple on that day (Num. 28:9–10). Now sacrifice had ceased, and in its place came something new. In Isa. 58:13, we hear for the first time that the sabbath is to be called a "delight, And the holy of the Lord honourable." From a day of rest it became a day of delight and joy, to be marked, it appears, by eating, drinking, and also, perhaps, by wearing of festive attire. Deutero-Isaiah refers four times to the keeping of the sabbath as a meritorious deed wherefor a man shall see the salvation of God (Isa. 56:2, 4, 6; 58:13), which indicates the great significance attached at that time to sabbath observance. In 56:6, observance of the sabbath by gentiles who join themselves to the Lord is stressed, which indicates that the sabbath, as a social institution, made a deep impression on the pagan environment. In the Greek-Roman world, also, the sabbath was one of the customs which spread rapidly in judaizing strata. The pagan world knew no day of rest for the laborer. To the gentiles, the sabbath became the very special symbol of the social-moral quality of the religion of Israel. It was in a sense the gospel of the good God and of the love of man. Heathens who labored with Jews and were given the day of rest were particularly susceptible to the attraction of this strange and wonderful religion.

Among the exiles there were fellowships of enthusiasts who performed special rites of mourning in memory of the destruction. These were they that mourned in Zion (61:3), her lovers who mourned for her (66:10), who walked gloomily with spirit dulled, putting ashes on their heads (61:3), of spirit contrite and humble (57:15). They were the ardent protagonists of the anticipation of redemption, unwilling to abide with captivity on foreign soil. But there were also among the exiles those who were unconcerned and the light-hearted, those who were at ease in the diaspora. Between these two groups there was strife (see below, Chapter II, Deutero-Isaiah). The mass of the people stood somewhere in the middle.

The new non-sacrificial worship developed in the diaspora by reason of inner necessity, and was considered a temporary surrogate for the true cult. And yet this new worship was not altogether a product of the era of catastrophe and exile. There had been need for worship outside the Temple from the time, in Josiah's reign, when the high places were removed and the cult restricted to the Temple in Jerusalem. After the Josianic reform, the people in daily life were cut off from the worship of God, which previously had been carried out by the priests in the local sanctuaries. The injunctions of Deuteronomy were intended to multiply the contacts of the people with the chosen sanctuary. But these contacts could not be continuous, daily. A hiatus developed and the need for a new worship, parallel to the temple cult. The destruction merely intensified this need. Moreover, it was now no longer possible to institute a kind of temple cult, parallel to the temple cult, and connected with it.

And so the new form of worship was destined to be retained and to develop. There was need to create a service in place of the temple ritual, even after the building of the second Temple. The new worship was in a way the necessary complement to the deuteronomic centralization of the cult.

The new worship

Thus, new forms of worship were created, in conformity with the feelings and attitudes of the diaspora, as a surrogate for the sacrificial service. This was the result in some measure of internal developments following the centralization of worship, but it was the result also of external pressure, the catastrophe. The sacrificial cult was still thought of as the true cult. In fact, however, due to the two factors, a higher form of worship had been created, a worship wherein prayer, confession, and song were the principal elements. This new worship was universalistic, supra-national, not attached to the holiness of any one place; and democratic, bound with no priestly-tribal sanctity. Even as the earlier restriction of the cult, because of divine election, had been an expression of the faith in one God, so now was the bursting of the territorial bond. The earlier restriction was symbolic of the one divine sanctity. The enlargement was an expression of the idea of the one divine rule in the world.

However, in addition to its intrinsic significance as a higher form of worship, the new cult was destined to be of decisive historical importance in the spread of monotheism. Israel's faith in one God could not have spread abroad if it had not developed supra-national forms of worship, if its cultic practice had continued to be confined to a single land and city. If Israel was to fulfill its historic mission, the territorial restriction of the cult had to be breached. The new ritual of worship was, therefore, in fact, no mere substitute. Rather, it was a creation of enduring historical significance, at once for the nation Israel, and universally.

The new rituals—the fasts, commemorative of the destruction, the gatherings for prayer, confession, and song, prayer itself as a fixed form of devotion, and in particular, the festival observances, national in character and now celebrated in the diaspora without a temple—all developed in the period after the completion of the Torah. The pentateuchal literature had already been written when this new kind of worship began to develop, although the Torah as a book had not yet been edited and completed. In the Pentateuch there is not a single command prescribing these new forms of devotion. All the rituals of the Pentateuch are connected with the land of Israel and with the Temple and sacrifices. Prayer is not a fixed required ritual. Even Deuteronomy, which separates the ordinary Israelite in his daily life from the temple cult, makes no provision for a service outside the Temple. Ezekiel also (40–48) does not mention the new forms. And yet the new worship took hold, to become in time, in fact, the essential cult. The concept of worship was transformed. Prayer, which formerly had been merely subsidiary to the cult, was now of independent value and no less important than sacrifice. This fact is reflected in ch. 6 of Daniel, wherein prayer is called service (v. 17).[33] Even Darius and his pagan officers think here in Jewish terms: the ritual which they impose is prayer-petition (vv. 8, 13). This entire development took place within the sphere of the oral law.

The book of Kings

That great historical work, the book of Kings, was composed approximately twenty-five years after the catastrophe, about the year 562, in the Babylonian diaspora.[34]

Kings is the fourth of the historical books included in the "former prophets." There is no basis for the widespread opinion that these four books were originally one historical composition, a deuteronomic book of chronicles. It is apparent that the several books were separate works, composed in different periods. Joshua is the book of the conquest and settlement, the period of greatest success and glory. It was evidently written in the beginning of the period of the judges. The book of Judges presents a picture of ups and downs, of sin and repentance, of many struggles. It tells the story of the early "theocracy," and of its fall. It exalts the monarchy, and we may assume that it was compiled in the early period of the monarchy. The book of Samuel is the history of the end of the period of the judges, and of the reigns of Saul and David. This book also describes essentially a period of great success, the reign of David. Like the book of Joshua, it knows no sin of the nation. Common to all three books is the absence in them of any reference to the fate of Israel in the period of decline and calamity. From Joshua's time to David, individuals or the nation are punished in their day for sins of private persons and kings, but then the sins are blotted out. No sin of that period casts its shadow to the time of the destruction. There is in these books no prophecy pointing to the fall of the nation.

The book of Kings is of another character. It is a pragmatic composition, quite different from the books which precede it. It tells the story of the approaching calamity. In this book for the first time, beginning with 9:6, there are prophecies of destruction. The author makes use of various historical sources: the book of the Acts of Solomon, the book of the Chronicles of the Kings of Israel, the book of the Chronicles of the Kings of Judah, etc. But he compiles, abbreviates, and edits his material with the intention of relating succinctly the history of the catastrophe. He begins his story with the chronicles of Solomon because the chain of events which end in the catastrophe began in Solomon's time. The division of the kingdom is the consequence of the sins of Solomon and his foreign wives. This was the initial lethal blow to the house of Israel. Jeroboam set up the calves, and the sin of the calves entails the fall of the Ephraimite kingdom. Judah's transgression was the high places, and her kings caused her to sin from time to time by idolatry. Manasseh was the most wicked king, and because of his deeds the destruction of Judah and Jerusalem was finally decreed. Because events prior to Solomon were not causally related to the catastrophe, the author included in his book only events dating from the reign of Solomon. He began with the monarch who built the Temple and ended with the king in whose reign the Temple was destroyed.

For the period after Solomon the book of Kings goes into detail only in those chapters which relate the acts and words of the prophets or which deal with significant cultic matters. Political history is dealt with very briefly. The essential purpose of the author is to draw the practical and moral lessons of his history. His view of history derives from the pentateuchal literature, rather than from classical prophecy; and of the literary prophets only Isaiah is mentioned. There is no reference to moral corruption in the sense of the prophets as a cause of the catastrophe. The fall was due solely to idolatry, as idolatry is viewed in the Pentateuch. The destruction was determined, in the author's opinion, in the time of Manasseh (II Kings 21:10–16; 23:26–27; 24:3–4). Accordingly, the rebellion of Zedekiah against the king of Babylon is not pictured as a sin. Rather it was decreed. God Himself turned Zedekiah's heart to rebellion (24:20). Thus it appears that the author is ignorant of Jeremiah's struggle, waged in the name of the Lord, against the revolt. Jeremiah is not once mentioned. The book of Kings is, therefore, a product of the old popular faith.

The book of Kings reflects the soul-searching of the nation after the catastrophe, and the mood of repentance of that period. It is the historical spiritual reckoning of the people. The author made use of a considerable historical literature and condensed it into a short book, intended to be a popular history understandable by all. Certainly the author also wanted to write history, to store up in the memory of the nation the record of its past at once glorious and tragic. Yet his primary purpose was pragmatic, to explain to the people the cause of the tragic fate of the kingdom which God had established, to describe and explain how and why the monarchy declined continuously to its final destruction. The author acts as guide and preceptor. He summarizes the past and points to the future. Let the nation read, so that it may know what had happened to it, and why. Then it would learn its lesson and know what it must do. The sin of idolatry had brought it to this pass; and only if it would purge itself of this sin would God restore it as of old. The book is a call for repentance and a fortifying of the belief in redemption. The hope of redemption is not specifically mentioned. Yet the background is certainly messianic. In the closing story of the release of Jehoiachin from prison, the author hints at the hope which animated him when he wrote his book. The release of the imprisoned king was the first ray of divine grace, a dim light amidst national servitude.

This historical book was composed at a time when the history of the nation Israel appeared to have ended. But this very book, which examines the past with a view to the future, is witness to the process of consolidation and renewal which went on beneath the surface. The book was sign and witness that the cessation of history was but temporary.

Against the idolatry of the gentiles

When, following the collapse of the Assyrian empire, a new pagan empire, no less powerful than Assyria, strode suddenly onto the stage of history, Israel was profoundly shaken. It had thought that Assyria's fall would mean the end of idolatrous power, and now this hope was disappointed. The terror and confusion of the time are expressed in Habakkuk's bitter outcry. Then, at that very moment, in Habakkuk's prophecy, there is born something utterly new and heavy with consequence, the first direct assault on paganism addressed to the gentiles (2:18–20). The words are visionary. But words of this sort are here spoken for the first time to the gentiles, and not merely in a vision. Then when the might of the new empire pressed heavily against Jerusalem and the shadow of calamity loomed, Jeremiah, the prophet of doom, declared war on the idolatry of the gentiles. Jeremiah also directed his preachments against idolatry to the gentiles (ch. 10). He even ordered the exiles to warn the gentiles that idolatry is faith in no-gods and that its end is nigh. Indeed, he phrased his warning in Aramaic, the language of the gentiles (10:11). Thus it was the prophet of doom who initiated the struggle whereby pagan idolatry was destined to be overcome. Then came the destruction. The people of the Lord were transported abroad. There was no Temple on earth.

And now, the Chaldean empire was about to collapse, and another pagan empire stood ready to conquer the world. At this moment, when the fate of the world was being determined by the contest of heathen powers and Israel lay prostrate, when one world empire followed another, the challenge to idolatry was renewed even more vigorously. Deutero-Isaiah directed his blows against the idolatry of the nations, challenging and deriding paganism beyond any earlier prophet. From that time the struggle never ceased. It was carried on in word and in deed throughout the generations. It was continued in Jewry and, subsequently, in Christianity and in Islam. Its protagonists in the word were the Jewish writers; in deed, the masses of the Jews. Everywhere among the gentiles they expressed contempt for idolatry and derided it, thus arousing hatred and murderous fury. But they also instigated a proselytizing movement among the gentiles. Their customs won hearts and found acceptance everywhere. Little by little the foundations of paganism were sapped, and the way was opened for the triumph of monotheism.

It is surprising, and certainly not without significance, that this struggle against the idolatry of the nations began at the moment when the political life of the nation was extinguished. It was the hour when the hope of the early fall of the pagan kingdom and the restoration of the house of David had failed, when the shadow of catastrophe enveloped the nation, and the people dwelt in exile amidst strangers.

Ancient monotheism, as it had crystallized in the Pentateuch, was of the nation and with no anticipation of becoming an inheritance to the gentiles. In the ancient Scriptures the hope is occasionally expressed that the gentiles will recognize the greatness of Israel's God, but without any real aspiration for universal rule. The creator of the vision of the conversion of the nations to the God of Israel and of the extinction of idolatry in the end of days is Isaiah. With his vision, Israel's faith acquired universal outlook, and the people of Israel their universal mission. But Isaiah's lofty vision was only a dream,

49

no call to action. The end of idolatry was to be the work of God, to be realized in the end of time. In the earlier writings, and also in the vision of Isaiah, the recognition of God by the nations is bound up with Israel's greatness. Israel's political or national success, or its miraculous deliverance from the clutches of heathen empire, and the fall of that empire, would cause the gentiles to recognize that the Lord, He is God.

History, however, would separate the problem of God from Israel's political fortunes. The heathen rule did not come to an end. Israel lived on in low estate, despised and subject to pagan rule. Finally, there came utter defeat and exile. Yet the belief in the end of paganism was unshaken. The basis of this belief was the conviction that the pagan world was a world of no-gods. Israel's heart was sick of hope deferred, but its faith was steadfast. Gradually it was realized that the contest between monotheism and idolatry was of a distinct order, that its issue was certain and did not depend on historical events. The triumph of idolatry was no proof that its gods were God, and even if its end was slow to come—this also was not decisive. Habakkuk was the first to express this thought. Therewith the question of idolatry ceased to be wholly eschatological. It became a subject of everyday logical argument. Idolatry was now—today—under all circumstances, stupidity; and this was, in fact, not a question of the end of days. Therein was expressed the absolute superiority of monotheism over paganism; and thereby the conquered Jewish nation found support and defense against the arrogance of the triumphant heathen enemy. This conviction was the source of the feeling of superiority and of election, and of the strength and courage of the nation. This insistence on the superiority of monotheism was particularly important in the diaspora, after the destruction. Monotheism was the one treasure left to the exiles: it was incumbent on them to defend it with all their strength; and they were able to defend the honor of their God now only by argument against idolatry.

Thus it was that after the political battle was decided in

favor of paganism, the battle for monotheism was waged on a new front, a spiritual offensive against victorious paganism. Precisely at the moment of political decline, there appeared the absolute value of monotheism in the world of the spirit, and its power to do battle with idolatry in exile, even before the event of "that day."

In the loyalty of exiled Israel to its God, and its zeal for His name, which had been defiled among the nations, this insight became the inheritance of all the nation. The conquered nation was sensitive to the scorn of the pagans, and given to answer in kind. The arguments, based on fetishism, and thus irrelevant to the essential quality of paganism, were quite naïve. And yet the conflict, the negation in the religion of Israel of the pagan apotheosis of matter, was definitely formulated. Moreover, in certain pagan quarters, the arguments found their mark. Everywhere the existence of a monotheistic diaspora living in pagan surroundings caused tension. Thus the struggle of exiled Israel against gentile idolatry was a people's war.

The struggle against paganism and the hope of redemption

On the basis of the foregoing, we must reject the tendency of Christian theology to view the struggle against gentile idolatry, the "mission to the gentiles," as a renunciation of the hope of national redemption. Such renunciation is assumed to have been due to the failure of political hopes, or to the recognition by gifted individuals that Israel's true mission was spiritual and religious, and their negative attitude to the anticipation of national-political redemption. According to this thesis, the battle against the idolatry of the gentiles was not an eschatological movement. It sought to turn the gentiles from idolatry by preaching and moral suasion, and had ceased to be the anticipation of the political downfall of idolatry in the end

of days.[35] But this thesis is erroneous. The struggle against
gentile idolatry was, in fact, only a corollary of the messianic
hope. It did not supplant it, and was not independent of it.
Christianity's struggle against pagan idolatry also was tied in
with eschatological promise. Jewry was able to undertake the
struggle only because it had come to terms with the catastrophe; it had justified the harsh decree. Indeed, if it had de-
spaired of redemption, it would have been incapable of doing
battle. By its struggle against paganism it expressed the fullness of its trust in its God, and its consciousness, for all the
catastrophe, of its absolute superiority over paganism. But
therewith it gave expression also to the certainty of its redemption from exile and the downfall of pagan dominion. The
contest with idolatry was not a result of renunciation of faith
in its unique destiny, its election and its national salvation;
rather, it sustained and fortified that faith. Moreover, though
doing battle now, in the present, with gentile idolatry, Jewry
foresaw complete victory only in the end of days, as a vision.
Even Paul, the apostle to the gentiles, imagined the process of
history in this manner. The struggle, therefore, was always
rooted in the vision of the end of days. We return to this
problem in the chapter on Deutero-Isaiah.

The influence of Judaism. The joiners

The war against gentile idolatry began within the Babylonian diaspora, even before Isaiah II. Deutero-Isaiah merely
gave sharper and more poetical expression to the scornful
attitude of the people. Furthermore, the struggle had already
borne fruit. In Isa. 56:3, 6–7 (also 14:1) we hear for the
first time of a new species of mankind, of "aliens, that join
themselves to the Lord, to minister unto Him, And to love
the name of the Lord, To be His servants." These are men
who have departed from idolatry, who believe in the God of
Israel and have adopted Jewish practices. They are called

"joiners," by which name they are designated also in Esther 9:27. The religion of Israel was beginning to reveal its inner power. The exiles, conquered and brought low, under the shadow of God's wrath, without cult, without sanctuary, in the very center of an arrogant, vibrant, and affluent paganism —the exiles were able to cause idol worshipers to forsake idolatry and to cleave to Israel's God. These joiners were a completely new phenomenon. They foreshadowed the institution of religious conversion, which was to eventuate only after several generations and without which the spread of monotheism would have been impossible.

Proselytism

Gerim (strangers, resident aliens) were no novel phenomenon in Israel. They are mentioned in ancient tales and law codes of the Pentateuch and in the narratives of the former prophets; nor were they peculiar to Israel. These early *gerim* were foreigners who joined themselves to Israel. They dwelt in the land, were assimilated into the national culture, and therewith came to worship the God of Israel. This was a national-cultural kind of conversion, in the wake of which came religious assimilation. This brand of conversion was accomplished in the course of generations, and occurred also among pagan peoples.

The religious proselytism of later Jewry was completely different. Religious conversion was not accomplished in the course of generations; it did not depend on residence in the land of Israel, and it was no by-product of cultural assimilation. Religious conversion is universalistic; it consists in one essential element, acceptance of the religion of Israel, and was carried out by a fixed ritual, whereby the conversion to the new faith was accomplished at one stroke. The convert, by means of the ceremony, was made as an Israelite in every respect, or in almost every respect. He was henceforth obliged to perform all the commandments, and endowed with all the religious perquisites of the Israelite, including the right of intermarriage. Conversion was a juristic-religious act, clearly defined with respect to meaning and consequences. Religious conversion was a new and original creation of Judaism which Christianity and Islam inherited, and of which paganism knew nothing. The pagan might serve another god, he might participate in the cult of a given temple, and become a member of one or another religious association. But he could not at one stroke "accept" a heathen religion. In the religions of Egypt, Babylon, Greece, Rome, etc. there was no specific ceremony by which the heathen could renounce his religion. The very concept of accepting a new religion was unknown to the ancient world. In Israel, also, the idea of religious conversion appeared only in later times. It was a creation of the oral law and developed only after the biblical period.

The concept of religious conversion, that is, the turning from idolatry to Israel's God, exists in Scripture, but only as an idea. There was no practicable possibility whereby the alien could become an Israelite by reason of religious association alone. Neither in the legal codes nor in the narrative sections does the Bible reflect the idea of conversion in its later sense. The basis of proselytism in the Bible is territorial or societal association; and there is no reference to any ritual whereby the faith of Israel is accepted.[36] The early *gerim* in Israel were not Israelites, and they were not rated as the "home-born." They were a special class, distinct racially and to a certain degree with respect to occupation from the Israelites. Even in the desert there was a class of *gerim* (Exod. 12:38; Deut. 29:10; Josh. 8:35; 20:9), but they received no landed inheritance along with the tribes. They were men without "nationality," of descent unknown and incompletely attached to Israel. Yet from the point of view of their cultural and religious beliefs they were "Israelites"; and Ezekiel commanded that land be given them in the future as an inheritance (47:22). Moreover, many of them, in particular wealthy and well-connected foreigners, merged completely into Israel. Also, patriarchal family groups, as the Kenites, were assimilated by way of territorial and cultural association. In addition there were bondsmen-aliens, as the Gibeonites and the Nethinim, who were incorporated into Israel's culture and religion by way of servitude. Also there were slaves. Slaves of priests were even privileged to eat "of the holy thing" (Lev. 22:11).[37]

The Priestly Code equates the "stranger" (ger) fully with the Israelite from the religious point of view. But the stranger is the resident alien who has become associated in the religion of Israel by way of national and cultural association over generations. Conversion in the Priestly Code is the result of residence among the Israelites and in their land. The ger is the man who sojourns in the land of Israel (Exod. 12:19, 48–49; Lev. 17:8; 19:33–34; 20:2, et al.).[38] But the Priestly Code contains no statute concerning the acceptance of Israel's belief, and no ceremonial by which conversion to the faith of Israel could be accomplished. In Exod. 12:44, 48, it is stated that only circumcised servants and strangers may eat of the passover. But the matter there discussed is only the fitness for eating. Circumcision is not a rite of religious conversion. In Deut. 21:10–14, ceremonies are prescribed whereby a foreign woman is prepared for Israelite marriage. This is the law of "a woman of goodly form," a woman captive, who is "converted" through captivity. Here again the territorial-social factor determines. The ritual symbolizes the detachment of the foreign woman from her nation, and is without religious element.[39] In the deuteronomic code, also, it is residence in the land which "converts" the alien (Deut. 23:8–9).

There are, of course, a number of instances in Scripture wherein non-Israelites acknowledge the God of Israel by reason of religious conviction.[40] But there is no instance of "righteous proselytes," as the term is subsequently understood, that is, men who accept fully the faith of Israel by a specific ceremony. Naaman comes to belief in Israel's God by conviction (II Kings 5:15–18). However, he undertakes but a single commandment: to sacrifice only to the God of Israel; and even this not in accordance with the law of Israel. Naaman does not become an Israelite; and there is no reference to any formal ceremony of conversion. And even here there is a trace of the residential kind of conversion: Naaman carries some soil of Israel away with him to construct an altar to the Lord.

Sui generis were the Cuthites at the beginning of the process of their judaizing (II Kings 17). Ostensibly they were *gerim* by religious conviction. It was the lions which God sent among them, forcing them to learn the law of God, rather than merely dwelling in the midst of Israel, which effected their conversion. Yet they also were proselytes of the land, since it was residence in the land which was the cause of their conversion. Moreover, their acknowledgement of Israel's God did not, in the first stage, involve abandonment of idolatry. (*Re* the Samaritans, see below.)

Likewise, there is in Scripture no indication that in the period of the first Temple there were any non-Israelites living outside the land of Israel who believed in the God of Israel and eschewed idolatry. The religion of Israel in the period of the first Temple exercised no influence on the gentiles. There were no *gerim* outside of the land of Israel, which implies that conversion could occur only by reason of residence and not by reason of religious conviction. Non-idolatrous peoples, monotheistic, existed only in legend, in the stories of the epoch of the early fathers of the world. Only in fiction and in vision are there nations which turn from idolatry to the God of Israel. These were the desideratum and hope of the pious and the poets or the promise of the prophetic visions of the time to come. Thus, in the days of the first Temple, there were legendary monotheistic nations and eschatological proselytes, but no actual religious converts. Religious proselytism in preexilic biblical writings was, therefore, only theoretical and legendary, and not practice. Proselytism existed as a desideratum and vision, but without any legal or cultic institutionalization. There was no need to determine legal forms for religious proselytism because it was completely nonexistent.

Age of judaizing

The statement, therefore, in Isa. 56:3, 6–7, concerning those who have joined themselves is evidence of a completely new historical phenomenon, the fact of non-Israelites, dwelling outside the land of Israel, who believe in the Lord. These men have become joiners solely for religious reasons. These are not proselytes by reason of residence or of fear of lions, nor are they legendary proselytes, converts by reason of miracles. They are non-Israelites who have joined themselves in love to an Israel which is exiled and in bondage, by reason of the inner power of the religion of Israel. In this sense they are religious proselytes.

And yet, it is an error to equate the fact of these joiners with the later Jewish institution of religious conversion. It is to be kept in mind that Judaism itself was at that time still in process of development. It had, as yet, no supra-national symbolism, and the Pentateuch was not yet completed. The phenomenon of religious proselytism was beginning to evolve —it had begun to exist in fact; and it sought for itself real forms. It was a time of transition and confusion. The catastrophe marked the end of the earlier kind of conversion by reason of residence; but conversion by religious rite was still to come. There was, as yet, no recognized class of joiners in Israel, and this kind of proselytism still surely involved a process of gradual approachment to Israel's faith. The joiners abandoned idolatry; they began to follow Israelite practice, attended the tales of the exiles, and associated themselves in their aspirations. But to the questions: how, when, and in what sense, did these aliens become "Israelites," there was no clear answer. The joiners are still called "aliens." The statement in Isa. 56:3, "The Lord will surely separate me from His people," reflects the misgivings of the joiners and the uncertainty of the period. These joiners were doubtless part of a wider circle of judaizers. Judaizers, that is, gentiles who approached Jewry and its beliefs, and practiced its customs, are mentioned in Esther 8:17. But the judaizers of Esther became Jews by reason of fear, whereas the joiners of Isaiah came to Judaism out of love.

We may conclude, then, that in this epoch there was judaizing, but not yet actual religious conversion. It is significant that in Isa. 14:1, as well as in Isa. 56:6–8, the joiners are assured that they will go up with the captivity of Israel to the land of Israel. Proselytism was not yet detached completely from its territorial aspect. Nonetheless, residence in the land of Israel here becomes an eschatological promise to the proselytes (see below, section Deutero-Isaiah).

This new class, the religious proselytes who are nowhere mentioned in the Torah, and for whom there was no legal status, wrought much confusion in Israel. This confusion, in the time of Zerubbabel, Ezra, and Nehemiah, had far-reaching consequences, as will be seen below.

Thus, the Babylonian exile was a period of profound agitation and of renewed creativity. The diaspora justified the sentence of destruction. Firm faith became its supreme and absolute value. The exiles began to develop a new kind of supra-national worship. They embarked on the struggle against paganism and instituted a new religious form of proselytism. In this period the foundation was laid and the conditions created for the role which Judaism would play in world history.

The return to Zion and popular religion

The coming to terms of the diaspora with the destruction was not acceptance of the exile. Acceptance of the destruction meant that Israel was unconditionally faithful to God; but the nation Israel did not surrender hope that God would restore His earlier favors: the land, the kingdom, and the glory. There was no affirmation of the exile. Even Jeremiah did not affirm it. He merely fixed a period of seventy years for it. The exile was of God's wrath; and the nation's yearning to be delivered from the wrath was a yearning to be delivered from the exile. The exile was an episode; the kingdom of idolatry would certainly end, and God would renew the days of Israel as of yore. The new worship was considered a temporary substitute. Repentance and the petitioning of God, though they had religious roots of their own, were tied in with the hope of complete redemption. The redemption was the goal of every deed of the diaspora.

Prophecy gave magnificent and sublime expression to the hope of full redemption. Prophetic vision is the golden background of the faith of Israel. It molded the world of dreams, the miraculous dreams which were imbedded in the soul of the nation. However, what happened in the real world was the issue not of prophecy, but of the older popular-priestly faith. Both the endeavor to create a new form of worship suited to passing needs of the diaspora and the effort to restore the legitimate cult in Jerusalem were rooted in the popular cultic religion, not in the idealism of the prophets.

The prophet foretold a return to Zion which would be grand and miraculous, a cosmic event. But the actual return in the days of Zerubbabel, Ezra, and Nehemiah was a shabby affair, by grace of the heathen monarch and his officials, and not accomplished by prophetic influence. Ezekiel's utopia was no blueprint for the return to Zion. Ezekiel did not envision the return as voluntary. It was both a sentence and redemption, to be wrought by mighty hand and outstretched arm. It would comprise all the tribes; and the tribes would take possession of the entire land, to the entrance to Hamath, etc. Ezekiel certainly was not speaking of a partial return under the protection of a pagan monarch; and he did not call on the people to return and to rebuild the earthly Jerusalem. His dream was of a miraculous visionary city; and his program did not serve in any wise as a model for the returnees, neither generally nor in its details. Both Jeremiah and Deutero-Isaiah urged the exiles to leave Babylon and to return to Zion (Jer. 50:8; 51:6, 10, 45; Isa. 48:20; 52:11). But the background of these incitements is the vision of Babylon's fall and a redemption which is complete and miraculous. These prophecies have nothing to do with the humble return by "grant." Haggai and Zechariah encouraged the returnees, and urged them to complete the rebuilding of the Temple. But the movement of return did not originate with them.

The return to Zion was a product of the spirit of repentance which animated the nation, of the longing for cultic holiness, the wish to be rid, and not merely in part, of idolatrous contamination; to reestablish, and not merely in meager and difficult circumstance, the legitimate cult in the holy land. Repentance had nurtured the wish to live according to God's will and the commandments of His Law, which would be possible only in the land of Israel. The hope of complete political liberation was surely part of these aspirations. The piteous return to Zion was thought of merely as preliminary to the redemption. There may have been some thought also of a temporary political reconstruction within the pagan empire. But the movement continued even when the dream of immediate political rebirth failed. It was nourished by the spirit of repentance and the yearning for cultic sanctity. Its roots went deep into the ancient popular-priestly faith. The great accomplishment of the epoch—the compilation of the Pentateuch—was also a product of the popular-priestly faith. No prophet took part in the compilation. Prophecy was the sphere of magnificent visions and sublime ideals. It certainly influenced the people, encouraging them by its flaming faith. But the primary agent in practical life was the power of the ancient religion of which the protagonists were the priests and the nation.

II

Deutero-Isaiah

SCRIPTURE gives no explicit biographical information concerning the author of the prophecies contained in chapters
40–66 of the book of Isaiah—not even his name nor where
nor when he lived. There is no caption for his prophecies, and
they include no dates. Except Cyrus, no contemporary historical figure is mentioned. We call him the Second Isaiah
(henceforth Deutero-Isaiah) because his prophecies were included in the book of Isaiah.[1] There are scholars who question
whether all of chapters 40–66 is of Deutero-Isaiah. Some deny
his authorship of chapters 56–66 and ascribe them to another
author whom they call the Third Isaiah (henceforth Trito-
Isaiah). But certain prophecies in chapters 40–55 also have
been denied to Deutero-Isaiah; and, further, chapters 56–66
are ascribed by some scholars to several prophets rather than
to a single prophet. These problems will be considered below.
The redactor of the prophecies of chapters 40–66 divided
them into three groups: 40–48, 49–57, 58–66. He closed each
group with a prophecy of retribution for the wicked, the first
two groups with the words: "There is no peace . . . concerning
the wicked" (48:22; 57:21; cf. 66:24). These closures are
thought to be the epilogues added by a later editor who
sorted the prophecies into sections of equal length. We will
observe, however, that the division is original and related
organically to the composition of these prophecies. The closing

chapters of the three groups (48, 57, 66) are similar in structure, each including castigation and consolation. In the first and third groups there are indications of distinct literary compositions. Thus the threefold division reflects a process of prophetic development. All these matters will be considered below.

§1. THE POLITICAL BACKGROUND

Deutero-Isaiah appears at the moment of the ascent of Cyrus and the fall of the Babylonian empire. The turn of events began about the year 550, and the agent was Cyrus, king of Anshan in Elam. The small kingdom of Anshan was part of and subject to the Median empire. The ruler of Media was Ishtuvegu or Ishtumegu, whom the Greeks called Astyages, and to whom Cyrus was vassal. Approximately in the year 553 Cyrus rebelled against Astyages and in 550 defeated him after he had been betrayed by the Median army. Cyrus conquered Ecbatana, capital of Media, and took Astyages captive. Thus the king of Anshan came into possession of the great Median empire, which in the year 612 had occupied half of the Assyrian world empire. Cyrus was also ruler of Persia, a small state, sister kingdom to Anshan, and was subsequently called king of Persia. In the war between Cyrus and Astyages, Babylon maintained neutrality with a certain preference for Cyrus. Nabonidus rejoiced at the calamity of Media, and even related that Marduk had prophesied to him three years before Cyrus' victory that Cyrus would defeat Astyages. It appears that Nabonidus availed himself of the occasion to occupy a small section of the Median empire, the city of Harran, wherein he built a temple to Sin. But with the conquest of Media the fate of Babylon was sealed. First after Media came the turn of Lydia. War broke out between Cyrus and Croesus, king of Lydia, about 546. It was then, it seems, that Nabonidus began to understand the danger which threatened his empire. Lydia, Babylon, Egypt, and Sparta concluded a pact of alliance against Cyrus. But the pact was not effective. Near Pteria, east of the river Halys, there was an inconclusive battle between Cyrus and Croesus, after which Croesus returned to Sardis, his capital, and entrenched himself there. Cyrus pursued Croesus without delay and defeated his army when it emerged from the city to do battle. Cyrus then attacked Sardis and took the city. Croesus was captured and his immense treasures fell (in 546) booty to Cyrus. The allies did not come to the aid of Croesus. After the conquest of Lydia, Cyrus overran great stretches of eastern Iran, and prepared for the conquest of the Babylonian world empire, wherein at that time there was no leader who might have measured up to a warrior such as Cyrus. Nabonidus was a priest and scholar, lover of antiquities and religious reformer. For some years he had absented himself from Babylon, during which time the important festivals were not observed, thus alienating, apparently, the influential priestly class. He made his son, Belshazzar, who was commander-in-chief of the army, head of state. Nabonidus brought the statues of the gods from the temples of the provincial cities to Babylon, apparently in order to protect the city, thus arousing the enmity of the provincial priests. The hour of Babylon struck about ten years after the fall of Media. In 540 Cyrus began war against Babylon. In the month of Tishri, 539, Cyrus' army clashed with the forces of Belshazzar near Upi (Opis), winning a decisive victory. On the fourteenth of Tishri Cyrus conquered Sippar without a fight. Nabonidus fled, and Belshazzar took refuge in Babylon. But Babylon opened its gates to the conquering army without resistance, apparently under the influence of the priestly class. Cyrus' army entered the city on the sixteenth of Tishri. Belshazzar was killed, probably at that time, and Cyrus himself entered Babylon on the third of Marcheshvan. Nabonidus was captured, and the Chaldean kingdom of Babylon was ended. Thus arose the world empire of the Medes and Persians.

Babylon's armies were defeated, its king taken captive, the son of the king, commander of its army, killed; but the city was not destroyed and its temples went unharmed. Cyrus appeared not as conqueror of Babylon, but as its legitimate king, the elect of Marduk, liberator of the empire from the yoke of Nabonidus "the tyrant." This is the way matters are described on the "Cylinder of Cyrus": a king, tyrannical and wicked, that is Nabonidus, ruled over Babylon. He made his yoke heavy on the people, devising evil all the day. He stopped the cult and did not serve Marduk. Marduk was wroth and left the land. Nabonidus brought the images of the gods to Babylon; and the gods were wroth and departed from their dwellings. Marduk heard the cry of the oppressed nation. Then he sought out a righteous king according to his heart, to strengthen his hands. He found Cyrus, proclaimed in his name, and made him king of the whole world. Marduk subdued the lands beneath his feet, and he, Cyrus, ruled them with righteousness and justice. Marduk observed his good deeds, and then ordered him to go up against Babylon; and he went at his right hand as friend and companion. He gave the city into his hand without a battle, turned the heart of the nation to him, and delivered the city from evil. The people of Babylon, Sumer, and Akkad kissed the feet of Cyrus and rejoiced at his coming. Bel and Nebo loved his dynasty. Cyrus was concerned for Babylon and its cities; he restored their temples. He served Marduk faithfully. At the command of Marduk he returned the gods, whom Nabonidus had taken from the cities of Babylon, to their dwelling places. He assembled their peoples and restored their habitations.

Thus matters are described also in the "Chronicle of Nabonidus" and in the "Verse Account of Nabonidus."[2] Cyrus was, therefore, the legitimate heir, by grace of Marduk, of the kingdom of Babylonia.

Turning point in the history of Israel

These political events marked a turning point also in the history of Israel. The kings of Persia make no mention of the Jews. Cyrus in the cylinder scroll names the city of Ashur, also Susa, Agade, Eshnunna, Zamban, and others, as places whose temples he restored, whose idols he returned; and states that he assembled their inhabitants and gave their dwelling places back to them. But Jerusalem is not mentioned. Our only source for the history of the Jews and their return is Scripture. The political background of the Jewish history of the period is available from outside sources; but there is no direct evidence. Unfortunately, the scriptural accounts of the period and of the Persian age in general are scanty and piecemeal, which increases the difficulty of understanding the prophecies of Isa. 40–66. The historical perspective of most of these prophecies is vague, on which account the scholar-poets have found ample opportunity for their imaginative flights. Some have gone so far as to rate the book of Ezra and parts of Nehemiah as legendary. They are the most fortunate of all, for they construct history with their pens, whereby the prophecies become clear of themselves. The system of these scholars is the well-known method of speculative exegesis and allusion. If, however, we are really to understand the prophecies we must first determine on the basis of the scriptural sources the specific nature of the historical situation.

The biblical sources for the history of Israel of the period are Ezra, Nehemiah, Haggai, Zechariah 1–8, Malachi. We shall consider later problems of the reliability and content of these sources. Here we establish only certain basic facts for which there is evidence in these books. In the year 538 Cyrus gave permission to the Jews to return to Jerusalem and to rebuild the Temple. The first leader of the aliyah was Sheshbazzar, to be followed by Zerubbabel and Jeshua. There was no "ingathering of the exiles." The immigrants laid the foundation of the Temple but were unable to build it. Foreigners whose center was in Samaria conspired against them, and by their machinations were able to interrupt the work of rebuilding. The Temple was built at last in the reign of Darius, about 520–516. The time of Haggai and Zechariah was most difficult for the Judean colony, a time of drought, weakness, and poverty. In the time of Ezra and Nehemiah the settlers struggled with the problem of mixed marriages. Both Ezra and Nehemiah opposed the mixed marriages; and the sure covenant included a general prohibition of mixed marriage (Neh. 10:31). The prophet Malachi also rebuked the people for them (2:11). The wall of Jerusalem was incomplete until Nehemiah finished it in 444 in the reign of Artaxerxes. In Nehemiah's time the nobles impoverished the people. Nehemiah forced them to cancel the debts, and put an end to exploitation and enslavement. The sins for which the prophets of the period, that is, Haggai, Zechariah, Malachi, castigated the nation in Judah were: negligence in their efforts to build the Temple (Haggai and Zechariah), absence of justice, kindness and mercy, oppression of the poor, false oaths (Zechariah), divination, harlotry, false oaths, oppression of the poor, disrespect for the Temple, negligence in temple offerings, and the tendency to religious nihilism (Malachi). There is not a single reference to the sin of idolatry in the books of Ezra, Nehemiah, or the prophets of that generation.

Which of all these matters are reflected in Isa. 40–66?

§2. COMPOSITION OF THE BOOK

The question of the unity of chapters 40–66

There is much difference of opinion with respect to the author, or authors, of chapters 40–66 and their dates. Budde thinks that chapters 40–55 are a unit; but in 56–66 he finds prophecies of various periods from the seventh to the third centuries. Duhm fixes the period of chapters 55–66 about the middle of the fifth century, that is, prior to Nehemiah, and the place of their composition Jerusalem. In these chapters he discovers accusations of his own invention against the Israelite-Samaritans: traitorous brethren who rejected the invitation of the Jews to share in the building of the Temple and in the cult of Jerusalem. Torrey argues for the unity of 40–66, but fixes the date of all the prophecies contained in them in the fourth century. Elliger argues for the unity of chapters 56–66 and, following Sellin, assumes that Trito-Isaiah was a disciple of Deutero-Isaiah and the redactor of his prophecies. He fixes his date at the end of the sixth century, approximately the time of Haggai and Zechariah, and the locus of his work, Jerusalem. Sellin is in agreement with these hypotheses. Eissfeldt tends, in general, to accept these dates, but thinks that there are fragments in these chapters of earlier and later dates. The section 63:7–64:11 is, perhaps, of the period shortly after the destruction; 57:7–13 is probably even earlier; and 65:3–6, 11, perhaps of the Hellenistic period. Glahn defends the unity of 40–66, but thinks that Deutero-Isaiah, "the prophet of the return to Zion," wrote chapters 56–66 while in the land of Israel, about the year 530, before Haggai and Zechariah. Klausner also thinks that chapters 40–66 are a unit, but distinguishes three periods in the prophecies of Deutero-Isaiah. He attributes chapters 56–66 to the third period, approximately the years 537–515. The prophecies of this period were surely written, he thinks, in the land of Israel, in part after the Temple had been built. Besides these, any number of other opinions with respect to this subject have been broached.

Historical horizon

The decisive problem is: what is the explicit historical background which is to be found in chapters 40–66 without resort to exegesis and allusion?

The situation subsequent to the destruction is reflected in the prophecies of these chapters. Jerusalem had been destroyed by Babylon of the Chaldees. The cities of Judah lay waste and Israel was scattered in all lands. The victories of Cyrus are mentioned in chapters 40–48. Cyrus is twice mentioned by name, 44:28 and 45:1. For Cyrus the prophet foretells victory over Babylon (43:14 and 48:14); and for Babylon calamity, loss of children, widowhood, and enslavement (ch. 47). Cyrus' victory will be the end of the exile, and the exiles will return to their land from Babylon and from other lands. There is in the prophecies no definite indication of Babylon's actual fate after the victory of Cyrus. But the disappointment of the prophet is evident in the fact that from chapter 48 onward he does not again mention Cyrus or the conquest of Babylon. This is conclusive proof that the prophecies of chapters 49 and following were written after the fall of Babylon.[3] The desire to build the Temple is also mentioned in the prophecies (66:1).

However, no Persian king, except Cyrus, and no event of Persian history after Cyrus, is mentioned in these prophecies. Likewise, neither in chapters 40–55 nor in 56–66 is there any explicit reference to the actual history of Israel after the victory of Cyrus, except for the hope of building the Temple. In particular, there is no mention of the history of the immigrants in the Judean "province" of which the center was Jerusalem. The actual situation in the land of Israel at that time is not reflected in any way in these prophecies; and there is nothing in them which would indicate that any of the prophecies were written in the land of Israel.

There is no reference to events of Nehemiah's time either in chapters 40–55 or in 56–66. According to 44:28; 45:13, Cyrus will rebuild Jerusalem. But there is no suggestion that another king (Artaxerxes) will rebuild the wall of Jerusalem. There is nothing of the problem of mixed marriages, the covenant, the laxity of the people with respect to the sacred offerings, etc. There are castigations concerning social injustice

(56:9–57:2; 58–59). But neither the eviction of the people from the soil nor the enslavement of sons and daughters is mentioned. Also there is nothing of Ezra's work.

In addition, the fact that in these prophecies there are verses, to wit: 60:13; 63:18; 64:10: 66:1, which prove that the Temple had not yet been rebuilt, invalidates the effort to date chapters 56–66 in the age of Haggai and Zechariah.[4]

Also incorrect is Glahn's opinion[5] that chapters 56–66 reflect the situation in the land of Israel from the time of the return to the building of the Temple in 530. Neither Zerubbabel nor Jeshua is mentioned in chapters 56–66. There is no reference to an effort to build a temple nor to the frustration of the effort by the machinations of antagonists nor to the rejection of the Samaritans. In 56–66, there is no indication of the local environment of the land of Israel, and no knowledge of actual conditions. There is no mention of the poverty or of the years of drought of which Haggai and Zechariah speak.[6] The evil of the day is described in 59:9 in a generalized metaphor: "darkness . . . we walk in gloom." Not only is the Temple not mentioned, not even the altar which the returnees built.[7] Zion is described in 56–66 exactly as in 49–55: it is a ruin, forsaken and hated, so that no man passed through (60:15; 62:4, 12), desolate (62:4). Zion is a wilderness, the holy cities are become a wilderness (64:9). Could this description possibly be that of a man who had returned to Jerusalem with the immigrants in the days of Zerubbabel, who saw the real Jerusalem as it is described, for instance, in Ezra 3? The dirge for the destruction in 63:7–64:11 parallels the dirge in 51:17–23. It is unrelated to the interruption of the rebuilding of the year 536.[8] Zion, to the author of 56–66, is still the "afflicted, tossed with tempest, and not comforted" of chapters 49–55.

There are, in chapters 56–66, many prophecies of the ingathering of the exiles. The descriptions of the return are not so detailed as in 40–55, but the prophecies of return correspond to those of 40–55 and are of the same tenor.

In 56–66, there is no differentiation in any prophecy of return between the exiles who have already returned and those who will return. These prophecies are 56:1–8; 57:13–14; 60:4, 8, 9; 62:4–5, 10–12; 65:9; 66:7–9, 18–21. The critics have tried by every means to blur their evidence, to rob them of their plain meanings, to fix them in a local Jerusalem frame of reference, to find allusions in them to an immigration which had already occurred and to various species of "Samaritans," etc. But their devices are quite dubious. In chapter 56, vv. 6–8 follow v. 1, the good tidings of the approach of redemption, which has not yet come, tidings which have parallel in 51:5. God will bring the "joiners" to His holy mount with all Israel. The sense of 56:8 is that He will gather the "joiners" of the gentiles along with the gathered of Israel,[9] which parallels the prophecy of Isa. 14:1. Also, with respect to the scope of the return, 57:14; 62:10–12 are very similar to 40:3, 10; 48:20; 49:22. They point to the return of the whole nation at one time.[10] There is no indication of an earlier immigration, and no differentiation between old and new immigrants. That the prophet does not prophesy a number of distinct movements of return is clear specifically in 60:4–9; 66:7–9. All the children of Zion will return together; Zion will bring forth her children "at once" (66:8). Even the immigration from the "isles afar off" (66:19–20) will occur in one act of redemption along with the migration from the lands close by. All this is visionary. The critics read the real immigrants of Judah and Jerusalem into these verses on their own.[11]

Also, the reproofs of chapters 56–66 do not reflect in any way the actual situation in the land of Israel. The adjustment of these reproofs to the actualities of the land is based on distortion of the history of the second Temple, which is itself the sequence to the distortion of the history of Israel prior to the destruction, wherewith the critics have been occupied these several decades. It is assumed that the syncretistic Israelite-Canaanite idolatry, which is an invention of the critics, continued into the period of the second Temple. This brand of idolatry, continuation of the preexilic idolatry, survived among the common folk into the period of the second Temple. Its protagonists were the Israelites and the half-Israelites, the "Samaritans," the "people of the land," who opposed the returnees and their purified religion. The rebukes of idolatry of 57:3–12 and 65–66 are directed against the Jewish and half-Jewish people of the land of Israel, who are "the Jewish-Canaanitish faction." These are the scoffers of 57:3, the brethren who cast out, of 66:5, those who were the cause of the interruption of the building of the Temple in 536.[12] The assumption that the Jews who had remained in the land were idolatrous depends essentially on the rebukes of chapters 56–66. Thus the critics are involved in circular reasoning. The assumption is the basis for the interpretation of the prophecies, and the interpretation is the basis of the assumption. But, in fact, there is in these prophecies no mention of a "Jewish-Canaanitish faction" nor of what is known from Ezra and Nehemiah of the deeds of the Samaritans. The Samaritans of history are non-Israelites, not "half-Jews," etc.; and, what is most important, they are not accused in the books of Ezra and Nehemiah of idolatry. Moreover, in the whole of Ezra, Nehemiah, Haggai, Zechariah, and Malachi, there is no allusion to the idolatry of the "Jewry of the land"; and also nothing about the sin of idolatry, which fact we have stressed above.[13] Likewise, there is in Ezra and Nehemiah no mention of clashes between the diaspora and the inhabitants of Judah, or between the returnees and the brethren who cast out. Thus both the assumption and the exegesis are fiction and distortion. Further, in chapters 56–65 there is contention between the faithful and those who deny, but not a word concerning opposition between the exiles and the people of the land. There is, therefore, in these prophecies no trace of the real struggle of the returnees with their non-Israelite antagonists. And even the imagined struggle with the "Jewry of the land" can be discovered only by means of interpretation and allusion. The land of Israel hypothesis of the rebukes is, therefore, to be rejected. To be sure, there is mention of idolatry in the land of Israel in 57:5–11; 65:7; but here the reference is to the sins of the fathers. We shall consider the reprimands in this chapter, and return to the problem of idolatry in the period of the second Temple in Chapter III.

In addition, however, to the fact that the history of the exiles who returned from Babylon to the land of Israel is not reflected in these prophecies, there is the even more striking fact that there is no indication of the actual return to Zion, the nature, that is, of the aliyah by permission of Cyrus. Our knowledge of the return is from the book of Ezra. But would we have been able to infer from the prophecies of Isa. 40–66 that there had ever been an aliyah of the kind there described; and, in particular, that the prophet himself had been associated in it? It is true that Deutero-Isaiah is the prophet of redemption. But there is no reason to designate him "the prophet of the return to Zion"; and he is not to be thought of as the preacher of the aliyah by grace of Cyrus in the time of Sheshbazzar and Zerubbabel. Deutero-Isaiah announces the redemption in glowing words. In colorful phrases he describes the glorious ingathering of the exiles in the sight of all the nations. Concerning the actual aliyah by grace of the pagan monarch he does not preach. He does not call on the people to make contributions for the return, to "help" with silver and gold, and with beasts (see Ezra 1:3–6). The real aliyah was a matter of a caravan, which had to cross the desert by a difficult and exhausting route, depending for protection on guards and cavalry. Could men have been aroused to undertake a trek of this kind by description of a splendid progress on broad highways through groves of cypress and plane trees and springs of water? Would it not, on the contrary, have been requisite to strengthen them to endure the hardships of the desert route? The challenges: "Go ye forth from Babylon" (48:20), "Depart ye, depart ye, go ye out from thence," (52:11–12) refer to the miraculous aliyah of all the people. They are unrelated to the actual return. The actual aliyah and its fate are not mentioned at all in chapters 40–66. Only its overall purpose is mentioned there: the hope of rebuilding the Temple.[14]

The crisis of the year 539

The foregoing implies that the historical horizon of chapters 40–66 is the period of the appearance of Cyrus, of his great wars, his victories over Media, Lydia, and Babylon, and a limited number of years after the conquest of Babylon in the year 539. This is the year of crisis of Deutero-Isaiah. His high hopes were not realized. The actual aliyah of history was not the solution of his dream. But his ardent faith in redemption did not give way. He continued to proclaim the tidings of salvation. Yet the spiritual crisis stamped his assurances after 539 with a new character. We may accept Glahn's judgment that Deutero-Isaiah continued to prophesy until about the year 530. But he says nothing of the aliyah or of the fate of the returnees. And we must assume that all his prophecies were spoken in Babylon. The crisis of the year 539 accounts adequately for the difference between the earlier and the later prophecies, to the end of the book; and there is no need to assume that the prophet himself went from Babylon to the land of Israel.

Linguistic unity. Diversity of literary forms

Chapters 40–66 are marked by unity of vocabulary and literary style. About this there is, in general, no difference of opinion so far as it applies to 40–55 as a whole. Also in 56–66 there are whole chapters and fragments which all the critics agree are written in the language of 40–55. These are primarily chapters 60–62. But in the remaining chapters, also, there is a linguistic and stylistic element which unites them with 40–55, a fact on which Glahn and Torrey in particular insist.[15] This is proven also, though indirectly, by Elliger,[16] who tries to prove that in 40–55 there are chapters and sections and expressions which belong, according to their language, to Trito-Isaiah, the author of 56–66 and disciple of Deutero-Isaiah and editor of his book.

But withal, there are in chapters 40–66 definite literary units distinguished from the other prophecies by ideology and idiom. These can be removed without causing a break or disturbing the sequence of the prophecies. Of this category are the four songs which, since Duhm, have been called the songs of the servant of the Lord. According to the accepted reckoning, they are 42:1–4 (or 1–7); 49:1–6 (or 1–9); 50:4–9; 52:13–53:12. The servant and his task are described in these songs in very characteristic manner, and the idiom also is distinctive, in particular, the idiom of the fourth song. The polemics against idolatry, 40:19–20; 41:6–7; 44:9–20; 46:6–7 are also distinctive; and some critics deny them to Deutero-Isaiah. The satirical lament for Babylon of chapter 47 stands apart, and it also has been denied to Deutero-Isaiah. Also distinctive are the passages 49:14–23 and 54:1–17, wherein Zion is the forsaken wife. The invectives of these chapters, in particular chapters 57–59, are unique, and also the lamentations for the destruction, 51:17–23; 63:7–64:11; and, finally, the prophecies of vengeance: 59:16–19; 63:1–6. Even more striking, chapters 40–48 are a section set apart from the rest of the prophecies by subject matter and also by vocabulary.

Biblical criticism explains this variety of the prophetic writings in its usual manner: the book is not the work of one prophet—rather, it evolved over a long period. Later authors (or at least one later writer, a disciple of the prophet) reworked the prophecies, added whole chapters, rephrased old prophecies, imitated the prophet and copied his style, carried on his work and included their own words in his writings. The critics undertake the task of separating the original and the copied styles by farfetched distinctions; and also of dis-

tinguishing what is original from the later additions and re-
workings.

With respect to these endeavors, the same question is to
be asked which we have asked in connection with the books
of other prophets: if later writers reworked the prophecies, rephrased them, if they added chapters and segments, why is
there an obviously uniform historical perspective? Why are
subsequent events not explicitly reflected? Why is Cyrus, and
only Cyrus, mentioned?

Further, these critical efforts to interpret depend on the
assumption that the prophet expressed a fixed and limited set
of ideas, and that he was confined within narrow literary and
stylistic bounds. There are favorite topics which he is forced
to hash and rehash, and a given number of words and expressions which are the limit of his vocabulary. Whatever tran-
scends these bounds is not his.[17] Does the fact that the prophet,
in a given period of his life, consoled fervently imply that he
could not rebuke harshly at other times? Obviously he could
not rebuke in the style of consolation. Thus he would naturally deride in satirical style and bewail in elegiac style.[18]
Also, the prophet did not compose *ex nihilo*. He was well-
versed in literature. Chapters 40–66 show the influence of the
first Isaiah, Jeremiah, Zephaniah, Ezekiel, Lamentations, and
of the psalm and wisdom literature. There is nothing surprising in the fact that in many prophecies the influence of
certain literary models predominates, of which no trace can
be recognized in the consolation prophecies. The linguistic
connection which links all the prophecies proves that they are
the creation of one prophet, a conclusion which will be confirmed by the analysis which follows.

The literary units and their combination.
Key words

The hypothesis that the prophetic books are composed of
small units, separate "oracles" which were combined by editors,

and not always in proper order, originated in the school of Gunkel. The critics of this school determine the individual units on the basis of literary types or according to indications of introduction and conclusion. The error of the system is its confusion of type or form units with units of composition. An author may combine various literary modes, thus parable, lament, rebuke, consolation, etc., in a single work. He may construct his work link by link, each formally separated from the other, yet all combined into a single composition.[19] On the basis of his assumption, Gressmann distinguished forty-nine units in chapters 40–55. Subsequently, Köhler discovered seventy units, Volz fifty, in addition to the servant songs, Mowinckel forty-one (outside of the servant songs), and Begrich seventy or more.[20]

In addition, Mowinckel tries to prove that chapters 40–55 were assembled, not by the prophet himself, but by a disciple-editor. Opposing the opinion of Budde, who argues that 40–55 were assembled according to a well-thought plan, Mowinckel thinks that there is no order or plan in this collection of prophecies. The prophet left behind separate prophecies, loose leaves, and the editor was unable to sort them out chronologically or by subject matter; wherefore he arranged them in mechanical, superficial manner on the basis of linguistic and subject associations. The primary ordering principle was of key words. The redactor placed prophecies one after the other if he found the same words in them, in particular at their beginnings or ends. Occasionally, in addition to this principle of arrangement, he arranged them according to topic. But there is no relationship to a regular progress in the work of composition.

For example, the first four units (40:1–2, 3–5, 6–8, 9–11) are placed together because of the key words: and proclaim; a voice calleth (proclaimeth); hark! one (a voice) saith: Proclaim; lift up thy voice. In fact, these passages also have common subject matter. 40:12–31 is also connected with the foregoing units by word repetitions, thus: mountains and hills (12) high mountain (9); he bloweth upon them and they wither (24); withereth . . . the breath of the Lord bloweth upon it (7). The question: who hath raised up? (41:2) connects the unit 41:1–4, 8–13 with 40:12–31: who hath measured? (12) who hath meted? (13), etc. Fear not . . . I help thee (41:14) connects 41:14–16 with 10 and 13: Fear not . . . I help thee. The holy One of Israel (41:14, 16, 20) connects 41:17–20 with the preceding verses. Vv. 41:21–29 are connected with 41:1–13 by the reference to Cyrus (2, 25) and by the reference words: first . . . the last (4), the former (first) things . . . things to come (22); and so forth. On the basis of this theory, Mowinckel argues that the servant songs (by his reckoning 42:1–4; 49:1–6; 50:4–11; 52:13–53:12) are not to be included within the framework of this first section because they are not connected with the units which precede them by key words. The songs can be removed whereby the sections which precede them are attached to the section which follows by connecting words. The same rule is applied to chapter 47. It is not connected by reference words to what comes before and after it. Therefore it is not to be attributed to Deutero-Isaiah, and was added to his book subsequent to the collection and reduction of his prophecies.

Mowinckel's concept is mechanical and not convincing. In the first place, non-rigid connections, such as these connecting words which he finds, can be found among almost all the prophecies. Even if the prophecies had been transmitted to us in confusion, as loose leaves, without any order, there would still be connecting words among them. Moreover, it is obvious that a technical editor, who might arrange prophecies according to use of the same words, would still bring together prophecies of a single dominant theme, because in them the use of the same words and the common subject matter would be very evident. A technical editor would naturally place after chapter 40:1–11 all the prophecies which deal with the return of the exiles and which describe the manner of the return, that

is, 41:17–20; 42:10–17; 43:16–21; 48:20–21; 49:8–13; 52:
7–12. There are continuity words among all these passages.[21]
And thus, on the basis of subject matter, the editor would
bring together the anti-idolatry polemical prophecies (40:
18–20; 41:7; 44:9–21; 46:6–7), the prophecies concerning
Cyrus, the two prophecies concerning Egypt-Ethiopia-Seba
(43:3; 45:14), the four concerning Babylon-Chaldea (43:14;
47; 48:14, 20), etc.

Repeated words. Artificial transitions. Stylistic breaks

And yet there is a degree of validity in Mowinckel's
thesis. He sensed the special literary quality of these prophecies,
even though he failed to see the matter in its entirety and did
not correctly assess its character. There are, indeed, reference
(catch) words which tie prophecy with prophecy. But it is not
because they were so arranged by an editor that the words
come close together. There are, in fact, many more of them
than Mowinckel noticed; and, what is essential, they recur
within the individual prophecies, and they pass from one
prophecy to another. There are words and expressions which
characterize entire sections. Throughout chapters 40–48, for
example, the "I" of divinity (I am the Lord, etc.) is stressed;
and the phrases "first . . . last," "the former things," "the new
things," and many others occur and recur.

This is not a matter of technical arrangement. Rather it
has to do with literary composition: this poet loves to repeat
words and phrases in a particular poetic unit, and also among
units which are more or less closely connected in a single
creative process. We have already considered Deutero-Isaiah's
way of repeating words and expressions. Word-plays are frequent, and he enjoys using words with several meanings.
Torrey cites twenty-eight examples, indicating the virtuosity of

the prophet in the use of words which recur in various senses.[22] But he is fond also of repeating words without changes of meaning. Köhler observed that the author of chapters 40–55 loved variation in the sense of repetition of words in different combinations and orders and also recurring (echoing) sounds, that is, the simple repetition of words in successive verses.[23] Köhler argues that Deutero-Isaiah sometimes repeats words and phrases for aesthetic reasons, but also at times because of the poverty of his vocabulary.[24]

In fact, however, the repetitions are not adequately explained by artistic intent, and certainly not by poverty of vocabulary. This prophet possesses a very rich vocabulary. But he was influenced in his writing, aside from the aesthetics of the matter, by word and subject association. It is as though the words direct him, a phenomenon similar to that found in Hosea 4–14.[25] Hosea also loves to repeat words, and to string words together with different meanings. But Hosea is able to bend words to his artistic purpose. He combines words in new phrases with consummate artistry; and he knows the secret of restraint in this respect. Not so Deutero-Isaiah. The repetitions in his prophecies are exaggerated in the extreme, and association takes precedence over artistic intent. If in Hosea 4–14 words are sown as "the growth of the field," in the present prophecies they are as agitated flocks of birds sweeping down on the poet; and there are word-flocks which vanish and subsequently reappear. It may be assumed that this reflects the passionate temperament of the prophet. Even his words seem to have temperament. They swoop down on him as though they would prevent him from seeking other words of his vocabulary. The peculiar character of the word repetition of these prophecies, whether with changed or unchanged meaning, is that it is frequently extremely mechanical, which implies that the second use is not really suited to the subject matter, and is wholly a matter of word association. This is the artificial transition or stylistic discontinuity which is characteristic of this prophet. It is the apex of the influence of word association.

79

Examples

The four segments of chapter 40:1–11 are knit together by the words "voice" and "proclaim"; also by "saith"
(1), "saith . . . And he saith" (6), "say" (10); and by "your
God" (1, 10), "our God" (4, 8). Vv. 6 and 5 are connected by "all flesh"; 7 and 8 by: "The grass withereth"
et seq. "But the word (ודבר) of our God" (8) goes back
to ". . . the Lord hath spoken (דבר)" (5). "High (גבה)
mountain" (9) goes back to "mountain and hill (גבעה)"
(4). V. 10 is linked to v. 9 by "Behold," and v. 11 to v. 10
by "His arm."

With respect to content: the tiding "Behold your God"
(9) carries on the good news of the appearance of "the glory
of the Lord to be seen by all flesh" (5); and the tiding
"Behold, the Lord . . . will come" (10) follows and gives
substance to the prophecy concerning "the way of the Lord"
and "A highway for our God" (3).

Vv. 12–31 (ch. 40) are connected with the preceding
not only by "mountains and hills" (12) and "He bloweth . . .
and they wither," but also by "the breath of the Lord" (7, 13),
the latter a typical connection which we shall consider below.
Further, "All the nations" (15, 17) continues the subject "all
flesh." In this segment there is a wealth of recurring words.
The interrogative "who" occurs six times. Then there are:
meted out with the span (12), Who hath meted out
(13); the dust of the earth (12), the foundations of the
earth (21), the circle of the earth (22), the judges of
the earth (23), root in the earth (24), the ends of the
earth (28); in a balance (12), the balance (15); His
counsellor (13), took He counsel (14); that He might
instruct (make Him know) (13), knowledge . . . that He
made Him to know (14), Know ye (21), Hast Thou . . .
known (28); and instructed (gave discernment to) Him

. . . of discernment (14), Have ye, understood (discerned) (21), His discernment (28); And taught Him . . . And taught Him (14); of right . . . the way (14), My way . . . my right (27); Behold . . . Behold (15); Behold, the nations (15), All the nations (17); are counted (15, 17). The negative (אֵין) is used in the phrases: not sufficient . . . not sufficient (16), past searching out (28), hath no might (29), and also in the expressions: as nothing . . . and vanity (17), to nothing . . . as a thing of nought (vanity) (23). Also: To whom then will ye liken . . . likeness (18), To whom will ye liken Me (25); The image . . . the craftsman . . . (gold)smith . . . the (silver)smith (19), craftsman . . . image (20); Hath it not . . . (21, four times), Hast not . . . hast thou not (28); Know ye . . . hear ye (21), hast thou (not) known? hast thou (not) heard? (28); that sitteth . . . and the inhabitants (sitters) . . . to dwell in (sit) (22); Scarce are . . . (24, three times); might . . . power (26), power . . . hath no might (29), renew their strength (power) (31); fainteth not, neither is weary (28), to the faint (29) and faint and be weary (29), they shall not be weary . . . and not faint (31).

In chapter 41, also, there are many words which are repeated and pass from one verse or strophe to another. But it is highly significant that the recurring words of chapter 40 reappear in 41. There are also words which occur only once in chapter 40, and which reappear in chapter 41. They are, therefore, to be seen as reference words (catchwords) of a larger literary section (see Appendix 1).

The remaining chapters of 40–55 bear the same imprint. They are woven together by a kind of linguistic network of recurring words.

Highly characteristic of these chapters are the contrived transitions and the breaks in style which we have discussed above.

We find a typical artificial transition even in the introduction to these prophecies. The voice which calls (40:3–5) proclaims immediately impending good news: Clear the way of the Lord, etc.; and, similarly, the bearer of good tidings to Jerusalem (9–11). In both passages the good tidings are the consolation and redemption which are shortly to come. But the subject matter of vv. 6–8 is quite different. Here are no good tidings of the moment, rather a timeless established truth, derived from the psalm and wisdom literature, specifically Ps. 103:15–17 (cf. 90:5–6), the everlasting mercy of God. The good news of redemption is indeed based on this religious truth. But the truth itself is not a "tidings," and not a matter to be revealed by a voice which calls. The manner of this "good news" is forced, dragged in by the proclamations which precede and follow it.

The breath of the Lord (v. 7) is a natural blast of wind which dries the grass; but in v. 13 the same words signify something completely different, to wit, the higher knowledge, the divine intellect. The metaphor of v. 7 is artificial and an instance of word association with v. 13. There are in Deutero-Isaiah very many cases of word association, wherein a word used subsequently determines its use in earlier passages. A phrase which the prophet has in mind apparently gets the better of him beforehand. Another example is to be found in v. 9: be not afraid! This admonition, addressed to the visionary bearer of good tidings to Jerusalem, is surprising and out of context. Why should he be afraid to lift up his voice? But in the subsequent prophecies, 41:10, 13; 43:1, 5; 44:2, the prophet turns five times to the fearful trembling "worm Jacob" with the heartening cry: Fear not. These are the words which bore down on him when he was speaking of the messenger of good tidings of chapter 40.

The transition in vv. 12–14 (ch. 40) by means of recurring words is quite artificial. The questions of v. 12 (who hath measured, etc.) imply a positive answer, that is, it is God. But the questions of vv. 13–14 (who hath meted, etc.) imply a negative answer, that is, no creature. It is the interrogative "who," with which the rhetorical questions begin, which unifies the passages. The word "meted" in v. 12 means

measured with a measure of quantity ("with the span," v. 12);
in v. 13, the meaning of "meted" is "searching out," "to
come to the bottom of" (cf. the last line of v. 28). This, also,
is word association and not a play on words. The connection
of vv. 19–20, concerning the making of the image, with the
rest of the text is quite tenuous, and some critics delete them.
In any case, the concept of the supreme majesty of God,
which the prophet expresses in vv. 12–31, is cosmic: there
is nothing in the world and its fullness to compare to God.
The idea that a graven image is not to be likened to Him
in power is dragged in and, in fact, is out of context. But
the prophet's subsequent polemic against image-idolatry
is already stirring in his mind; and from the (cosmic) question: To whom then will ye liken God? he passes to the question: Or what likeness will ye compare unto Him? And after
the word "likeness," the image and the casting are dragged
in. The transition is artificial; but it is characteristic of Deutero-Isaiah, and vv. 19–20 are not to be deleted (re 41:6–7,
see below).

An incongruity similar to that of vv. 6–8 occurs in
v. 21 (ch. 40). The prophet here argues that Israel ought
to know and to understand who is the Creator of the world.
This insight is the recognition of a religious truth, and not
the knowledge of an historical occurrence. But the prophet uses
the expressions: Know ye not? hear ye not? Hath it not been
told you from the beginning? etc.[26] The telling from the beginning refers to an event which is foreseen by the prophetic
spirit before its occurrence; and the expression is out of place
when applied to the awareness of a truth having to do with the
creation of the world. The words: know, hear, been told (v.
21) are used, in fact, in various combinations in chapters 40–
48 to express the witness of prophecy to the validity of Israel's
faith (see 41:22–23, 26; 42:9; 43:9, 12; 44:7–8; 45:19, 21;
46:10; 48:3, 5–6, 14, 20). For the use of the word-phrase
"from the beginning" (מראש), compare 41:4, 26; 48:16.
Clearly there is here a stylistic discrepancy and, in addition, a
reflex association: the witness of prophecy is already at work in

the mind of the prophet, and the expression is forcing its way out. The word appears also in v. 28, but there in context harmonizing with the subject matter.

In 40:28; 41:5, 9, we find the recurring expression "the ends of the earth" in adjacent prophecies. But the expression fits the subject matter only in 41:5. On the other hand, the expression, "Creator of the ends of the earth" is very awkward; and the phrase, "whom I have taken hold of from the ends of the earth," as applied to Israel, is inappropriate, since Egypt, in relation to Israel, is not "the ends of the earth." This, then, is another case of word association and stylistic incongruity. The exegetes have long argued that the expression, "let . . . renew strength" (41:1) is unsuited to the subject matter, and some scholars would emend it.[27] In fact, however, this is an association of words derived from 40:31, and should not be emended.[28] We find similar transitions and stylistic breaks in the remainder of the chapters. See Appendix 1.

Chapters 56–66

We have remarked that in chapters 56–66 there is a literary quality which unites them with 40–55; and that a supposed gap between these sections can be staked out only by artifices and casuistic analyses. In addition, it should be observed that 56–66 are marked by the same stylistic peculiarities which mark 40–55. In these chapters, also, there are many recurring words which are repeated both within the chapters and from chapter to chapter;[29] and also the forced transitions and stylistic incongruities which characterize chapters 40–55.

Examples, chapter 56: Keep ye . . . and do . . . that doeth . . . that keepeth . . . and keepeth . . . from doing . . . that keep . . . that keepeth (vv. 1–6); justice . . . and My favor (justice) (v. 1); that holdeth fast by it . . . and hold fast by My covenant . . . and hold fast by My covenant (2, 4, 6); That keepeth the sabbath from profaning it . . . that keep My sabbaths . . . that keepeth the sabbath from profaning it

(2, 4, 6); the alien that hath joined himself to the Lord . . .
the aliens that join themselves to the Lord (3, 6); a memorial
(hand) and a monument (name) . . . an everlasting memorial
(name) . . . the name of the Lord (5–6); who gathereth . . .
I will gather . . . beside those of him who are gathered (8);
All ye beasts . . . all ye beasts (9); come . . . come (9, 12);
are all blind . . . all dogs . . . They all turn to their own way
(10–11); without knowledge (do not know) . . . know not
where they have enough . . . cannot understand (know)
(10–11); dumb dogs . . . the dogs (10–11); cannot understand . . . none considering (understanding) (11; 57:1).
Chapter 57: And no man layeth it to heart . . . nor laid
it to thy heart (1, 11). Against whom . . . against whom (4);
children of transgression . . . that stay the children (4–5);
that inflame (הנחמים) . . . pacify myself (אנחם) (5–6);
in the valleys . . . the valley (5–6); among the smooth
stones (בחלקי) . . . thy portion (חלקך) (6); Thou hast
offered (העלית) . . . wentest thou up (עלית) . . . hast thou
set up (ותעלי) (6–8); Hast thou set thy bed . . . Hast thou
set up thy symbol . . . nor laid (set) it to thy heart (7, 8, 11);
Hast thou set thy bed . . . Thou hast enlarged thy bed . . .
whose bed thou lovest (7–8); whose hand thou sawest
. . . renewed of strength (hand) (8, 10); and (be) in fear . . .
fearest not (11); And as for Me, thou hast not remembered
Me . . . Therefore thou fearest Me not (11); clear the way
. . . of the way of My people (14); Take up (הרימו) . . .
the High (רם) . . . in the high (14–15); inhabiteth . . .
Holy . . . I dwell (inhabit) in holy (15); contrite . . . of the
contrite ones (15); humble spirit . . . the spirit of the humble
(15); to revive . . . to revive (15); will I be wroth . . . I was
wroth . . . I was wroth (16–17); in the way . . . his ways
(17–18); will heal him . . . And I will heal him (18–19);
Peace, peace . . . There is no peace (19, 21); But the wicked
. . . concerning the wicked (20–21); troubled (cast up) . . .
And (they) cast up (20).

We find a similar continuous linguistic web in the remaining chapters; and, likewise in these chapters, very many

artificial transitions and also incongruities. Thus, the keeping
of the sabbath in its holiness and the keeping of the hand
from doing evil, which are qualitatively distinct concepts, are
joined in 56:2 (That keepeth the sabbath . . . And keepeth
his hand) by the associate word. The verb-root, ענג (in
hithpael), occurs in the sense of mockery only in 57:4, and
is used in this verse only because of word association with
55:2, 58:14, and 66:11 (in the sense, delight). The phrase:
The restorer of paths to dwell in (58:12) is awkward. The
passage relates to the establishment of permanent settlements,
which is not a matter of paths (and there is no resemblance
to Job 24:13); and is the consequence of the association
משובב (restorer) . . . תשיב (turn away) (58:12–13).
Wholly artificial is the transition: And the Lord saw . . .
That there was no justice, and He saw that there was no man,
and was astonished . . . Therefore His own arm brought salvation to Him, And His righteousness, it sustained Him
(59:15–16). This indicates the reflex influence of the hymn
of vengeance of 63:1–6: And I looked, and there was none
to help, and I beheld in astonishment, and there was none to
uphold, Therefore Mine own arm brought salvation to Me,
etc. Word association is responsible for: And he saw that
there was no . . . (59:15–16), and also for the mention of
"justice, And righteousness," in 59:14. The רוח (breath)
of the Lord of 59:19 is the natural breath, which is the movement of the air, and the רוחי in the following: My spirit
that is upon thee (v. 21) is the holy spirit. This is an artificial
association similar to that of 40:7, 13.

The clause: The rams of Nebaioth shall minister unto
thee (60:7) is passing strange because the root-word, minister (שרת), is not used with respect to sacrifices. Some
critics substitute ישחרונך (shall seek thee) or: ירשתך (be
thy possession); others delete the word phrase "shall minister unto thee."[30] In fact, however, this is a word association deriving from v. 10. As a bridegroom putteth on a
priestly diadem (61:10) is an expression *sui generis* and fol-

lows the imagery of v. 6: But ye shall be named the priests of the Lord. The play on words, I have stained (אגאלתי) ... (my) redemption (גאולי) (63:3-4) is graceless enough. The figure: That caused His glorious arm to go at the right hand of Moses (63:12) is incongruous. There is no scriptural parallel to the causing of an arm to go. The figure derives by reflex association from the phrase: that led them (caused to go) through the deep, of the following verse. The expression: Even from Thy holy and glorious habitation (63:15) is singular, since the word glorious (or beauty) (תפארת) is used only with respect to the Temple here below and its sanctity, and never with respect to the heavenly habitation (see Isa. 60:7, 13; 64:10; Ezek. 24:25; Ps. 78:61; Lam. 2.5; II Chron. 3:6; cf. Exod. 28:2, 40.) Here, again, the cause of the prophet's use of the word is the association of the words glorify (פאר) and glorious, which are so prominent in chapters 60-64 (see in particular 64:10). The word לשבועה in 65:15 means: for a curse. But the והנשבע of the next verse refers to an oath which implies an affirmation of faith. The "former troubles" of 65:16 are followed in the next verse by "the former things" in the sense of the whole of the old creation. The expression: Even so I will choose their mockings (66:4) is awkward, and incompatible with the end of the verse. The sense is: I will requite them according to their mockings. The verb, I will choose (66:4), derives from the expression: According as they have have chosen their ways (v. 3); and from: And chose that in which I delighted not (the last line of v. 4). (See also 65:12; 56:4.)

Chapters 56-55

Chapter 56 is linked specifically to chapter 55, just as the other chapters of 40-66 are linked one to the other, and in very striking fashion, by many reference words. Thus: an everlasting memorial . . . That shall not be cut off (56:5) follows: for a memorial, for an everlasting sign that shall not be cut off (55:13). The root כרת recurs in the phrases: by My covenant . . . everlasting . . . That shall not be cut off (יכרת) (56:4–5) and: And I will make (a covenant) (ואכרתה) . . . an everlasting covenant (55:3). And choose the things which please Me (56:4) follows: accomplish that which I please (55:11). The name of the Lord (56:6) follows: to the Lord for a memorial (name) (55:13). My salvation is near (56:1) reflects: while He is near (55:6). The content of 56:1 is parallel to 51:4–5. The motif of 55:5 is the "joiners." Behold . . . a nation that thou knowest not . . . shall run unto thee because of the Lord thy God, etc. Even them will I bring . . . And make them joyful (56:7) follows: with joy . . . (ye shall) be led forth (55:12). The conclusion: who gathereth the dispersed (56:8) is similar to the termination of chapter 55.

The liberal-Protestant severance of chapters 56–66

In view of the foregoing, the question arises: why did Duhm divide chapters 40–66 precisely at 55:13, and make of 56–66 a third book? To this there is but one answer: in chapter 56 there is reference to the sabbath and also to the anticipation of the renewal of the cult in the Temple. Duhm is one of those critics who strongly maintain the extreme position that the true prophet is a liberal Protestant who negates the ritual commandments. The Christian scholars look upon Deutero-Isaiah as the founder of prophetic universalism and one of the harbingers of Christianity. How, then, can a prophecy concerning the sabbath and the Temple be the message of such a prophet? It is this consideration which, we must conclude, is determinant.[31] The critics, accepting this theological naïveté as a scientific discovery which fixes an epoch, have agreed that chapters 56–66 are to be separated from 40–55. However, the uniformity of style of the whole of 40–66 and, in particular, the links between 56 and 55, prove that there is no basis for the separation. It is true that there are differences in subject matter between the earlier and later chapters. But there was a severe crisis in the life of the prophet. The hope which he attached to Persia had been disappointed. On this account it is natural that there is a great difference between his earlier and later prophecies.

Chapter sequence. Compilations and sections

There is in this collection of prophecies no such "plan" either as a whole or in parts, as Budde thinks. Here, as in the books of (the first) Isaiah and Ezekiel, the prophecies are arranged according to the chronology of their composition, and express the thought of the prophet as it developed in successive periods.[32] In Isa. 40–66, the prophecies are grouped into three collections, distinct one from the other, and yet interwoven and unified by content and language patterns. The grouping is evidence of chronological ordering; the groups reflect composition of the prophecies in distinct stages.

Most strikingly, the first group, chapters 40–48, forms a distinct unit. This unit comes first in the book and also chronologically, for in it alone is there mention of the conquests of Cyrus and of the downfall of Babylon. After chapter 48, neither Cyrus nor the Chaldeans are mentioned. Further, it is unique in many respects. Only here do we find polemic prophecies against the stupidity of idol worship (from 40:19 to 48:11). Here only is the argument from the fact of prophecy (from 41:4, 22 ff. to 48:16). Only in this section is God extolled as the Creator of the world (from 40:12 to 48:13; in later chapters the only praise of this kind, 51:13, 16, is a sort of afterthought). There is in this section no moral chastisement, nor any prophecy of national vengeance. Also the symbol of Zion, the abandoned mother, is absent. The object of consolation is Israel. Further, this section is linguistically distinct. Understandably, we find only in it the phraseology which has to do with the polemics against idols, the proof by prophecy, and the doxology by reason of cosmogony. This section is marked by the frequent, emphatic I am the Lord, or, in absolute sense, I am God (some twenty times, beginning with 41:4 to 48:17), which, from chapter 48, occurs only a few times. It is strange that the word אף (scarce) occurs only in this section (twenty-four times from 40:24 to 48:15), and then completely vanishes.

The third group, chapters 58–66, also stands out as a distinct section. This is a scroll of censure, judgment, and retribution. Only in this collection do we find chapters of moral rebuke, 58–59, 66:1–4. There is no rebuke because of idol worship, but there is rebuke on account of the worship of spirits (Fortune and Destiny, 65:11), because of black rites in gardens and graveyards, and because of the eating of flesh of abominable things (65–66). In this section only are there detailed prophecies of God's warfare with the enemies prior to the redemption, a warfare which will also be judgment of the wicked of Israel (59:15–20; 61:2; 63:1–6; 65–66).[33] Only in this section is there complaint at the delay of the coming of redemption (59:11; 63:7–64:11; see also 58:3).

The second section (chs. 49–57) serves as transition between the first and third. The figure of Zion the bereaved mother appears in 49:14–21; 54:1–17, and is continued with thematic variations in chapters 60–62 and 66:7–12. Vehement nationalistic prophecies of vengeance occur in 49:23, 26; 50:9; 51:8, 22–23 and continue into the third section. Censure because of the sins of the current generation comes in 50:2; 55:7; 56:10–57:21, and continues into the third section. There is no polemic against the stupidity of idol worship, but in 57 there is rebuke because of Israel's going astray after gentile idolatry (in the past, as we shall see below). There is a definitely societal theme only in 56:10–57:2; and moral rebuke is contained only in the third section. The sanctuary and the sacrifices are mentioned for the first time in 56:7, and thereafter frequently in 60–66.

From the foregoing we may conclude that the traditional division into three compilations is original and reflects the process of the development of these prophecies. This is to be seen also in the connection between the concluding verses of the first two sections and the prophecies which immediately precede them. The word "peace" in 48:22 follows "thy peace" in v. 18. The word "peace" in 57:21 follows "peace, peace" in v. 19. The word-phrase "concerning the wicked" in 21 follows "But the wicked" in 20. All three sections close with a warning to the wicked.

In addition, various units can be distinguished in chapters 40–66 on the basis of dominant themes. Chapters 40–41 are united by the recurring words: as nothing, as nought, as vanity (40:17, 23; 41:11, 12, 24, 29), words which predominate only in this section. The expression: fear thou not, or: be not afraid (40:9; 41:10, 13, 14; 43:1, 5; 44:2) recurs in chapters 40–44. The words, my servant, servant, etc., always in the singular, occur nineteen times from 41:8 to 53:11. The expression, the servants of the Lord, appears in 54:17; and thence to the end of the book, servants are spoken of in the plural. My servant Jacob, and Israel My servant, are to be found only in 41:8; 44:1, 2; 45:4; 48:20. Chapters 42–49 are a segment marked by the repeated occurrence of the words: blind, deaf, etc. (42:7, 16, 18–19; 43:8). The root word יצר (potter, to form, etc.) occurs in various forms many times from 41:26 to 54:17; but it is predominant in particular in chapters 43–46 (43:1, 7, 10, 21; 44:1, 9, 10, 21, 24; 45:7, 9, 11, 18; 46:11). The words "joy" and "gladness" are to be found from 51:11 to the end of the book (55:12; 56:7; 60:15; 61:3, 7, 10; 62:5; 65:13, 18–19; 66:5, 10). Chapters 51–52 include prophecies with double opening phrases (51:9, 12, 17; 52:1, 11). The motif, "glorify," "glorious," is predominant in chapters 60–64 (60:7, 9, 13, 19, 21; 61:3, 10; 62:2; 63:12, 14, 15; 64:10).

Units such as these stand out beyond the various categories of individual prophecies and their groupings, and alongside the webs of recurring words, which connect the prophecies. This could not have happened if the prophecies had been collected and arranged on the basis of some extrinsic criterion, or if the editing had been confused, without order.[34] Of necessity it reflects the sequence of composition of the prophecies and definite changes which took place in the thought of their author during the stages of their creation.

The units

It is extremely difficult to determine the structure of the individual prophetic units of chapters 40–66. Gressmann's criterion, to fix the units on the basis of opening and closing words, is misleading, for in some compositions the prophet uses the opening and closing words repeatedly. We have already remarked that there are no captions in the book and no indications of the historical situation, and that the historical background of most of the prophecies cannot be recognized at all. The speech of Deutero-Isaiah is rhetorical and general, which makes specific attribution difficult. Certainly the prophecies do not consist of brief "oracles." They are not responses to men who seek answers from God. The prophet consoles, encourages, seeks to influence men's hearts, expresses thoughts and adduces evidence, things which are not adapted to brief "oracles." Because of the absence of captions, and on account of the torrential nature of his speech, it is difficult to determine most of the prophetic units, and we are able for the most part only to surmise.

Chapter 40 is a composite unit. It includes four proclamations of good tidings (1–11), a paragraph of meditation concerning cosmogony and derision of idolatry (12–26), and a cry of encouragement to Israel (27–31). It is a unit in that the tidings of consolation derive from the recognition of God's unity and omnipotence. Chapter 41:1–16 is the first prophecy concerning Cyrus, along with prophetic interpretation. Vv. 17–20 are the first description of the return of the exiles.

Vv. 21–29 are a unit of two parts, of which the topic is the proof from prophecy. Each part closes with a statement of the nothingness of the gods. Vv. 1–9, chapter 42, are the first of the songs of the servant of the Lord. Vv. 42: 10–43:14 are a composite prophecy concerning the redemption of the "blind nation." Vv. 43:16–44:5 are a prophecy concerning the former and the new things. Chapter 44:6–28 is a prophecy of redemption, and includes a polemic against idolatry. Vv. 1–13 of chapter 45 are a composite prophecy concerning the deeds of Cyrus. Vv. 14–25 are a prophecy of redemption of Israel and the world. Chapter 46 is a composite unit comprising a prophecy of the ruin of the gods of Babylon and derision of idolatry. Chapter 47 is a satirical lament for Babylon. Vv. 1–11, chapter 48, are a rebuke for Israel. Vv. 12–21, which are composed of three links, are the final prophecy concerning Babylon and Cyrus.[35]

Vv. 1–13 of chapter 49 are the second servant song. Vv. 14–26 are the first prophecy which includes the figure of Zion as the abandoned mother. It ends with a prophecy of vengeance. Vv. 1–2, chapter 50, are a prophecy of censure and of encouragement. Vv. 4–9 are the third servant song. Vv. 10–11 are a prophecy of rebuke. Vv 1–8, chapter 51, comprise three prophecies which begin respectively with the words: Hearken to Me, Attend unto Me, Hearken unto Me. From 51:9 to 52:11 there is a succession of prophecies of which the first words are repeated: Awake, awake; I, (even) I, etc. The lament for the destruction of Jerusalem of 51:17–23 is a paragraph to itself; and therewith the whole of 51:1–52:12 can be considered a single composition, of which the content is consolation and encouragement. Chapters 52:13–53:12 are the fourth and final song of the servant of the Lord. Chapter 54:1–17 is the second allegory of Zion the abandoned wife. Chapter 55:1–13 is a cry of repentance and of the promise of redemption. Chapter 56:1–8 is a prophecy of the approach of salvation, and reassurance to the aliens who join themselves to the Lord. Chapters 56:10–57:2 are a reproof of the watchmen who are blind. Chapter 57:3–21 is a rebuke to the scoffers and consolation to the contrite and the mourners.

Chapter 58 is the first moral chastisement of the compilation; and chapter 59, which is a rebuke and lamentation, the second. Chapter 60 foretells the glory of Zion, 61 the glory of the mourners of Zion, and 62 the glory of Zion and Israel. Vv. 1–6, chapter 63, are a vision of the downfall of "Edom," and 63:7–64:11 an elegy-psalm for the desolation of Jerusalem and the Temple. Chapter 65 is rebuke of those who betray and consolation for the faithful. Chapter 66 is a variegated prophecy which includes rebuke of the faithless, consolation of the faithful, and visions of the final judgment, the splendor of Jerusalem, and the ingathering of the exiles.

§3. CENSURE AND VISION

Prophet: neither scribe nor theologian

Deutero-Isaiah is a prophet, not an "author." He spoke directly to the people and did not spread his message solely by handbills.[36] Certainly, like other prophets, he also copied his prophecies into a book, for by that means only could he influence wider circles and reach the exiles in their various settlements. The "nation" to whom the prophet could speak person to person could never be more than a limited group. Even in the court of the Temple, not everyone there assembled could hear the prophet's voice. And it was unlikely that there would always be, among the listeners, someone who would remember what had been said and be able to report it accurately by word of mouth to those who had not heard it. The words of the prophets were spread abroad by means of scrolls, written by the prophet himself, or by a scribe at his dictation. This is realistically described in Jer. 36. The scroll of prophecies which Baruch wrote down "from the mouth of Jeremiah" was read on the fast day in the area of the Temple and the king's palace three times in three places, before three different assemblages. The words could reach wider circles only by means of proclamation and additional readings. The prophetic literature was fashioned of such original written scrolls; and thus also the book of prophecies of Deutero-Isaiah. The prophet spoke directly to an audience in the district where he lived, and put his words in writing in order to reach the diaspora settlements; and from his scrolls came the book.

The prophecies of Deutero-Isaiah bear the stamp of oratory. The prophet consoles, encourages, judges, rebukes, argues, and replies to objections. In his consolation speeches he addresses Israel in general and not just his present listeners.[37] This message is always good tidings to Israel in all its habitations and to Zion, the symbol of Israel's hope. On the other hand, in his reprimands of 56:9–58:14; 65–66, he is speaking to specific groups. We may assume the correctness of the hypothesis that he would appear before a congregation of exiles where they were wont to assemble for prayer on the sabbaths and holy days.[38]

Deutero Isaiah is not to be thought of as a theologian who expressed his own cogitations about God and His works.[39] There are religious propositions in the prophecies of Deutero-Isaiah. God is Creator of the world, and this is the basis of the prophet's faith in historical providence. Deutero-Isaiah argues the stupidity of idol worship and substantiates his words by the witness of the truth of prophecy. But religious-ethical ideas are to be found also in the writings of earlier prophets.[40] The prophetic form, that is, the expression of ideas as the word of God, is decisive. Thus, in the prophecies of Deutero-Isaiah also, the religious ideas are not presented as the result of the logical cognition of the prophet, as the fruit of his consideration of the attributes and works of God. Instead, they come as intuitive awareness by reason of direct revelation of God's word, and are spoken as the word of God.

95

Even what appears to be expression of the thought of the prophet is, in fact, the word of God. The passage 40:12–26, which includes cosmogonic praise of God and argument against idolatry, is spoken apparently in the third person concerning God. But v. 25 (To whom then will ye liken Me?) shows that the whole passage is, in fact, presented as God's word; and, similarly, the argument against idolatry in 46:5–7 (To whom will ye liken Me, etc.). The polemic against idolatry in 41:7; 44:9–20 is encased in a framework of God's word. The cosmogonic adulations of 45:7, 12, 18; 48:13; 51:15 are phrased as God's word, spoken in the first person. Similarly, the proofs by reason of true prophecy in 41:21–29; 42:9; 43:9–10; 44:7–8; 45:21; 46:10; 48:3–16 are phrased as the word of God. Deutero-Isaiah is, therefore, prophecy and never propositional theology.

Visions and imagery

Was Deutero-Isaiah an ecstatic, a beholder of visions? In his prophecies there are none of the usual prophetic descriptions of visions. There is no description of the revelation of God and His angels, such as in Isa. 6 or Jer. 1, or in the visions of Ezekiel and Zechariah. Nonetheless, Deutero-Isaiah was certainly a seer, gifted with prophetic insight. He heard mysterious voices. In the introduction to his prophecies he relates the experience of prophetic hearing. He hears God say: Comfort ye, comfort ye My people (40:1–2). He hears: one (a voice) calleth in the wilderness (3–5).[41] "Hark! one saith: 'Proclaim!'" (v. 6). And Deutero-Isaiah also sees visions. He does not describe the appearance of God or the angels in the prophetic vision; but visionary figures act in his prophecies. The visionary figure is not conceived as a supernatural being; rather it is an image which performs a function in the prophetic vision of the nature of the sentinel and the watchman of

Isa. 21:6–12. In 40:1–7 Deutero-Isaiah describes, it is true, only what he hears. But there are individual figures in the background. God orders someone to comfort His people and to speak to the heart of Jerusalem. Someone calls in the wilderness: Clear ye the way of the Lord, etc. In v. 6, the prophet himself converses with "the voice."[42] This is no realistic description; therefore it cannot be assumed that the reference is to real heavenly beings. These are sublime images with no more substance than visionary shadows. The visionary figure comes openly on the stage in 40:9: thou that tellest good tidings to Zion.[43] Clearly this is no vision of an angel. The prophet envisions a female herald and a high mountain. He commands her to ascend the mountain and to proclaim the good news of redemption to Zion and the cities of Judah. In 52:7–9, the messenger and the watchmen are vision-figures, and, similarly, the watchmen "that are the Lord's remembrancers" (62:6–7), whom the prophet has set upon the walls of Jerusalem. Visionary also is the questioner of 63:1–6 (Who is this that cometh from Edom . . . Wherefore is Thine apparel red . . .) Also the servant of the Lord of the servant songs is to be thought of as a vision-figure. This is, in fact, the key to understanding of these songs, as we shall observe below. And the court of justice, also, in which the case of Israel and its God versus the nations is tried, and which hears evidence and argumentation, is visionary, as will be seen in the following.

Universalism prior to Deutero-Isaiah

Deutero-Isaiah, contrary to the opinion which is prevalent among biblical scholars, is not the creator of universalist monotheism, nor of the vision of the turning of the gentiles from idolatry. Universalism is a basic, deep-rooted element in the religion of Israel. The universality of the divine regimen, belief in one God who is sole ruler of the whole world, is a concept which is found in every stratum and every source, with no exceptions, of the biblical literature. Belief in the universalism of God's grace and in God's revelation to all mankind in the beginning dominates the earliest accounts of creation (Gen. 1–11). To be sure, there is also the concept of Israel's election and the special grace of revelation to the patriarchs and to Israel at a later period of human history. But, even before the age of literary prophecy, the poets and narrators expressed the hope and desire that all nations should come to know the God of Israel. Isaiah, Micah, Zephaniah, Habakkuk, and Jeremiah envisioned the turning of the nations from idolatry in the end of days, and from them Deutero-Isaiah received the vision. Biblical criticism arrived at its erroneous conclusion, that Deutero-Isaiah was the founder of universalism, only because it followed vain paths in its efforts to determine the course of development of the biblical literature and the religion of Israel.

Deutero-Isaiah unacquainted with pagan religion

Deutero-Isaiah, like the other prophets, received monotheism as part of the inheritance of the people of Israel, an ancestral faith. He grew up in the monotheistic atmosphere of the nation, which was the religious climate of the diaspora as well. Along with the other biblical writers, he does not negate the reality of the gods; and he also indicates no awareness of the true nature of gentile idolatry. He regards paganism as belief in the divinity of idols which are the work of men's hands, as fetishism; and this is the basis of all his polemics against idolatry. His monotheism is of Israel and only Israel. There is no justification for the assertion that Deutero-Isaiah proclaimed that the gods were "cast down from their thrones,"[44] or that he rejected the claim of the gods that they were rulers of the world.[45] Deutero-Isaiah does not mention the gods even with a single word. There are no gods in his world, even as there are none in all of Scripture. They have no "thrones" and make no "claims." There are only idols to which the nations give honor due to God. The gods had ceased to be in Israel many generations ago. Deutero-Isaiah did not create monotheism. He inherited a faith long since established in Israel.

Likewise, there is no basis for efforts to attach the thought of Deutero-Isaiah to the spirit of the age, to the influence of the Babylonian civilization as it developed during the Persian period, that is, to the influence of Zarathustrian thought; or even to relate it to intellectual currents which appeared at that time in areas of Hellenistic culture.[46] The universalism of Deutero-Isaiah is rooted in the universalism of Israel, which is ancient and prophetic and unrelated to intellectual currents of the pagan world. The God in whose name Deutero-Isaiah speaks is unknown to the gentiles. There is no reference in his prophecies to groups in the gentile world which are spiritually akin to him; and also, there is no polemic whatsoever against the concepts of pagan faith.

Some critics discover in the style and content of Deutero-Isaiah's prophecies traces of an acquaintance with the Babylonian scriptures and the Babylonian mythological rites; and even "countless proofs" of a "direct Babylonian background" of his prophecies.[47] But the literary resemblances to Babylonian writings do not justify the conclusion. They are explained adequately by the common rhetoric and manners of speech of the ancient near east.[48] Moreover, the content of the prophecies proves that Deutero-Isaiah, like the other biblical authors, knew nothing of pagan religion.

The accuracy of Deutero-Isaiah's description of the making of idols is confirmed by Babylonian writings. It is evident also, from 46:1–4, that the prophet had observed the cultic processions of the Babylonian holy days.[49] But, like Ezekiel,[50] he reveals knowledge only of the externals of paganism and not of its beliefs. Thus he says nothing of its tenets; and his judgments of pagan beliefs are supplied in every instance by the biblical critics themselves. This is clearly evident in the proof by prophecy to which Deutero-Isaiah appeals so many times in chapters 40–48. Some critics contend that this proof is directed against the Babylonian belief in the oracles of their gods. Indeed, Astarte and Nebo also boast that their words are true and valid forever.[51] But the fact is that Deutero-Isaiah never says that the oracles of the gods are false. He argues that the gods do not foretell at all; they do not declare, they do not announce, there is none that heareth their utterances (41:26). And this is because they are graven images, molten images, and are unable to announce utterances. (Cf. 41:24, 28–29; 42:8–9; 44:7 f.; 45:19–21; 46:5–10; 48:3–5.) This is the argument also of Habakkuk: . . . dumb idols . . . can this teach? Behold it is overlaid with gold and silver, And there is no breath at all in the midst of it (2:18–19). This indicates that Deutero-Isaiah was completely unaware that the gentiles believed in oracle-gods, and attributed oracular utterances to them. And, on the other hand, he refers to the Babylonian belief in men who can foretell, in sorcerers and astrologers (astrologers, the star-gazers, 47:13). However, he, like the other biblical authors, thinks this divination is magical wisdom (44:25; 47:9–10, 12–13). God frustrates the "tokens," makes the magicians mad, makes their knowledge foolishness (44:25). Yet withal, this witchcraft is "wisdom," and its reality not wholly denied. Deutero-Isaiah, however, does not realize that the lore of the wizards and the astrologers is part of belief in the pagan gods. His knowledge of idolatry, therefore, is superficial and vague. We will return to the subject of the appeal to prophecy.

Earlier and more recent biblical critics have found indication of an attack on the dualism of Zarathustra or the early Persian religion in Isa. 45:7 (I form light and create darkness, I make peace and create evil).[52] In fact, however, there is no reference in this passage to any Persian doctrine. YHWH is described as the God of light and darkness in other scriptural passages without any Persian connection. The spirit of God hovers over the primeval darkness, and light is created by

God's word; God divides the light from the darkness (Gen. 1:1–5). He creates the lights of the day and the night (*ibid.*, 14–18). He makes the morning darkness, brings on the shadow of death in the morning, and darkens the day into night (Amos 4:13; 5:8). The gates of death are revealed unto Him; He brings light and darkness (Job 38:17, 19–20). He knows the going down of the sun; He makes darkness, and it is night (Ps. 104:19).

Opinions differ as to whether the first Persian kings were Zoroastrians. The opinion of those (including Nyberg)[53] who say that they were not Zoroastrians is persuasive, and for this there is convincing evidence in the stories of Herodotus. But in any event, there is no polemic in Scripture against the religion of Zoroaster or the ancient Persian folk religion. No Persian god is mentioned in the Bible, and there is no reference to any specific belief of the Persians. Deutero-Isaiah does not refer to the gods of Persia, nor does he reveal any knowledge of Persian beliefs; which fact cannot be set aside by any exegesis.

The historic significance of Deutero-Isaiah

The historic significance, to the nation and for world history, of the prophecy of Deutero-Isaiah is that it gave sublime expression to the great decision reached in that epoch in the soul of the nation. Deutero-Isaiah gave expression to the resolution of the crisis of national disaster, the enduring faithfulness, independent of any material and political circumstances, of Israel to its God; and also to Israel's absolute faith in the eventual triumph over paganism. The significance of the prophecy of Deutero-Isaiah is not the affirmation of the idea of monotheism, but the evidence implicit in the prophecy of the potency of the idea. The fateful question was whether the religion of Israel could survive in the contest with pagan cultural influence. To this question, answer is given in

Deutero-Isaiah, an answer for all generations. The prophet opened his prophecy with the good tidings of consolation and redemption, good tidings which are not solely of nationalistic import. This was at once an historic witness and a religious commitment. The prophecy of consolation is witness to the fact that there was indeed a people who looked forward to redemption, whose gaze was upward to its God, a people not brought by national calamity to the point of belief in the gods of its conquerors, a people from whose hearts the memory of Zion, ruined and desolate, had not been expunged by the brilliant pagan civilization. This was the nation to whom the prophet was sent. If there had been no nation, the prophet would not have been sent. If there had been no anticipation of consolation, the prophecy of consolation would not have been heard. There was at the moment no political-factual basis for the tidings of redemption, no Jerusalem fortified and defending itself; neither king, ministers, nor generals; no nation, army, military establishment; no one to stand guard. There was only faith. The nation hoped because it believed that its God was the one omnipotent God of the universe.

In the prophecy of Deutero-Isaiah the hope rises to the level of absolute confidence. It betokens the new covenant between Israel and its God, which was made after the national catastrophe, at the moment of divine wrath, on foreign soil, after the loss of all those favors of God with which Israel in earlier times had been endowed. The prophet affirms this covenant according to God's word. With soaring spirit, in joyful consciousness of firm faith, he promises the return of divine favor. Israel has not abandoned its God, and God has not abandoned Israel. The covenant is eternal, and in it is the assurance of the glory of Israel in the time to come.

The prophet's passionate enthusiasm, the golden dreams, the heavenly Jerusalem which he envisions, all these are expressions of the absolute faith of the prophet and of the people. The gap between vision and reality is wide. The Jerusalem of carbuncles and sapphires, to which all nations shall flow, on the one hand; and on the other, the actual Jerusalem destroyed, burned, enslaved! By the contrast between vision and actuality Deutero-Isaiah expresses the sublimity of his faith and trust, superior to every circumstance of time and place. This was to be a symbol and example to Israel in every generation.

World history and its goal.
The servant of the Lord

From the point of view of ideology, Deutero-Isaiah continues the work of the great prophets. The idea of world history is predominant in his prophecies, and he conceives its direction to be toward the development of the kingdom of God on earth. His universalism also is the universalism of divine grace in the time to come. In his prophecies the concept of religious conversion is, as we shall see, adumbrated for the first time; and therein this universalism reaches its climax. We also find in his prophecies the idea of peace in the end of days. He believes that the covenant with Israel and the holiness and glory of Jerusalem are forever. The law and justice will go forth from Jerusalem to all peoples. His rebukes bear the stamp of the prophetic censure. For him, also, the moral factor is decisive; and he opposes the appraisement of the cult as of independent value. He attacks idolatry more than did his predecessors because of the intellectual climate of the period. In the expression, "Servant of the Lord," wherewith he designates Israel, he creates a symbol of the absolute loyalty of the nation to its God.

The struggle of empires

The events of the years 546–539 are the historical background of the first collection of prophecies, 40–48. It is useless to attempt to determine the chronological order of these prophecies and to relate them specifically to the stages of the struggle for world dominion of that period.[54] In all of them there is one pervading mood. It appears that Cyrus had already conquered Media and triumphed brilliantly over Lydia. The struggle with Babylon had begun. Babylon was preparing to defend itself, but was not strong enough to attack, and that fact determined its fate. There were corroding forces at work in it, defeatists and traitors. It was felt that its fate had been sealed. The mood of anticipation of a change of guard in world rule is the spiritual background of chapters 40–48.

The great political convulsion of the period ended the prolonged slumber of the Jewish captivity. What was its prospect in this titanic struggle? What would happen to it when the Chaldean monarchy collapsed, that empire which had put an end to the political life of the Jewish nation? Would the land of the enemies devour it? Or did it still possess will and hope to return to its homeland and to renew the life of the nation? It was this agitation of the captivity which gave rise to Deutero-Isaiah. His prophecy discloses the breath of life which began to stir in the silence of the captivity.

The political events roused Deutero-Isaiah to prophesy to his nation. Violent warfare raged among the pagan empires. The world order of Nebuchadnezzar was collapsing and a new order impended. Would this new order be nothing other than the result of force, of armies and armaments, of troops and commanders of troops? The prophet distinguishes two spheres, the sphere of revealed forces and that of hidden forces, in what comes within his and the world's perspective. Revealed is warfare among pagan nations, lust for domination. They battle for dominion, for treasure, silver and gold, for land, for the wealth of nations. But in this materialistic warfare the prophet discerns a meaning which is spiritual and hidden. A divine plan, unknown to the belligerent nations, is at work. The prophet believes that the kingdom of Babylon will fall and that the armies of the victorious commander will accomplish its end. But he believes also that the end of Babylon is divinely decreed; and that the significance and purpose are unknown to the victor. On the surface there is a struggle among pagan powers, a contest in which the nation Israel plays no part, not even as ally of one of the contestants. There are Susa, Ecbatana, Sardis, Babylon, Sparta; but Jerusalem is no longer a political force. Yet the prophet believes that Israel and Jerusalem are determining factors in the realm of the concealed. For beyond the warfare of the pagan powers he sees another struggle; and in this, the war of Israel against the whole pagan world, it is Israel which stands in battle array. This is the warfare of the religion of Israel with paganism. To the prophet, this spiritual contention is the battle for the true values of human life. In this decisive struggle victory is assured to Israel; and in this victory lies the true significance of the collapse of Babylon. To the prophet, the purpose of the great events, the end which is not visible to the combatants, is the establishment of Israel and Jerusalem. The destruction of Babylon is merely the prelude to the rebuilding of Jerusalem. In the first of his prophecies, in words of surpassing beauty, he resolves the mystery of the political events: Comfort ye, comfort ye My people.

Was this the interpretation of a dreamer of dreams or of a seer of hidden things? We may say that this solution is at once dream and the sensing of a hidden reality. The political struggle ended in an event which the prophet had not expected, in the founding of a new heathen empire. But the other, the spiritual battle was also real; and in it Israel was destined in the course of time to win victory. History would demonstrate that this struggle was a sphere to itself, completely apart from the battle of political powers. In his dream the prophet envisioned the spiritual contest as directly tied in with the political. In his vision, a more realistic historical situation is reflected.

Israel and the nations

Thus, for all their visionary haziness, the prophecies of Deutero-Isaiah reflect a clear and reliable picture of the situation of Israel in the world at that time. The political battle for national independence had ended, and Israel was confronted by no political foe in the pagan world. There was no longer an enemy standing at the gate as in the times of Ahaz, Hezekiah, Josiah, Jehoiakim, and Zedekiah. Also, the characteristic warfare of the diaspora had not yet begun. The pagan world opened its gates to the Jewish exiles and permitted them to to take root and to flourish in the lands of the gentiles. There were no exilic persecutions; and wherever Deutero-Isaiah mentions a foe, despoiler, and robber, he is referring to enemies of the past. In 42:22–25, he describes events of the destruction, not persecutions of his time. Israel was for a spoil and to the robbers, its young men captive and in chains, and imprisoned,[55] encompassed by violent battle. All this was because it had sinned against God. Thus also in 43:28; 47:6; 48:10; 49:16; 50:1; 51:17–52:4; 54:6–9; 57:17; 62:8–9; 63:15–64:11. Moreover, there was no prospect of renewal of the political battle for liberation, no realistic hope of successful rebellion and military victory against the pagan government. Deutero-Isaiah symbolizes this impotence by the epithet "the worm Jacob," wherewith he designates Israel (41:14).

And yet, it was felt that the battle was not ended, and that there was still a foe. There was something fateful in the circumstance of the Jewish captivity, pregnant, harbinger of clash and battle. This was the only exile community in the world which sealed itself off, refusing to worship the national gods; the only community in exile which did not take root in the land of exile and acquire it as a new homeland. The gaze of the captivity was toward Zion. The diaspora assimilated; but it was not absorbed. These exiles remained exiles, strangers. And further, the exile community was aggressive, embattled. Their battle was not political-military; rather something completely novel in the world, religious warfare. The exiles were scornful of idolatry; they derided the worship of idols and spurned the national gods. In Deutero-Isaiah there is striking example of this. The prophet openly mocks idolatry,

scorns it without reserve, and stigmatizes it as shameful stupidity. This estrangement and this aggression gave rise of
necessity to reaction on the part of the idol worshipers.
The characteristic irritation of the exile appeared, explosive
with animosity and hatred. In the Hellenistic period this
tension between the Jews and their environment would appear
openly in all its force and consequences. Unquestionably, however, it was born in the period we are now considering. The
phenomenon was strange to the indigenous peoples. There was
then no antisemitic propaganda, no antisemitic movement, and
no antisemitic legislation. But the seeds of antisemitism had
already been sown and had begun to sprout. The antagonism
between the two worlds, Israel and the nations, was in the air.
Rejection produced counter-rejection. Just as in the Hellenistic
world, the scornful attitude toward idolatry was felt then in
every contact with the Jews. In that period all aspects of life
were permeated with religion, so that the denigrating attitude
necessarily involved continual irritation in all contacts. The animosity was, it appears, openly expressed first among the upper
classes. We may assume that the Jews who served in the
royal court were forced to participate at times in pagan ceremonies; and that they were unable to hide their feelings. This
was the background of accusations and machinations, a state
of affairs which is reflected in the tales of Shadrach, Meshach,
and Abednego in the fiery furnace in the book of Daniel (ch. 3)
and of Daniel in the lions' den (ch. 6). These are stories or
legends, but there is a grain of truth in them. In both these
episodes high Jewish officials are hounded by gentiles of their
own class because of their disrespect for royal idolatry. In
the beginning of the Persian period, in the reign of Artaxerxes,
antisemitism began to crystallize. Haman appeared. Already
there were mortal enemies everywhere seeking the lives of the
Jews. But even earlier, there were antisemitic tendencies. The
struggles of the diaspora began only some considerable time
after the destruction; but they were preceded by a climate of
antisemitism. The self-segregation of the diaspora and its war

against idolatry necessarily gave rise to the excitation of animosity and anger.

Deutero-Isaiah gave expression to this opposition of the two worlds.

Case against the nations. The visionary court

Israel was no longer engaged in politico-military warfare with its one-time foes. There was no longer any pagan political enemy; and the distinctive exilic type of persecutions had not yet begun. But even at that time, a half-century after the destruction, without state, land, or army, Israel existed as a national-religious community, distinct from and in challenging posture against the gentile world. There was no actual warfare; but there was "controversy." Deutero-Isaiah expresses the antagonism between Israel and the pagan world at that time by the metaphors, lawsuit and judgment. There is controversy and judgment between Israel and the nations. Parallel to this lawsuit is the case of Israel's God against the pagan gods, wherein the prophet himself pleads vigorously. And these two are in essence a single case: Israel and its God against the nations and their gods. The contention is not a struggle for domination and material goods. Israel contends for God. Israel is the witness of God in this case at law; and in that Israel strives for God, the prophet dubs Israel the servant of the Lord.

Yet, this struggle was no academic disputation. It was bound to turn into actual strife, arousing zealotry and hostility. There were those who were "incensed" with Israel, opponents who contended with him (40:11–12; 45:24). The worm Jacob feared (41:14; 43:1 et al.); the diaspora felt itself isolated amidst the nations, and stood in battle array against them. There were those who taunted and reviled Israel (51:7), and Israel was despised of men and abhorred of nations (49:7). There were those who reviled the name of Israel's God (52:5); and the reaction to blasphemy was counter-blasphemy. There were oppressors, vengeance seekers; and Israel was afraid because of the fury of the oppressor (51:13). With the tension of strife came the exilic contempt and the exilic fright. The prophet encouraged Israel. Because Israel fights the battle of God, God will stand at Israel's right hand and will vindicate Israel in the heavenly court of justice. Israel will be redeemed from exile and from the fury of the oppressor; and the name of Israel's God shall be glorified. Deutero-Isaiah, in his prophecies, phrases and rephrases this figure of the twofold, interlaced religious-national lawsuit of Israel and its God against the nations and their gods.

Deutero-Isaiah certainly is referring, even in 40:13–14, to God's role as counselor-judge and guardian of right: there is no counsel like unto Him, and no one who knows "the path of right" like Him.[56] In 41:1–7, God summons the nations "to judgment." The issue is, who rules the world: God or the idols? In 41:21–29, God calls on the gods to "produce cause." The juridical argument is the proof from true prophecy. The gods cannot declare the future things; wherefore, they are not God. Among them there is no "counsellor" who knows how to plead in the law court and to give an answer (28), no one that is "right," found justified in the lawsuit (26).

The lawsuit, the proof from prophecy, and the argument that idolatry is without substance appear together in this section. The proof, therefore, by appeal to prophecy and the polemic against idolatry, wherever found in these prophecies, are to be viewed as arguments before the visionary court in the "cause" of God against the gods (40:18–26; 41:1–7; 42:8–9; 43:9–13; 44:6–20; 45:18–21; 46:5–11; 48:14–15). In 43:9–13; 44:6–20, God, the peoples, and Israel are assembled for judgment against the gods; and Israel is God's witness, who testifies to the true prophecy. In 44:9 (according to the traditional version),[57] those who fashion graven images are themselves witnesses to the nullity of the gods.

And because God and Israel are one party in this action at law, Israel is assured of victory in its particular action, its suit as a nation, against the nations. Israel will be God's witness also in that the redemption of the worm Jacob from pagan bondage will be a sign that Israel's God is God. By Israel's redemption the name of Israel's God will be honored above the gods 41:17–20; 42:5–8, 14–17; 45:1–7, 14–16; 46:1–11).Therefore God stands by Israel in its action against the nations. Israel, however, is impatient and complains that God is not attentive to its case in law against the nations. The prophet encourages Israel to trust in the discernment and power of God (40:27–28): Israel is the chosen of God, and God will uphold him in his contention. All that were incensed against him shall be ashamed; they that strove with him shall be as nothing (41:8–13). The Lord is pleased to vindicate Israel in its contention in order that Israel may make the teaching great and glorious (42:21).[58]

V. 3, chapter 43, is also to be explained in this sense: God will give the visionary judges a "ransom"—Egypt, Ethiopia, and Seba for Israel.[59] The lawsuit theme appears also in 45:9–13: "Woe unto him that striveth with his Maker, As a potsherd with the potsherds of the earth!" etc. These words do not refer to Israel, as though there was complaining against the prophet because he assigned to Cyrus the office of Israel's redeemer. Such a complaint is a fictitious invention of the critics, with no basis in Deutero-Isaiah. In view of the proclamation, 45:1–7, that Cyrus is established only for the sake of Israel, there is no reason for complaint. The one who strives with his master is the heathen litigant in the visionary court. The pagan world carries on the lawsuit; it is in opposition to the plan of God and His works. And to the pagan peoples the prophet says: Do ye ask Me about the things to come? Concerning My sons and the work of My hands do ye command Me?[60] God, the Creator of the world, He it is who has roused Cyrus in order that he may restore Zion and send forth the exiles of His people. And further, with respect to Zion (14–17): distant peoples shall fall down to Israel's God; the makers of idols shall be ashamed, they shall go in confusion—

apparently they will leave the visionary court when they are put to shame. There follows (19) the assurance, in the name of the Lord, that "I speak righteousness, I declare things that are right," and at the end of the chapter the assurance to Israel that it will be justified in the Lord, that all they that are incensed against them shall come in confusion (24–25).[61]

The lawsuit motif appears also in two of the servant songs, in 49:2–4 and 50:4–9. God has made the mouth of the servant like a "sharp sword." He has hidden him "in the shadow of His hand," and the servant is confident that God will uphold him in his right (49:2–4). God gave the servant "the tongue of them that are taught" in order that he might argue in the court; He will justify him against every adversary; who shall condemn him? (50:4–9). (*Re* this interpretation, see further below.) In 54:17, Zion is assured that she will put every tongue that shall rise up against her in the wrong.

Included in this metaphor of the lawsuit of Israel with the nations is the figure of Israel imprisoned. Israel is a prisoner who anticipates a just judge and deliverer. Israel's despoilers cast him into "the prison houses" (42:22). Israel is in the dungeon; they are those that sit in darkness (for this expression, *cf.* Ps. 107:10, 14) Their redeemer will bring them out of the darkness opening the blind eyes (42:7; 49:9). He will say to the north: "Give up!" and to the south: "Keep not back!" (Bring out from the prison house, 43:6.) A little while and the bowed (bent-down) prisoner shall be loosed of his chains; he will not go down dying into the pit, nor shall he any longer eat the prisoner's bread (51:14).[62] The servant of the Lord is imprisoned ("taken away," 53:8),[63] placed in a pit ("cut off out of the land of the living"),[64] numbered with the transgressors (53:12). Concerning chapter 53, see below. Also the question of Israel's "sale," the right of the gentiles to rule over them, is related to the case at law. Israel is a "servant of rulers" (49:7), Israel is "sold." But God takes the side of Israel and argues that Israel was not sold to His creditors (50:1). Israel was sold and "taken away" for nought; wherefore the verdict of his redemption is that he is to be redeemed for nought from beneath the hand of the gentiles (52:3–5).[65]

The victory of Cyrus. Redemption of Israel. Significance of the events

Deutero-Isaiah looks upon this warfare, the struggle of Israel and its God with the nations and their gods, as the essence of the historical events of the period. The issue of this struggle was for him, as we have said, the hidden true purpose of the political events, the battling of the nations for world dominion. Cyrus will be the victor of the political events, of the warfare of the nations for world dominion.* The basis of Deutero-Isaiah's certainty is stated in his polemic against idolatry. Idolatry is a stupid belief in no-gods. Therefore, the history of the pagan nations is not divine history. It is not "history" at all, since it consists in events without value, without significance or meaning. Only insofar as it bears on the history of Israel is it "history." The meaning of the events of the period is to be sought, therefore, in the fate of Israel, in the outcome of the "lawsuit" of Israel and its God. Indeed, this is also the destiny of the nations.

The basis of Deutero-Isaiah's judgment of idolatry is the argument of fetishism, with the auxiliary argument of the absence in paganism of predictive prophecy. These two arguments derive, in fact, from lack of acquaintance with paganism. Nor is it to be assumed that Deutero-Isaiah came to monotheism by way of these theoretical propositions. Both monotheism and the concept of idolatry as worship of stone and wood are, as we have emphasized, ancient ideas which prevailed in Israel from the beginning of its existence as a people. Only their polemic use in the "action at law" against the nations was novel; the feeling of a specific need to reiterate them in the

* Translator's note: one line is lacking at this point in the original Hebrew.

years which followed the terrible national catstrophe, the time of depression and bewilderment in the face of pagan pride of victory. The proof by appeal to prophecy was merely a passing argument, without basic value.[66] It was implied apparently by Deutero-Isaiah's certainty that his prophecies concerning Cyrus would shortly be completely fulfilled. His concept of history was, therefore, rooted in the world outlook of Israel. The universal history of Genesis also is formulated on the basic premise that it is belief in one God whereby the chronicles of man become "history," a record of significance, worthy to be preserved and remembered throughout the generations of man. The book of Genesis relates primeval human history which, in the view of the author, was monotheistic until the generation of Abraham. Thereafter Abraham and his seed were chosen, and endowed with monotheism as an inheritance. From that time history is the history only of Israel. The annals of other nations are merely a framework or branch of the chronicles of Israel. This is also the prophetic concept of history. Isaiah evaluates the role of Assyria from this point of view; Jeremiah evaluates the role of Babylon from this point of view; and, similarly, the other prophets. Isaiah conceived the idea that the eventual goal of history is to bring the nations together under the grace of God, to monotheism which had been confined to Israel. Micah, Zephaniah, Habakkuk, and Jeremiah took this concept from Isaiah; and Deutero-Isaiah followed in their footsteps. The election of Israel was the basis of its superiority over the gentiles. The religious superiority of Israel was an historical fact even now, despite the destruction and subjugation. Therefore, the significance of all the world historical events was what happened to Israel. Nonetheless, Israel's salvation will be also a "light unto the gentiles."

The consolation prophecies

Deutero-Isaiah, like seers before and after him, viewed his troubled time as a time of eschatological events. He thought his was the age of redemption; and this explains his relationship toward Israel and the gentile peoples in chapters 40–47. Israel had drunk the cup of destruction to the dregs. But Israel in its exile was still the people of the Lord, the servant of the Lord. The purpose of what was happening, therefore, was not punishment of Israel but its redemption. The decision in the suit of the Lord against the gods would be a decision also in the contention of Israel with the nations. Therefore Deutero-Isaiah represses retribution and emphasizes mercy. In his first prophecy, he proclaims to Jerusalem that her guilt is paid off; that she hath received of the Lord's hand double for all her sins (40:1–2). In 42:18 he does not mention the sin of Israel; he speaks only words of comfort and encouragement. In 42:24–25 and 43:22–28, he refers to the sin of Israel in the past and to the punishment which was meted out. All this is, of course, the very foundation of his world outlook. Israel is the chosen of the Lord, the servant of the Lord.

Withal, however, Israel is exiled and subjugated. The guilt is Israel's. God chose Israel, but Israel rebelled against its God. This censure may have been the prophet's response to the complaints of his contemporaries. In 43:25 and 44:22, the prophet limits his earlier good news of the guilt being paid off. Sin still besets Israel. Nonetheless, he promises eschatological forgiveness; and, in any event, there will be no further punishment. God blots out the transgressions of Israel for His name's sake, in that His name is called upon Israel. He will redeem Israel so that His name shall be honored. In 42:18–20 and 43:8, the prophet chides Israel: it is blind and deaf. This rebuke is, apparently, the prophet's reaction to his contemporaries' doubts concerning his good tidings. They do not see what he sees; they have not learned the lesson of the past. We find very stormy castigation only in 48:1–11; and this, also, is directed against those who doubt and lack faith. Israel swears by the name of the Lord and makes mention of His name "But not in truth, nor in righteousness." Nonetheless, he turns to them because they are sons of the

holy city, and they stay themselves upon the God of Israel—
at least, so they say.[67] God has revealed events before they
occur to Israel by the mouths of His prophets, because Israel is
treacherous and sinful, and tends to disbelief. God restrains
His anger for His name's sake. And now, behold, He refines
Israel in the furnace of affliction, all this for the sake of His
name and His glory.[68] In this severe rebuke also, there is no
threat of punishment. There is only the assurance of redemption.

Cyrus and the kingdom of idolatry

Deutero-Isaiah evaluates the events of the gentile world
also from this point of view. Cyrus is not, for him, "the rod
of the Lord's anger" appointed to punish Israel, as Assyria
was for Isaiah and Babylon for Jeremiah. The guilt of Israel
had been paid off; and if there was yet sin in Israel, God had
nonetheless pardoned. The purpose of the political upheaval
was the redemption of Israel, and not new tribulations. Cyrus
was the rod of anger against Babylon, the enemy of Israel and
ravager of Israel's land. There was no historical account to be
settled between Persia and Israel, and Cyrus was not the
ruler of an enemy kingdom. Isaiah had foreseen that the salvation of Israel would come with the rout of Assyria in the
hill country of Israel. Jeremiah made the redemption of Israel
dependent on the fall of the Babylonian empire. But Deutero-
Isaiah did not regard Cyrus as the leader of hostile paganism.
He viewed the ascent of Cyrus as one act in the drama of redemption. Cyrus would execute the divine plan for Babylon
and, in addition, rebuild Jerusalem.

Deutero-Isaiah does not describe in detail the manner in
which he pictured the progress of events. But the opinion that
he prophesied world dominion for Cyrus and thereby, by implication, renounced hope of the restoration of the kingdom
of the house of David is not correct.[69] This thesis depends on

the separation of the political-secular from the religious-spiritual sphere, and is simply a liberal-Protestant exegesis. Deutero-Isaiah does not speak at all of the kingdom of Cyrus; and the comparison with Jeremiah's prophecies concerning Nebuchadnezzar[70] is irrelevant. Jeremiah conceived the idea of the pagan empire, an empire which God would establish and whose dominion He would impose on the world for a period determined from the beginning.[71] But this was a cruel, conquering, pagan empire. Judah and Jerusalem were within its realm. It was appointed to punish Israel, and its end was fixed in advance.

This is not the theme of Deutero-Isaiah. What, indeed, would be the role of an empire which was not idolatrous and not of Israel in the world view of Deutero-Isaiah? In fact, the prophet speaks only of the victories of Cyrus and not of his empire. He says nothing about Persia and Media, the dynasty of Cyrus, the period or the territorial limits of his dominion. There is a purpose for the victories of Cyrus, to wit, the punishment of Babylon and the restoration of Jerusalem. All the victories are given him for the sake of Israel, the elect of the Lord (45:4); and, further, that Cyrus may know that He is the Lord (45:3), that the whole world may know that He is the Lord (45:6). Deutero-Isaiah says nothing of the fate of Cyrus' empire after Cyrus' completion of his assignment. The redemption of Israel, for which Cyrus' victories are the prologue, will be accomplished by mighty wonders: the transformation of the wilderness into springs of water, the glorious procession, a theophany of the glory of the Lord in the sight of all flesh, accompanied by the voice of song of all creation. The kingdom of God will be establshed in Zion (52:7). Does this leave room for a secular, political universal empire? Did Deutero-Isaiah imagine that Cyrus would be the real ruler in Zion like Nebuchadnezzar? Did he imagine that the city, to which peoples from afar would fall down (45:14), of which kings would be the foster-fathers, and lick the dust of its feet (49:23), that that city would be a province of the

Persian empire? And what would have been the logic of such a dichotomy: a kingdom of God in Zion and a kingdom of the "vicar of God" in Persia? The everlasting glory of Zion after the redemption would leave no room for a Persian world empire; and there is in the prophecies of Deutero-Isaiah not one word concerning such an empire.[72]

The end of the empires

Deutero-Isaiah certainly did not prophesy a universal Israelite empire in an eschatological future. This fact is very significant,[73] but it is not to be explained in the sense of the Christian separation of the political authority from religious-spiritual leadership. It is rooted in the ideas of the prophets and, primarily, the ideas of the greatest of them—the first Isaiah. These prophets did not think of the political state as an independent entity. The supreme authority was the word of God. The prophetic ideal was the kingdom of God, the kingdom of righteousness and justice. This was the basis of the first Isaiah's negation of war and of dominion acquired by warfare. This ideal implied the negation of world rule generally, of empire; for secular world empire is nothing more than the domination of one people over another by reason of the "right" of war. The prophetic ideal is the end of the rule of the sword, of free peoples and free kingdoms. The prophets do not "render unto Caesar what is Caesar's." Rather, they deny "Caesar." For this reason, Deutero-Isaiah does not prophesy an imperium of Israel over the nations; and for the same reason he has no place for a non-Israelite world empire. Thus, there is no basis to assume that he renounced the hope of restoration of the kingdom of the house of David. If he thought of every nation as a kingdom, he certainly thought of Israel as a kingdom; and in 55:3–4 he referred explicitly to the restoration of the house of David (see below). The restoration of the kingdom did not, however, occupy a central position among his

117

descriptions. We shall consider the reason for this in the following.

Cyrus not a redeemer

Likewise, the hypothesis that Deutero-Isaiah assigned to Cyrus the task of a "messiah" (45:1), of the redeemer of Israel, and that this prophecy outraged his contemporaries and caused them to kill him,[74] is merely a bizarre confusion of ideas. There is no redeemer (גואל) in the Bible who is called "messiah"; and in Deutero-Isaiah's time the word messiah (משיח, anointed) was not a technical eschatological title which might have been applied to some individual. Isa. 45:1 could not have "outraged" anyone. Further, the idea of a human redeemer does not occur in Deutero-Isaiah nor anywhere else in Scripture, concerning which see below. In Deutero-Isaiah, God alone, and no "messiah," is the redeemer of Israel, leader of the exiles on the way, source of the miraculous way of redemption. The designation, Redeemer, is given only to the Holy One of Israel. The redemption will make known the name of the Lord to all peoples "from the rising of the sun and from the west." The victories of Cyrus are, however, the prologue to this miraculous divine drama; and in that Cyrus is chosen to carry out a task in this drama, he is the anointed of the Lord. The Lord anointed him as king and dispatched him against Babylon. In the days of Elijah and Elisha the Lord had anointed Hazael to be king over Aram and sent him against Israel (I Kings 19:15–17; II Kings 8:7–15). Thus, Hazael was a "messiah." Subsequently the Lord appointed the king of Assyria and made him the rod of His anger (Isa. 10:5 f., et al.). The armies of Media which destroyed Babylonia were the "consecrated" of the Lord, His mighty ones, the host of His battle, and the Lord was their "musterer" (ibid., 13:1–18). In the time of Jeremiah, the Lord enthroned Nebuchadnezzar as the universal king and, according to Jeremiah, called him "My servant" (Jer. 25:9; 27:6). It is in this sense that Deutero-Isaiah regards Cyrus, the destroyer of Babylon, as the "messiah" of the Lord. He was anointed, however, not to punish Israel, but for a definite role in the era of redemption.

No battles of the end of days

In accord with his appraisal of the pagan monarch who triumphed at that time, Deutero-Isaiah did not prophesy, in his first period, an eschatological battle with the pagan world, a final judgment of the nations, and the theophany of the avenging God. He did not, like Isaiah, prophesy the defeat of the nations on the mountains of Israel nor, like Jeremiah, chaos of the nations, they who drink the "cup of the Lord," who are drunk with fury. Only Babylon would drink that cup, not the whole pagan world. The Lord appears as a "man of war" who does battle against the enemy only in 42:13; and in this instance, also, the reference is certainly to the struggle with Babylon. Israel's redemption is for the gentile world as a whole a time of loving kindness. The Lord will be known to the peoples not in blood and fire but in loving kindness. His glory will be revealed to all flesh (40:5); the miraculous redemption will be for a sign to all the nations, and all peoples will sing a "new song" to the Lord (42:10), an expression taken from the psalm literature (see Pss. 33:3; 40:4; 96:1; 98:1; 144:9; 149:1). In this instance, also, as in many of his prophecies, Deutero-Isaiah made use in an eschatological vision of a metaphor which in the psalm literature is without eschatological connotation.[75] Peoples from the end of the earth, those who go down to the sea, the isles and the inhabitants thereof, the wilderness and the cities thereof, the sons of Kedar, the inhabitants of Sela—all will declare the praise of the Lord (42:10–12).[76] Israel will return to its land from the east, west, north and south (43:5–6). Far-off nations will come and fall

down to Zion and say: Surely God is in thee, and there is . . .
no other God (45:14–15). This will be the end of idol worship; the idol worshipers will be ashamed because they trusted
in their idols (42:16–17; 45:16–17). In the vision of (the
first) Isaiah the end of idolatry will come in the day of the
Lord of hosts, a day of the terror of the Lord (Isa. 2). According to Deutero-Isaiah, the end will come with the glory
of the redemption of Israel. The redemption of Israel will be
salvation for the gentiles, a new "song" for them. And the
prophet turns in his fervor to them even then, in the vision,
and says, "Look unto Me, and be ye saved, All the ends of the
earth" (45:22).

Both the redemption and the return of the nations are
parts of the universal miraculous drama of the end of days.
Deutero-Isaiah, in his Cyrus prophecies as well as his other
prophecies, is altogether eschatological. The opinion that he
acted as a "missionary," as a religious apostle among the
gentiles,[77] or even that he sent a message (45:1–7) to Cyrus,
which Cyrus rejected,[78] is an invention of the critics. Deutero-
Isaiah prophesied the turning of the pagan world to God. But
it never occurred to any Israelite, either before or after Deutero-Isaiah (not even to Paul, the apostle to the gentiles), that
such a deed would be accomplished by missionary-preachers
(concerning which, see Appendix II). The conversion of the
gentiles would come as a result of the theophany of the redemption of Israel. The deeds of Cyrus also are set within this
framework of the universal eschatological drama.

Dream and reality

Deutero-Isaiah's vision of the approaching redemption
and Cyrus' role therein bears very little resemblance to the
actual return to Zion. The prophecy that Cyrus would conquer
Babylon was fulfilled; and Cyrus did give permission to the
exiles to rebuild the Temple in Jerusalem. But Deutero-Isaiah

never imagined that the Temple would be rebuilt in a Jerusalem subject to an alien monarch, in a city which was the residence of a governor who was the real ruler. Nor did he foresee a humble return by permission of the alien king. We have already noted that he never preached a voluntary emigration by permission of the king. He prophesied a universal emigration, the simultaneous return of the exiles from every land, a miraculous redemption wherein the whole world would see the finger of God. In such a miracle-redemption Cyrus could not perform the office of a "messiah" or a "redeemer." Cyrus' role was not to effect the redemption. Rather, he was the leader of the nations which, under the influence of the divine miracle-redemption, would return to God. Cyrus is pictured as the leader of the nations which will fall down to Zion and pray to its God; as the first among the kings, of whom the prophet subsequently said: "Kings shall see and arise, Princes, and they shall prostrate themselves" (49:7). "And kings shall be thy foster-fathers . . . They shall bow down to thee with their face to the earth" (49:23); and much more in this vein. As champion of the pagan world, who will bow his head to Israel's God, he will send forth His exiles and rebuild His city. If this expectation is "naïve,"[79] it is not more so than the other anticipations of these prophecies. If we put the expectation in the framework of reality it is naïve. But if it is eschatological, it becomes an expression of firm faith, not confined by the actual situation.

The anticipations of Deutero-Isaiah were not realized. The advent of the miracle of redemption was delayed, and the heathen world did not cast off its idols. Cyrus did not destroy Babylon, nor did he exile Bel and Nebo. On the contrary, he proclaimed himself king by grace of Marduk.

But we do not value the prophets for their knowledge of future events, rather for their sublime religious-ethical ideas. Thus the gap which developed between reality and the vision in no way detracts from the eminence of Deutero-Isaiah. His expectations were the result of his profound awareness of the superiority of the religion of Israel over idolatry. His vision was essentially a vision of what ought to be, the aspiration for an ideal reality, a promise and a charting of the course. He expressed the right of the supremacy of the spirit. The kingdom is not the rule of the man of war and the iron fist; rather it is the right of Zion, the city of God, to which free peoples bow down in that it is the city of God from which shall go forth law and justice. Cyrus is victor over idolatry in the real world. But this in no way detracts from the worth of the idealistic vision.

Moreover, there is reflected, in fact, in the prophecy of Deutero-Isaiah an historical reality which was, it is true, to become manifest only in the course of generations. There was a sensing for realities in both the universalistic and the nationalistic elements of his prophecy. Deutero-Isaiah's vision of the conversion of the gentiles sprang from his awareness of the superiority of the religion of Israel. For this awareness there was objective basis. The vision proclaimed the victory of Israel's faith over idolatry; and the process of this victory began in fact in his generation, though its traces were as yet scarcely visible. Even at its inception, the prophet envisioned the final issue of the struggle of the Jewish nation against idolatry, which began in that period. The defeat of idolatry did not come in his time, as he had expected, nor in the manner he had imagined. Nonetheless, he sensed that concealed within the religion of Israel there was power to overcome idolatry.

Likewise, the prophet expresses in his prophecy the feeling that this spiritual force has a nation-protagonist, the people of Israel, the servant of the Lord. The spiritual superiority of the nation Israel as compared to the pagan world is rooted in the superiority of the religion of Israel. The prophet voices the conviction that no destruction and no exile can sever the historic bond between Israel and the faith in one God. No reality, however bitter, can root out the faith in its future from the heart of the nation and subjugate it spiritually to the pagan peoples. Subsequent history has demonstrated the validity of this conviction, at once universal and national.

The new pagan kingdom

Events of the years following the conquest of Babylon in the year 539 were a bitter disappointment to Deutero-Isaiah. Cyrus' victories were the prologue to the founding, not of the kingdom of God in Zion, but of a new pagan empire. Cyrus was the heir of the Babylonian world-empire, not its destroyer. Paganism was not overcome; it survived in all its splendor. Israel was still what it had been: conquered, exiled, and dispersed, the worm Jacob. Certainly the prophet was desolate and confused at that time. About six months after the conquest of Babylon, Cyrus granted the exiles permission to rebuild the Temple in Jerusalem. Deutero-Isaiah says nothing concerning this permission, the aliyah, its deeds and fate, the men who led them, what they accomplished in Jerusalem. We know nothing of his attitude with respect to this permission or of his relationship to the aliyah. But it is obvious that to him this permission and this return were not "redemption," his redemption. Cyrus did not become an enemy and persecutor; but his monarchy, even if less cruel than Assyria and Babylon, was still a mighty and tyrannical oriental empire. Cyrus did not restore the kingdom of the house of David even as a dependent, vassal state; he did not restore political freedom to Israel. Jerusaelm was still subjugated, a petty provincial city in the new pagan empire. Thus Cyrus' permission changed nothing of the situation of Israel in the pagan world. The "contention" of Israel and the nations continued.

The prophet did not discard his prophecies concerning Cyrus, and neither did his disciples or "editors"—which indicates that the prophecies have come to us as they were, without "revisions."

Deutero-Isaiah surmounted his disappointment and his bewilderment and, in fact, was confident even at that time. The contention was the cause of God; and victory was certain. The prophet expressed this certainty in his first prophecy following the disappointment. Israel says: "But I said: 'I have laboured in vain, I have spent my strength for nought and vanity; Yet surely my right is with the Lord, And my recompense with my God'" (49:4). Israel will yet be justified in "judgment." Nonetheless, Deutero-Isaiah, from chapter 48, does not again mention Cyrus or Babylon. Cyrus was not a "foe," but his assignment was ended. Babylon had ceased to be a kingdom, and was no longer an enemy. Persia and Babylon were swallowed up now in the pagan world which carried on its dispute with Israel. The nationalistic theme of revenge and retribution becomes more and more prominent in the prophecies. The pagan world was heir to the sin of Babylon; it continued the subjugation of Israel. The ancient eschatological idea of God's judgment of the nations reappears now in the prophecies of Deutero-Isaiah. But he still does not speak of a new pagan empire, in the manner of Jeremiah or Daniel. He specifies no terminal dates. The reign of idolatry is a passing phenomenon. Its end will come in the day of vengeance and retribution.

Reproof

Deutero-Isaiah found a way out of the confusion and consternation which followed the fall of Babylon. Sin was the cause; Israel was not yet worthy of redemption. This was the well-worn way of religious thought, both before and after Deutero-Isaiah. With this thought there came a turning point in the prophecies. Even as redemption was delayed, the element of rebuke became predominant in his prophecies; and in his final prophecies he is primarily admonisher. In 50:2, he explained what had happened: "Wherefore, when I came, was there no man? When I called, was there none to answer?" This rebuke is unrelated to the return by permission of Cyrus; it surely antedates that permission. There were always individuals ready to return. But there was no redemption because the nation was not whole in its desire for redemption, in faith in redemption, in true repentance. It lacked the assurance and the fervor of the prophet. There was absence of faith and fear of "the fury of the oppressor." The exiles were more concerned with their everyday troubles than with the great historic confrontation with idolatry; and this, in the eyes of the prophet, was a forgetting of God (51:12–13). The sin, therefore, which prevented redemption was above all the absence of trust and of true devotion to God.

Rebuke is to be found also in chapters 40–48. We have observed that in his earlier prophecies Deutero-Isaiah refers in particular to the sins of the past. Only in 46:8, 12 does he speak of "transgressors" and the "stout-hearted" who are skeptical of redemption. In his view, Israel as a whole is the servant of the Lord; and even in the songs of 49:1–13 and 50:4–9 the servant symbolizes all Israel.

Now, however, he comes to distinguish two types: the humble faithful, and the offending brothers. With this, his admonition becomes more pragmatic and is directed to the actual situation. In 50:10–11, he draws a line between those who fear the Lord, who obey "the voice of His servant" (the prophet), to whom salvation is assured, and those who "kindle a fire," who "shall lie down in sorrow."[80] In 51:1, 7, he addresses his words specifically to those "that follow after righteousness, . . . that seek the Lord, . . . that know righteousness, The people in whose heart is My law"; the consolation of redemption is restricted to them. In 56:7 he calls on the wicked and the men of iniquity to forsake their ways and their thoughts, to return unto the Lord, the God of compassion and pardon. In 56:1–2, he calls on them to keep justice and do righteousness and assures salvation only to those who do this, who keep the sabbath, and who keep their hands from doing any evil. It appears that a dichotomy of this sort within the nation is expressed also in the servant song of 52:13–53:12, as will be seen below.

In 54:17 the plural, servants of the Lord, appears in place of the singular, servant of the Lord; and from this verse to the end of the book we find this distinction: redemption is assured to the servants of the Lord, but the day of judgment to the offending brothers. The general consolation of redemption of the earlier prophecies is now partial. The redemption will not be wholly loving kindness, neither for Israel nor for the nations. As with the prophets who preceded, redemption is now combined with judgment: the judgment of the transgressors in Israel, and of the nations which have enslaved Israel. This turn in Deutero-Isaiah's prophecy is the consequence of his consciousness of sin, the sin of Israel and of the nations, a consciousness which overwhelmed the prophet after the bitter disappointment of the year 539.

Zion, the widow-mother

With this turn in the prophecies of Deutero-Isaiah toward reproof and a dichotomy, there appears a new figure, Zion the widow-mother, the afflicted and bereaved—a figure derived from Lam. 1–2. Zion is mentioned repeatedly in chapters 40–48, but always in connection with the good tidings of consolation and rebuilding (40:2, 9–11; 41:27; 44:26, 28; 45:13, 14). In those passages the prophet does not portray ruin and desolation, or speak of enemies. Zion is a city consoled. But from chapter 48 Zion is described in somber colors, "afflicted, tossed with tempest, And not comforted" (54:11), the symbol of the suffering of the nation; no longer a city, but a metaphor. This is not the Zion of (the first) Isaiah, "the faithful city Become a harlot" (1:21), and certainly not "this city" of Jeremiah, the city of anger and fury "from the day that they built it" (32:31), and also not the city of Ezekiel that "sheddest blood," the city of sin and fury (22:3). Nor is it the city of Zerubbabel and of the returnees, whose sons had returned to rebuild her, a city wherein there are, even if in poverty and misery, a nation and its princes.

The Zion of Deutero-Isaiah's prophecies from chapter 49 on is unreal, transfigured, a kind of heavenly Jerusalem. The prophet describes her suffering and affliction, and also the anger of the Lord with her and His rebuke. But he does not speak of her sin. It is always the nation which appears in the descriptions of sin, but never Zion. Zion is the holy city, the symbol of the holiness with which the Lord endowed the land of Israel, a holiness without blemish. Zion symbolizes Israel as the people of God, God's elect. Its captivity is captivity of holiness, symbolic of the "exile of the Shekinah." From 49:14 to the end of his prophecies, Deutero-Isaiah pictures Zion as completely ruined, its first lament: "The Lord hath forsaken me, And the Lord hath forgotten me" (49:14). This expresses the disillusionment of the prophet himself, but also his firm faith. Zion is abandoned; her destroyers and those that made her waste and those that swallowed her up are yet in her midst (49:17, 19). Her children are gone forth, she is bereaved and solitary (49:21). The prophet bewails the ruins in the style of the book of Lamentations, with which he was certainly acquainted and influenced by its vocabulary.[81] The prophet beholds Zion in the midst of the fury of the destruction. In his vision her sons are fainting "at the head of all the streets." Zion is still drunken of the fury of the cup of staggering. She lies in the dust, captive and imprisoned (51:17–52:2).

The abandoned widow-mother is now the principal subject of the prophet's outpourings of compassion and consolation. He prophesies glory and praise for her in the future. And with these predictions, there are now, for the first time, prophecies of general revenge in place of the earlier prophecies of vengeance specifically against Babylon. The Lord "will contend with him that contendeth with thee, . . . And I will feed them that oppress thee with their own flesh; And they shall be drunken with their own blood, as with sweet wine" (49:25–26). The Lord will take the cup of staggering out of Zion's hand and will put it in the hand of them that afflict her, that trample her (51:22–23). The uncircumcised and the unclean shall no more come to the holy city (52:1). The rest of the prophecies of the period include material of similar content (see below).

The creation of this symbol of the widow-mother is connected, apparently, also with the predominance of the element of reproof in the later prophecies of Deutero-Isaiah. Earlier, the prophet had used the figure of "the servant of the Lord" to symbolize Israel, the chosen and faithful. But the figure was ambivalent from the start. The "servant" was "blind" and "deaf" and rebellious. As his censure became more severe, the prophet sought a sublime symbol for the holiness element in Israel—a symbol untouched by censure. In chapter 53 he attempts to transform the "servant" into such a figure. But beginning with chapter 54, Zion the mother-widow completely supplants the figure of the "servant." From this we learn that the "servant" in all the prophecies is always the image of Israel.

The songs of the servant of the Lord

The songs which are known as "the songs of the servant of the Lord" are, from a certain aspect, a distinct unit in the prophecies of Deutero-Isaiah. This is particularly true of chapter 53, which Christians have interpreted even from early times as a prediction of the fate of their messiah. This chapter was always a matter of contention between Jews and Christians. The controversy continues even in the scientific literature of our time, and it encompasses the entire sequence of the servant songs (42:1–7 or 1–9; 49:1–9 or 1–13; 50:4–9; 52:13–53:12). Most Christian scholars, even if they disagree with respect to the interpretation of these prophecies, find in them, and in particular in chapter 53, the Christian idea of vicarious suffering, the suffering of the righteous who suffers for the sins of others and atones for them by his suffering. Even nonorthodox Christians think there is an historic tie between chapter 53 and the role and fate of Jesus, who was acquainted with this prophecy and realized it in his life and death. Jewish scholars deny the Christian-messianic element of this interpretation; but some of them acknowledge that the concept of vicarious suffering is indicated in chapter 53.

Opinions are many, and the controversy continues. The varying interpretations, however, can be divided into two classes: the individualist and the collectivist.

The individualist explanation

Those who interpret the servant as an individual argue that he is pictured as a person, either the visionary messiah-redeemer or as an historic person, to whom the prophet appointed the office of messiah-redeemer. These critics agree that the servant of the prophecies of Deutero-Isaiah, other than in the servant of the Lord songs, is Israel. But in these songs he is an individual, not Israel. The two servant figures are incongruent. Outside the songs, the term "servant" is merely a metaphorical description of the nation, an ordinary poetic personification. In the servant songs, on the other hand, he is described in genuinely individualistic terms; he is a subject with personal experiences, with a "biography." And further, outside the servant songs, he sins; in the songs, he is innocent of transgression. Outside the songs, he suffers for his own sins; in the songs (in ch. 53), he suffers for the sin of others. Outside the songs, he is passive; in them, he is active, a struggling figure with a dual mission, national and universal. Outside the songs, the servant is redeemed; he does not redeem. Within the songs, his role is that of messiah-redeemer; he redeems Israel from exile and the gentiles from the sin of idolatry (42:1, 3, 6–7; 49:2, 5–6, 8–9; 50:4–9; 53:5, 10–11).

Outside the songs, it is the redemption of the servant-Israel which causes the gentiles to acknowledge the God of Israel; the universal role of the servant is eschatological. In the songs, on the other hand, the servant spreads the knowledge of God by speech among the gentiles. He is a missionary, and in chapter 53 he takes on himself affliction and death in order to atone for the gentiles and restore them to God. Outside the songs, the nations are the "ransom" for the servant (43:3–4); in chapter 53 the servant is the ransom for the nations. Thus the servant of the songs is a real person, a messiah-redeemer.

Identity of the servant

The critics who interpret the servant as an individual do not agree with respect to his identity. Some try to understand him as an historical person, to identify him with Zerubbabel or Jehoiachin, who were the bearers of the messianic hopes of their generations (Sellin). Others assume that a man of unknown name is described in the songs, a political leader on whom Deutero-Isaiah based his messianic hopes, and who suffered and was killed. The idea of the suffering messiah was born of this experience (Kittel, Rudolph). Attempts have been made to identify the servant with Deutero-Isaiah himself. He suffered and was killed because of his prophetic activity; but before he died, he sensed that he must die a martyr's death (Mowinckel, Begrich). Some hypothesize that, although the servant who was killed was Deutero-Isaiah, it was a disciple, Trito-Isaiah, not the prophet, who composed the songs wherein the fate of his master is described (Sellin, Elliger). Others think that the songs are only a messianic vision of the time to come. The servant is a king and prophet, redeemer of Israel and judge of the nation, who will teach the gentiles faith in the Lord. The idea that the messiah will suffer and die and be resurrected in order to fulfill his destiny was born of the suffering of the exile (Gressmann).

Other critics discover in these songs the influence of non-Israelite mythologies and rites. Something of the figure of Tammuz-Adonis, the god who dies and returns to life, inheres in the figure of the messiah who is killed and rises again. According to Gressmann, annual lachrymations, similar to those for Tammuz, were observed in Israel, in memory of Josiah, the righteous king. He had died a tragic death, and there was expectation of his resurrection as redeemer among the people. This belief influenced Deutero-Isaiah. Dürr discovers in the servant songs the influence of the ceremonial ritual of the Babylonian New Year's day, in which ritual the king was humiliated. The priest would remove from him the symbols of royalty, tweak his ears, slap him on the cheek (or buttocks), throw him to the ground. The belief in the redemptive efficacy of the afflictions of the king was known among the exiled Jewish community. The prophet described the king-messiah in manner to correspond with the Babylonian king-priest. He anticipated the advent in the glorious future of the king-priest-redeemer, who would atone by his sufferings for the sins of the nation. According to Engnell, the servant songs are rooted in "the kingship ideology" which pervaded the whole orient, including Israel. In the cult the king fulfilled a "messianic" office. He acted in the ritual drama as the god-priest. As Tammuz, he suffered and died, was buried, and rose again; by his suffering, he restored the power of the world. This cult existed in Israel also. Many of the psalms of the lowly one who is in pain and nigh unto death are to be understood as songs of the king in the ritual drama. The servant songs are liturgies in the manner of the cultic psalms. The servant is a king, the son of David, priest and messiah-redeemer.

The collectivist interpretation

The foregoing and similar interpretations are rejected by those critics who interpret the servant as a sodality. In their opinion, the servant of the songs is to be explained in accordance with the other prophecies of Deutero-Isaiah; and in them the servant is always Israel. The allegorical personal element is more pronounced in the servant songs. But this is not decisive. The allegorical personal theme is also prominent in the prophecies concerning Zion, the widow-mother. Moreover, in the servant song, 49:3, the term "My servant" is expressly applied to Israel. (The critics of the individualist school delete the word Israel, which is lacking in one manuscript.) The death and resurrection of the servant in chapter 53 are merely allegories of Israel's exile and redemption. The exile is national death and the rebirth is national redemption. The "grave" also (53:9) is merely a metaphor for the exile. This is the symbolism which we find again in Ezekiel's vision of the dried bones (ch. 37). The passage (Isa. 53:10): "That he might see his seed, prolong his days," can be given a naturalistic explanation only on the basis of the collectivist hypothesis. Otherwise, it is impossible to explain why the resurrection of the servant is not mentioned explicitly in chapter 53; for if the servant had been an individual this would have been an extraordinary miracle. Thus the prophet was thinking not of a real resurrection but of the redemption of the nation, about which he speaks so many times in his prophecies.

To be sure, Israel is burdened with sin, whereas the servant of the servant songs is free of transgression. But the servant is Israel transfigured. Some critics say that the servant symbolizes the ideal as opposed to the real Israel, the concept as opposed to the fact. And it is also said that the servant symbolizes the chosen few who are faithful, the class of prophets, or the company of scribes, or the prophet and his followers.

Budde, a leading spokesman for the collectivist interpretation, rejects these opinions. The servant endures suffering, and certainly the misfortunes affected the real nation and not merely as an idea—the whole nation, and not just a chosen few. The fate of the servant shocked and astounded the peoples. Could the peoples have distinguished and been aware of a small group within Israel? The servant is the whole of the actual nation; but the figure is of Israel as it ought to be, and as it will be in the better future which is anticipated when the time shall have been fulfilled. It is true that in chapter 53 the people speak of the events of Israel's past, and say of Israel that he suffered without sin, and indeed for their (the nations') sins; and that his sufferings have brought redemption to them. But in all the other prophecies of Deutero-Isaiah, Israel suffers for its own sins; and there is no parallel in Scripture to the idea that Israel suffers for the sins of the gentiles. Israel, therefore, in chapter 53 is described as he appears to the gentiles, not as the prophet views him. Israel is the only people in the world which knows the Lord; the nations are steeped in the sin of idolatry.

Thus, in the estimation of the nations, Israel is a righteous people, whereas they themselves are laden with sin. The nations were worthy of punishment for the sin of idolatry, but they were relieved of punishment. Israel, however, was banished from his land and brought to the portals of death. This means that Israel suffered in their stead; and the suffering of Israel brought spiritual redemption to the gentiles. Israel could fulfill its mission of spreading the religion of the Lord throughout the world only by being exiled and dispersed among the nations, and by the termination of its separate national existence. It had to come into continuous contact with the gentiles so that it could preach the word of the Lord to them and combat idolatry. Israel had "to die" in order to become "for a light of the nations." Thus the fate of Israel is seen in the prophecies of Deutero-Isaiah from two points of view: the causal and the teleological. Israel sinned, and his sin was the cause of the exile. But there was purpose to the exile, to wit, the spiritual redemption of the gentiles. In comparison to the gentiles, Israel was a righteous nation; and the nations viewed its exile only from the point of view of its purpose. Israel suffered for their sins and for their sake; by Israel's bruise they would be healed. Chapter 53 is the expression of this view. The collectivists reject the argument that, according to 49:5–6, the servant fulfills the function of redeemer for Israel itself. In their opinion, the Lord, not the servant, is the subject of the verbs "to bring back . . . to raise up . . . to restore."[82] Those, however, of the collectivists who think that the servant represents the faithful few agree that the subject in these verses is the servant. But in their opinion, the prophet, in fact, ascribed the role of the redeemer of the whole nation to the faithful few.[83]

Chapter 53

Christian scholars, those both of the individualist and the collectivist schools, are agreed, as stated above, that the concept of vicarious suffering is expressed in chapter 53; and scholars of both schools are of the opinion that the idea which is realized in the life and death of Jesus is foreshadowed in chapter 53. In this chapter, it is Israel which redeems the world by his sufferings and death; but the concept is realized in its full meaning in Jesus. For this reason, these scholars consider chapter 53 the supreme scriptural creation. There are Jewish scholars, also, who accept this evaluation of chapter 53, even though they reject the application to Jesus.[84]

The individualist interpretation

Because the servant songs are allegorical and of multiple references, the problem of their character and meanings is not to be solved by examination of the songs apart from their context. To assess their character we must first explicate a number of general historical-ideological subjects.

Every individualist interpretation of these songs rests on the assumption that there had been a belief in a messiah-redeemer in Israel from early times. The "messiah" of chapter

53 is a messiah who suffers and is killed. It is universally held that this figure of a "messiah" is not original. It is rather a new and very late reworking of the figure of the political messiah who saves and redeems, which had previously been widespread in Israel. But there is no basis for this hypothesis. The idea of an eschatological redeemer is completely absent from Scripture.

The scholars discover messianic passages in the Bible either by way of theological exegeses (as in Gen. 49:8–12) or by confusing the idea of the future king with the idea of the redeemer. The "shoot out of the stock of Jesse," who is promised in Isa. 11:1–10, is a king-judge, endowed with gifts of the spirit. But he is not a redeemer, vanquisher of the dominion of idolatry and founder of the kingdom of the future. The ideal king is himself one of the mercies of God of the end of days. Also in the passages Isa. 9:5–6; Mic. 2:13; 5:1–3; Jer. 23:5–6; 30:8–9, 21; 33:14–26; Ezek. 34:23–24; 37:24–25 a king-redeemer is not mentioned. Throughout the Bible the only redeemer is God. Scripture knows no king-redeemer, no prophet-redeemer of the time to come, no national messiah, and no universal messiah.[85] And it is very significant that in Isa. 40–66 also, if we enclose the servant songs for the time being in brackets, there is no mention of a human redeemer, neither king nor prophet. Yet there are many portrayals of the redemption, which are quite clear. Deutero-Isaiah speaks of the renewal of the kingdom of the dynasty of David (55:3). But he does not speak of a messiah descended from David who will accomplish the redemption. And further, even the figure of the ideal king does not appear in his prophecies. It is possible to find the "messiah" only in the obscurity of the servant of the Lord songs. But there is no human redeemer in Scripture generally, and none in Deutero-Isaiah in particular. It follows that it cannot be assumed that he is to be found in the servant of the Lord songs. And certainly it cannot be assumed that a messiah who suffers and is killed is described in chapter 53. The absence of the idea of a human redeemer in Scripture proves that the individualist interpretation of the songs is altogether erroneous.

The opinion that in Israel the king performed a "messianic" function as a suffering or dying god-priest in a cultic drama presentation is poetic-exegetical fiction, for which there is in Scripture not a single bit of evidence which is explicit and clear. But even if it be assumed that the king did perform this function, the role would have been cultic and not eschatologic. The king would have been an annual messiah-redeemer, not a symbol of the redeemer of Israel from pagan subjugation in the end of days. No such redeemer appears in any of the many eschatological prophecies. And, inasmuch as the servant songs are eschatological, it cannot be assumed that their subject is a king-redeemer. Moreover, the title "king" is not once applied to the servant; and there is nothing to indicate that he is of the house of David. With respect to the influence of the ritualistic drama, see below.

The conversion of the gentiles not the purpose of the exile

Against the prevalent version of the collectivist interpretation it is to be emphasized that nowhere in the Bible is the turning of the gentiles from idolatry considered the "purpose" of the exile and the dispersion. Nowhere is there indication of such an idea as this, that Israel is exiled in order to bring the gentiles to a better way. In the biblical view, the cause of the exile and its purpose are linked together. Israel's transgression is the cause of the exile; and its purpose is to purge Israel of sin and thus remove the cause. There is no further purpose, no mission to the gentiles.

This whole concept which Budde and his associates discover in chapter 53, to wit, that Israel had to "die," to cease being a nation, in order that it might preach to the gentiles, is derived from the doctrine of that modern assimilating Jewry which affirms the diaspora, and justifies it as a purposive providential dispensation without which the Jews could not have carried out their mission among the gentiles. But this is a confusion of historical data. In the Bible there is no such idea. Isaiah, Zephaniah, and Jeremiah prophesy the return of the gentiles without any reference to exile. It is true that factually the exile was a factor in the beginning of the struggle against the idolatry of the gentiles; and also that the dispersion served as a conduit of influence. But we must distinguish between historical fact, as it appears to later generations, and the earlier ideology. No biblical author thinks of the struggle against idolatry as the purpose of the exile or its justification. Indeed, the writers of the Bible, including Deutero-Isaiah, do not make the repentance of the gentiles dependent on the exile, but on the redemption, or, more exactly, on the salvation, that is, the fall of the kingdom of idolatry. Even before the destruction and the exile, there was expectation of the end of the kingdom of idolatry. And it is to be emphasized, even from an objective point of view, that the exile was by no means a condition necessary to the spread of monotheism among the gentiles. Buddhism and Islam spread without exiles. In fact, the exile was a hindrance to the expansion of Judaism. It was because of the exile that Judaism itself could not spread among the gentiles and was forced to make way for the two religions, to which it gave birth, but which separated from the religion of an exiled nation, as I have explained elsewhere.[86]

On the contrary, the biblical authors anticipated the spread of the religion of Israel itself among the nations, and foresaw correctly that this would be realized not by means of the exile, but by means of the national salvation, the glorious return to Zion.

No mission to the gentiles

In contrast both to the collectivist and the individualist exegeses, it is to be emphasized that a "mission to the gentiles" and the sperading of the religion of Israel among them is not in Scripture considered the "destiny" of Israel or Israel's religious obligation. Some Christian scholars complain against Israel that it did not carry out the office, with which supposedly the prophets charged it, to preach the word of God to the gentiles; that it entrenched itself within a wall of commandments and relinquished the "mission" in favor of Christianity.[87] But this complaint is based on an erroneous assumption. It is correct that the prophets viewed Israel as an instrument in the hands of God to bring to the gentiles the true faith in the end of days. God would reveal Himself to the gentiles in the history of Israel, in its wondrous redemption. In this sense it is permissible to speak of the "mission" of Israel or of its task in universal history. But the prophets never imposed on Israel the "mission" to preach belief in the God of Israel to the gentiles and to convert them from idolatry by propaganda. More than that, the prophets imposed no such "mission" even on themselves; and they never went forth to preach monotheism to the gentiles (see Appendix II). The conversion of the gentiles from idolatry is in Scripture a desideratum and aspiration or an eschatological vision; but Israel is not commanded to preach its faith to the nations and to convert them from paganism. To be sure, we know that the Jews did, in fact, combat gentile idolatry in its own territories. But here, again, we must distinguish between historic event and contemporary ideology. The warfare of the Jews against paganism was the natural consequence of their religious consciousness. Their God was the God of the whole world; and this thought aroused in them the hope that the gentiles, also, should come to know and worship Him.

The polemic against idolatry of the period after the destruction of the first Temple was caused by the feeling that the destruction was a profanation of God's name. The vanquished were sensitive to the derision of the conquerors and sought to retrieve the honor of their God and their honor, and to prove their religious superiority. The Jews did, in fact, do battle and preach and receive the "joiners." But they did not think that this task was imposed upon them; and certainly they did not think that this was the sole purpose of their election. They were chosen for themselves and in God's mercy; but they wanted to associate the nations in the gift of God which had been given to them. Moreover, we must remember that the missionary propaganda of the Jews in the later days of the second Temple, and also the preaching of Christianity in its early years, were directed, in fact, to individuals among the gentiles and not to the gentile nations as a whole. The missionaries aspired to win "souls" for the true faith and to save individuals from perdition. But they did not believe that they could by missionary activity convert nations from idolatry and bring them beneath the wings of the Shekinah. They could imagine such a universal conversion only as an eschatological act of God (see Appendix II).

The servant has no active mission

This implies that the "servant" of the 'Ebed YHWH songs has no active mission at all. He is not a national messiah, a redeemer of Israel; such an idea is completely lacking in Scripture. He does not convert the nations from idolatry by missionary activity; in the Bible (and in the early Christian Scriptures) the conversion of the peoples is an eschatological ideal, a divine act, which is not conceived as the result of missionary activity. The Bible nowhere makes the conversion of the nations the work of a human "redeemer." And no such mission is imposed on the people of Israel. Israel is not appointed "for a light of the nations" by means of preachments. It will be "for a light of the nations" only because a new theophany will occur in its history in the end of days.

The confession, 53:1-10

According to the prevailing collectivist interpretation, vv. 1-10, chapter 53, are to be understood as confessions spoken by the gentiles. Israel is free of transgression in that it knew God; but the nations are sunk in the sin of idolatry. They are deserving of suffering and death because of this sin; but, in fact, the servant bears the suffering and death in their stead. The premise of this exegesis is that idolatry is in the Bible accounted a sin to the gentiles, and for this they are deserving of punishment. But this premise is erroneous. Idolatry is not accounted a sin to the gentiles, and nowhere in Scripture are the gentiles punished for it. The gentiles are brought to judgment only for moral sins or for wrongdoing against Israel, but not for idolatry. The idea that idolatry is sin for the gentiles is adumbrated in Jer. 10:25; 50:38, and in Dan. 5:23.[88] But even in these passages it is not stated explicitly, and in any case, it is not current in the Bible. Furthermore, it is most significant that in Deutero-Isaiah idolatry is stigmatized as stupidity, but not accounted a sin to the gentiles. The gentiles will be "ashamed in their idolatry," they shall "be turned back," etc. But there is no threat of punishment for idolatry. This evaluation of gentile idolatry in Scripture invalidates completely the opinion that in chapter 53 it is the gentiles who are the speakers and confess the sin of idolatry. In fact, there is no allusion in chapter 53 either to the idolatry of the gentiles or to their turning from idolatry, as we shall see below.[89]

53:1–6 if spoken by the gentiles

Furthermore, if the confession of 53:1–6 were spoken by the gentiles it would be completely dishonest; and it is unthinkable that the prophet would have attributed such words to them.

In the confession, the speakers say they esteemed the suffering servant as "smitten of God"; however, they now realize that he bore their iniquities. These words, if spoken by gentiles, are surprisingly oblivious both of the historic situ-

ation and of the biblical view of the relationship between the
gentiles and Israel. The confession does not allude, even by
one word, to the historic role of the gentiles in what had
befallen the "servant." These gentiles confess only that they
had held the servant in contempt because they erred; they had
thought that God had punished him on account of his own
transgressions. They had not harmed the servant, even by the
breadth of a hair. On the contrary, they were not there at all;
they did go astray like sheep, they had turned "every one to
his own way," and what the Lord did, He did on His own
(v. 6). Thus, the confession puts a kind of dishonest alibi-plea
in their mouths. It changes rapacious wolves into straying sheep.
In this confession there is no hint whatsoever of the fact that
it was these very "sheep" who smote and afflicted and devoured
Israel greedily.[90] The speakers do not confess that only now
is it known to them that they are the rod of God's anger.
They also do not make confession that they had spurned Israel
and Israel's God; nor do they mention that they have not
known Israel's God, and that they worshiped "wood and
stone." The monotheistic statement "Whereas we did esteem
him . . . Smitten of God" (4) would, in the light of the historical situation and also according to scriptural ideas, be a
surprising prevarication if spoken by the gentiles. The nations
thought that they, by their strength and their mighty hands,
or that they and their gods had smitten Israel. And if, according to Isa. 53, the sin of the nations were idolatry, they could
not have esteemed Israel to be smitten "of God." This confession would be wholly dishonest if spoken by the gentiles.

Vicarious suffering

The overwhelming majority of the critics, both of the
individualist and the collectivist schools, find in chapter 53 the
concept of vicarious suffering, that is, suffering of one person
for another, suffering which atones and releases, suffering

borne by the righteous for the wicked in order to atone for him and exempt him from punishment. According to the individualist exegesis, the suffering servant is the messiah-redeemer who atones by his suffering for the sins of Israel, or of the world. According to the prevalent collectivist exegesis, the servant is Israel which endures the suffering and the exile in order to atone for the sin of the idolatry of the gentiles. On the other hand, there are critics who say that the concept of vicarious suffering is not biblical and not Jewish at all and, accordingly, that it is not to be found in chapter 53. Dalman has shown that the concept is present in later Judaism. But does it have roots in the Bible, and if it does, in what form?

Suffering without personal guilt

Certainly the idea is current in the Bible that men suffer for the sins of others; and in this broad sense the concept of "vicarious suffering" is biblical. If God visits the sin of the fathers on the children, if mankind is condemned to die in all generations because of the sin of Adam and Eve, if the whole community is punished for the sin of part of the community or even individuals within it, men suffer for the sins of others.[91] However, the biblical concept of suffering without personal sin is rooted in the concept of collective retribution.[92] According to the biblical outlook, sin besets not only the individual, but also the group of which the individual is part, his family, city, tribe, people, state, or even, as in the case of Jonah, the ship in which he journeys. From this point of view, every individual of the community shares in the sin of a part of it. Accordingly, the sufferings which affect the whole community are punishment for sin, but not the suffering of the innocent instead of the sinners, and in order to atone for the sinners. Thus, by reason of the idea of collective sin and retribution, these are not "vicarious sufferings," suffering of one for another, but suffering for collective sin.

Saul's crime in putting the Gibeonites to death besets the whole nation, and therefore famine strikes all. But the famine is esteemed punishment and not atonement. God is reconciled to the land only after the killing of the sons of Saul, since Saul himself is punished, according to the biblical view, through his sons (II Sam. 21:1, 3–6, 14). The sin of Achan lies at the door of all Israel, and the defeat before Ai is viewed not as "vicarious suffering" in the stead of Achan but as punishment for the sin of Israel. Only the killing of Achan and his family removed the anger of God from Israel (Josh. 7:11–12, 26). The death of Josiah also is not considered an atonement, but rather as punishment, part of the punishment decreed against Israel. The generation of the destruction bore the iniquities of its fathers (Lam. 5:7) because the transgression crouched also at its door, and in it the fathers were punished. God cuts off from the land of Israel "the righteous and the wicked" (Ezek. 21:9), not in order that the sufferings of the righteous may atone for the wicked, but because the nation-community associates the righteous and the wicked in sin and in punishment. To be sure, the idea of punishment in order to atone for others is implied in Num. 25. The impalement of the chiefs of the people turns the fierce anger from Israel (4), and the killing of Zimri turns the wrath from them (11). But here it is not the suffering of the righteous but specifically the punishment of men heavily laden with sin.

No nation punished for the sin of another

Thus, according to the biblical view, the righteous man shares in the sin of the community and is punished for this sin (even if it is not a personal sin) along with the entire community. Also, he may be punished for the iniquity of his fathers by reason of the association of sin and punishment encompassing generations, and because his punishment is accounted punishment of his fathers.

143

But we do not find in Scripture the idea of responsibility without association in the collective sin. The members of the community are responsible one for the other, but they are not liable for sin and punishment except on the basis of community association. The sons suffer for the sin of the fathers; but they do not bear the guilt of the fathers of other men. Subsequent generations of a people are punished for the sin of their nation but not for the sin of a foreign people. The idea that one community sins and another is punished in its stead is completely foreign to Scripture. There is nothing in the biblical idea of retribution (and in the moral sentiment generally) to support the idea that Israel or the children of Ammon or Moab are punished because the Philistines or the Pathrusim or the Casluhim sinned. Accordingly, there is no reason to seek in Isa. 53 the absurd idea that the sins of the nations brought the punishment of exile on Israel.

The doctrines of sacrifice and retribution

The idea of specifically vicarious suffering is to be found in Scripture only with respect to sacrifice. To be sure, the idea that the sacrifice is the surrogate for him who sacrifices is not prominently expressed, but it is adumbrated here and there. Abraham offers up the ram "in the stead of his son" (Gen. 22:13). The idea that the paschal lamb takes the place of the first-born who had formerly been sacrificed that night is reflected in the story of the passover night (Exod. 12:13). The concept of substitution appears also in the ordinance wherein the firstling of an ass is ransomed by a lamb (Exod. 13:13; 34:20). The custom also of laying hands upon the head of the sacrifice (Lev. 1:4; 3:2 et al.) derives apparently from the idea of substitution: by the laying of the hands the sin is laden on the head of the sacrifice which is innocent of transgression. The idea is implicit also in the ceremony of the scapegoat sent to Azazel; by means of the laying of hands and the confession "all the iniquities of the children of Israel" are put upon the head of the goat (Lev. 16:21); and the goat is sent "unto a land which is cut off" (22) in the stead of the children of Israel.

Mic. 6:7 speaks explicitly of the sacrifice of sons: "Shall I give my first-born for my transgression, The fruit of my body for the sin of my soul?" The son, therefore, was offered for the sin of the father and in place of him. This concept of sacrifice also is rooted in the idea of collective retribution. The sacrifice is of the person who sacrifices, a possession of the sacrificing individual or the community, associated with him or them in legal responsibility or through family relationship, a part, as it were, of him. The association is expressed in the ceremony of the laying on of hands.

Indeed, the Christian concept of the crucifixion of Jesus as atonement for the sins of the world is rooted in the idea of sacrifice (Matt. 26:26–28 and the parallel passages, John 1:29, 36; 1 Cor. 5:7; Eph. 5:2; Heb. 7:27–10:20, et passim). But in Hebrew Scripture the idea of vicarious sacrifice, insofar as it is present, is limited strictly to the cultic sphere, and has no place in the doctrine of retribution. The God who exacts retribution never makes someone who has no part in the sin a "sacrifice" in order to atone for it. An individual who is himself innocent of transgression is included in the sin of the social group of which he is part. He is punished in its punishment; and his suffering is considered punishment, but not atonement and sacrifice. There are attempts in Scripture also to explain the sufferings of the righteous in other ways. Job is not punished on account of communal sins; but his suffering is nonetheless not an atonement and not vicarious. According to the prologue, his suffering is a trial. In the poetic dialogue-cycles, there is no explanation for Job's sufferings; they remain a divine mystery. In Prov. 3:11–12 it is said, "For whom the Lord loveth He correcteth." The authors of the book of Psalms also struggle with the problem. But the suffering of the righteous is never explained as the suffering of a "sacrifice" who atones for the wicked and releases them from punishment. There is also suffering of the righteous at the hand of man, of the wicked. But this suffering is thought of, not as atonement, but as wrongdoing which calls for requital. The psalmists pray for the theophany of the avenging God to judge the wicked for their misdeeds against the righteous. If "in restitution" (Isa. 53:10) is interpreted as guilt-offering, it is an isolated trope in Scripture and cannot prove very much (see below, p. 133).[93]

Justice and mercy. No sacrificial redeemer

A fortiori, the idea that God would appoint a righteous one as "sacrifice" and "messiah" for an eschatological remission of sin is alien to the world of biblical imagery. The scriptural measure of justice is satisfied by the communal punishments which befall Israel whereby the nation is purged of sin, brought to repentance, and its remnant made ready for redemption. Divine mercy is the complement of divine justice; in the end of days God will pardon the iniquity. But the communal retribution which befalls the righteous also, or the wicked, in the final judgment day is sufficient to the attribute of justice. There is no basis in the biblical world view for the idea that justice requires in addition the suffering of a particular individual, a suffering "messiah." Certainly God's mercy does not depend on the "sacrifice" of a "messiah." In the workings of justice and mercy there is no place for "messianic" vicarious suffering. The measure of retribution of the end of days is full to overflowing, and there is no further debit to be paid by a special "sacrifice." The retribution is potent to purge of sin and does not depend on the further suffering of a "messiah." And in any event, the divine mercy can balance the "account," without an additional special satisfaction. Also, in Deutero-Isaiah, outside chapter 53, there is no indication of an eschatological defect in the workings of divine justice and mercy. There is retribution and also eschatological forgiveness; but there is nothing of the idea that the forgiving depends on some "messianic" sacrifice. Israel sins and is punished. The measure of punishment is filled and overflowing; Jerusalem has received double for all her sins (40:2). Again: God will blot out the transgressions of Israel in the hour of redemption (43:25; 44:22). In other prophecies Deutero-Isaiah threatens the wicked with vengeance in the day of judgment. But in all this concatenation of ideas there is no role for the redemptive suffering of a messiah.[94]

The pagan cultic drama

It cannot be assumed that the idea of a suffering messiah found its way into Isa. 53—there specifically and nowhere else in Scripture—from some semitic or even Israelite cultic drama by way of the Tammuz cult or the influence of the Babylonian new year ritual. Baudissin and Dürr argued that there was no element of atonement in the rites of Tammuz. The death and rebirth of Tammuz reflected processes of nature only. But Dürr's view that Isa. 53 reflects a figure corresponding to that of the king of Babylon, who is humiliated and smitten in the ceremony of the New Year's day and who atones for the people by his suffering, is also unacceptable. The figure described in chapter 53 bears no resemblance either to Tammuz or to the king of Babylon. Theirs are the splendid existences of gods and kings, and their sufferings a passing shadow. Their sufferings are annual events, of short duration, with termination anticipated and publicly known in advance, cyclically recurrent suffering and its end. The servant of chapter 53, on the other hand, is a man of pains, acquainted with disease, without comeliness, despised and afflicted constantly; and his grandeur is a miracle, astounding, unanticipated, a unique event. The suffering of Tammuz is his death, whereas the servant endures pains and sickness and contumely in life. The suffering of the Babylonian king is histrionic. The king plays a fixed role in the ritual drama, whereas the suffering of the servant is real, his destiny. Tammuz and the king are not "saints" who suffer for the sins of others. In the Tammuz cult there is, as remarked, no element of atonement, and the king of Babylon also is no saintly one who atones by his suffering for others. He is pictured as associated in the sin of the nation; and in the cultic drama he symbolizes the sin-laden nation. In chapter 53, on the other hand, the righteousness of the servant is an essential element. The idea, therefore, that the recurrent temporary sufferings of the cultic drama could have been the archetype for this description of the fateful suffering of one innocent of all wrongdoing, to the end of eschatological pardon, is impossible. We have already remarked that, since the idea of a personal messiah was completely absent in the biblical period, there was never in Israel a protagonist of a messianic role of this character.

Conclusions

From the foregoing we are able to draw general conclusions with respect to the servant of the Lord songs. The individualist interpretation is completely unacceptable. The servant is not the political redeemer of Israel, nor the religious redeemer of the gentiles, nor the redeemer who saves the world by means of his sufferings; all this inasmuch as there is no personal redeemer anywhere in (the Jewish) Scripture. Redemption is solely of God. Likewise, there is in Scripture nothing of the vicarious suffering of a "sacrificial" redeemer, of a saintly one who endures suffering of atonement in order to release the wicked from judgment. The servant, therefore, is Israel, as in the other prophecies of Deutero-Isaiah.

The servant is not charged with any active mission to the nations, this in accord with the fact that there is in Scripture no prophetic mission to the nations to turn them from idolatry. The conversion of the gentiles is wholly eschatological; and the servant songs are to be understood accordingly.

The conversion of the gentiles is not the purpose of the exile. Israel does not suffer exile in any sense for the sake of the nations. The exile cannot be thought of as atonement for the sin of idolatry of the gentiles for two reasons: first, idolatry is not reckoned as a sin to the gentiles; second, one people does not suffer vicariously for the transgressions of another. Therefore, both the servant and the speakers of 52:13–53:6 must be Israel, despite the difficulty of this interpretation.

The servant of the Lord—a visionary figure. *The ideas of Israel*

In the servant songs the servant is portrayed as a person. Because the servant is, as we have said, a visionary figure, this is not merely an ordinary metaphor, one more of the visionary images of Deutero-Isaiah. The servant is a man-figure who appears on the visionary scene and fulfills specific tasks. He appears and acts against a "theatrical" background in the prophetic vision, wherefore the prophet describes him in personal terms, and endows him with a "biography." Nonetheless, the servant is only one of the figures which represent Israel. Indeed, the servant of the servant songs is innocent of transgression, whereas elsewhere the servant-Israel is burdened with sin. However, Israel is an ambivalent figure both in biblical tradition generally, and in Deutero-Isaiah in particular. Even in the narratives of the Pentateuch, Israel is both chosen and rebellious, accepting the law and making the calf, the subject of God's favor and of His wrath. And thus in every generation! Israel, only, of all the families of the earth, is known of God, and yet Israel betrays and rebels continuously. Israel is the vineyard of the Lord of hosts, but the vineyard brings forth wild grapes (Isa. 5:1–7). Israel is the beloved of the Lord, and he sacrifices to the Baalim (Hosea 11:1–2). He is the Lord's hallowed portion and he defiles His land (Jer. 2:3, 7). Likewise, in Deutero-Isaiah, Israel is chosen and beloved, the servant of the Lord, but also a transgressor from the womb (48:8), blind and deaf (42:19; 43:8). In the songs the servant is symbolic of one particular Israel—Israel the righteous, not Israel the "ideal," the unreal, and also not the "true" Israel, the future Israel. The historic Israel of that day and of the past was, in fact, equivocal, actually both faithful and rebellious, righteous and wicked. Similarly, the prophet saw Israel of the Babylonian exile in two guises. It was faithful, separating itself from idolatry and yearning for Zion. But there was in it also an inclination to take root in the lands of the gentiles. Not all of Israel was possessed of that zeal which the prophet demanded; Israel did not yearn with whole heart and soul to go forth from the lands of the gentiles. The servant was not just a few nor a prophetic few, as opposed to the mass. In fact, there was no clear line of demarcation between the righteous and the rebellious Israel. There were rather two tendencies, two poles, two aspects; and at times the line was drawn within the souls of men. The servant of the songs is one aspect of the real and historical Israel, Israel insofar as he is righteous and faithful.

And withal, these two extreme positions tended, in the life-time of Deutero-Isaiah, to crystallize into two distinct and op-posed "parties." On the one side were the humble, the lowly, the contrite, the brokenhearted, the mourners of Zion whose heads were covered with ashes (57:15; 61:1–3). These bore the burden of the national suffering; they symbolized the heart-break of the nation, the pain of the "exile of the Shekinah," the passionate yearning for Zion. They were the captives and the bound, those to whom redemption and liberty were prom-ised (61:1). On the other side were those who were forgetful of the holy mountain, who betrayed, who were inclined to fol-low after idolatry, to whom Zion was become strange and re-mote (65:11–15). Between the two extremes stood the mass of the moderates. They, too, in fact remained faithful, but without the extremism of the humble and the chosen. Deutero-Isaiah, in his final prophecies, gives expression to the opposition between the two extreme "parties." In these prophecies the symbolic singular "servant" is replaced by the plural "servants," who are the actual humble ones. The transition occurs in 54:17. But until he abandoned the figure of "the servant" the prophet sought, particularly in 52–53, to portray in the servant the class of . humble ones—servants. The description of the servant includes the elements: the "crushed," the humble, the mourner, the brokenhearted, the imprisoned and bound, him who is despised in the eyes of the nation. The servant is still the symbol of Israel; but the line of demarcation has shifted toward the humble. Now there appears on the scene in 53:1–6 a kind of chorus figure which speaks—it also —in the name of Israel. These are not those who betray; rather they are the nation, the mass, symbolized indeed, in a way, by the humble, and yet not identical with the humble and the contrite. The chorus and the humble-contrite are bound by community of fate and of reward. Israel is both, appearing now on the visionary stage in two figures—the servant and the "chorus." This is, as we shall see, the setting of the confession of the chorus.

It is on this basis that we must explicate the songs of the servant of the Lord.

The first song: 42:1–9

The servant appears on the visionary stage in the guise of the humble one; and with him God and the prophet. Vv. 1–4 are the words of God, who points to the servant and says, "Behold My servant, whom I uphold." The description of the servant in v. 1 resembles the description of Israel in 41:8–10; 44:1–3; 59:21. He is frail and submissive, unable to cry out and cause his voice to be heard in the marketplace. He lacks strength to break a crushed reed or to quench a dimly burning wick. But withal, he shall not fail nor be crushed; and the day cometh when he will make the right to go forth among the nations, and the isles shall wait for his teaching. Israel is weak; his voice is not heard in the council of nations. He has ceased to be a political force. But he is the elect of God, and a day will yet come that there shall go forth from him instruction and right to the nations. This is the vision of Isa. 2:2–4: "For out of Zion shall go forth the law . . . And shall decide for many peoples." This is not a reference to missionary activity in the diaspora, but to the kind of influence described in Isa. 2:2–4, the influence of Israel restored in its homeland on the nations. After v. 4 God departs from the scene, and the prophet speaks to the servant in God's name, explaining the words spoken by God in vv. 1–4. In v. 6 he uses the same words which he addressed to Israel in 41:9–10, 13. God has called the servant, taken him by hand, and made him bearer of a covenant of the people, that is, the covenant-people of the Lord,[95] and since the teaching shall go forth from him to the peoples, for a light of the nations. The subject of v. 7 is not the servant but God (the determining model for this verse and for 49:8–9 is 51:16):[96] "I the Lord . . . To open the blind eyes, To bring out the prisoners from the dungeon, And them that sit in darkness out of the prison-house. I am the Lord. . . ." The opening of the eyes is here the bringing forth of "them that sit in darkness" from the prison-house; and the whole is a metaphor for the redemption of Israel from the servitude of the exile. (Cf. 42:16; 43:8; 49:9.) Freeing of prisoners and opening of eyes are attributes of God, as in Pss. 79:11; 102:21; 107:10–14; 142:8; 146:7–8.

The second song: 49:1–13

The servant and the prophet appear on the visionary stage. In vv. 1–6 the speaker is the servant; and the servant is portrayed here in terms used elsewhere for Israel. God

formed him from the womb (49:1-5; *cf.* 44:2, 24), made
mention of his name (49:1; *cf.* 43:1), made his mouth like
a sharp sword, hid him in the shadow of His hand (49:2; *cf.*
51:16), and formed him to be His servant (49:5; *cf.* 44:21).
In v. 3 it is stated explicitly: "Thou art My servant, Israel,
in whom I will be glorified" (*cf.* 44:23). The background
of vv. 1-4 is the metaphor of the lawsuit and judgment. The
servant pleads the case of his God, and God helps him to
win His case. God made his mouth like a sharp sword so
that he could speak in the gate.[97] God protected him, concealed him like a polished shaft in His quiver, and appointed
him that He might be glorified in him. To be sure, the servant's anticipation of his salvation was still unrealized; and he
was nigh on despair, "But I said: I have laboured in vain,
I have spent my strength for nought and vanity" (4).

This song is the first of Deutero-Isaiah's prophecies after
the disappointment of his hopes in Cyrus, and in 49:4 he gives
utterance to his cry of despair. But his despair is of the moment
only; his faith is not destroyed. The servant says: "Yet surely
my right is with the Lord, And my recompense with my God"
(4). He believes that the Lord will see to it that he is victorious in the "judgment" and give him his reward.

Vv. 5-6 explain vv. 1-4 realistically. The servant continues: . . . The Lord that formed me . . . to be His servant, now saith to bring Jacob back to Him, and that Israel
be gathered unto Him.[98] However, I will now be even more
honorable in the eyes of the Lord,[99] for He saith: It is too light
a thing in My eyes, because thou art My servant to raise up
the tribes of Jacob, And to restore the offspring of Israel.[100]
Therefore, "I will also give thee for a light of the nations,
That My salvation may be unto the end of the earth." Because
Israel in exile remained faithful to its God and contended for
His cause, its redemption will be an event of worldwide significance. The God of Israel will be glorified in the glory of
Israel; from Israel the right will go forth to the nations, and
knowledge of Israel's God will reach unto the end of the earth.

The prophet speaks in vv. 7–13. V. 7 explains v. 6. Israel will be "for a light of the nations" in that the humiliated and subjugated nation will be glorified and raised very high. Kings and princes shall prostrate themselves to Israel, and its splendor will witness to all mankind the Holy One of Israel who chose Israel. The beginning of the glory will be the wondrous redemption. The Lord will give answer in an acceptable time, He will help us in the day of salvation, and make us a covenant of the people, To raise up the land, and to cause Israel to inherit the desolate heritages, etc. (8–13).[101]

In this song also, the servant does not function as the redeemer of Israel.

The third song: 50:4–9

Lawsuit and judgment are the setting of this song. The servant appears on the stage, and he alone speaks. His God hath given him "The tongue of them that are taught . . . to sustain with words him that is weary." Because of the last expression the role of the servant has been understood as that of a teacher of the word of God to "the weary"—to the faint and confused of Israel or of the gentiles. Christian scholars find support for this interpretation in Matt. 11:28. However, in the rest of the song there is no reference to "the weary," or to the task of the servant as a teacher. From vv. 7–9 it is evident that the servant is being judged along with the litigants and that he trusts in his God who "justifieth" him. Graetz proposed the emendation: "to answer" (לַעֲנוֹת) for "to sustain" (לָעוּת). However, "him that is weary" (יָעֵף) also requires emendation, and should be read: him that is counselor (יָעַץ). The counselor is an officer, the judge who presides in the court (cf. Isa. 1:26; 3:2–4; Job 12:17; 3:14; Mic. 4:9; Ezra 7:28; 8:25). The Lord gives the servant a tongue of wisdom so that he will be able to respond by word to the counselor in the courtroom.[102] God instructed him morning by morning as an instructor teaches pupils.[103] The agonies of the preparation are described in v. 6: "I gave my back to the smiters, And my cheeks to them that plucked off the hair," etc. Israel has been refined in the furnace of affliction and exile to the end that he be faithful to his God and fulfill the task of the servant of the Lord who contends for Him (cf. 48:10). Therefore, Israel is confident that he will be acquitted in the lawsuit. The Lord will help him, and who shall condemn him? His opponents "shall wax old as a garment, The moth shall eat them up" (cf. 41:10–12; 54:17).

This song, also, is an expression of assurance that Israel will triumph in the historical "lawsuit" wherein, against the pagan world, he contends for his God.

The fourth song: 52:13–53:12

The servant appears in the form of a meek one, contrite and humiliated, marred of visage, despised, a man of pains; and with him, God, with arm outstretched and laid bare upon tho servant, His light shining upon him. The prophet also appears and, finally, a "chorus," to participate in the visionary conversation. God speaks in 52:13–15, the chorus in 53:1–6, the prophet in 7–10, and God once more in vv. 11–12, which conclude the colloquy.

The aspect of the servant is of dual significance. His marred and tortured visage symbolizes the lowly estate of Israel and the affliction of his exile. But the arm of God is laid bare upon the servant, which points to his elevation and glory in the future. The vision symbolizes both the suffering and the compensation. The glory of the servant is the promise of the future in 52:13–15; 53:10–12. The speakers, however, of 53:1–6 refer to it as a present reality. For the appearance of the servant in the light of God is the sure guaranty and the miraculous beginning of his glory: and behold, it is already reality!

Here, as in 42:1, God points to the servant and says: "Behold, My servant shall prosper, He shall be exalted and lifted up, and shall be very high," etc. God proclaims that, even as many had been appalled at the humiliation and subjugation of Israel, so shall nations and kings be astounded at the splendor of his visage in the future, which to them will be something wondrous and unforeseen; and they shall shut their mouths because of great astonishment.[104]

We have already discussed the general problem of the identity of the speakers of 53:1–6. They are certainly not gentiles. The gentiles do not appear on the scene; and they do not see the glory of the servant in the prophetic vision. In 52:15 it is said of them that they will perceive the glory of the servant in the future and that they will be astounded, for this "had not been told them"; they "had not heard" of it. But the speakers in this song hear the word of the Lord and see His arm revealed upon the servant (53:1). The gentiles become silent from pure amazement (52:15); but the speakers speak out and confess.

From what is said in 53:4–6 it is possible at first glance to infer that the speakers had not suffered at all; and that only the servant, he who was innocent of transgression, suffered the agonies which they in their transgressions had deserved. The critics who identify the speakers with the gentiles take this as decisive proof for their exegesis. They point out that the agony of the destruction and exile befell all Israel, every class within it; wherefore, these speakers, who were exempted from suffering, could not possibly have been of Israel. Only gentiles could have spoken thus.[105]

But this interpretation attributes to the speakers statements which do not accord either with the historical situation or with the dominant imagery of Scripture. Who, then, could these gentiles have been? They who suffered no illnesses, no pains; who were not punished for their transgressions; who dwelt in tranquillity at that time when Israel was conquered, subjugated, exiled from his land, and "dead" for their sake? Assyria and Babylon had destroyed and exiled many nations— not just Israel. Assyria had been a universal power of destruction. The whole earth had been given over to Nebuchadnezzar. Assyria destroyed nations and cut them off (Isa. 10:5–15; 36:18–20; 37:10–13). The king of "Babylon" made "the world as a wilderness," all the world rejoiced at his fall (Isa. chs. 13–14). Nahum celebrated the fall of Assyria as a festival of liberation of all peoples (3:1–19). Habakkuk expressed his anguish at the ascent of the Chaldeans, whom he looked upon as a new destroyer of nations (chs. 1–2). Jeremiah viewed the Chaldean monarchy as a universal empire which would enslave all nations (25:9–11; 27:6–13; 28:14). But the cup of destruction passed also to Assyria and Babylon, both in fact and in prophetic vision. The "gentiles," therefore, could certainly not have said that by the suffering of Israel they were relieved of all disease and pain. They themselves suffered and were punished for their transgressions.

It is, therefore, impossible to explain 53:4–6 in the sense that the servant alone bore the punishment of the speakers. Indeed the phrase: "And with his stripes we were healed" (v. 5) implies that the speakers also had suffered disease and been healed by merit of the suffering of the servant. We must interpret all these verses in conformity with this. Indeed, the diseases which he bears are diseases which were ours to bear; and his pains were really ours to endure. He was punished for our iniquities and our transgressions. We, all of us, have sinned, but the Lord visited our punishment on him.

This does not mean that he alone bore all the punishments and sufferings, but that his sufferings were on their, not on his, account. Their diseases were visited on him, etc. Words such as these are natural when spoken by a "chorus" which represents the average sinful Israelite, as opposed to the humble, righteous servant.

The speech of the chorus

In the Septuagint, chapter 53 opens with the cry: Lord![106] This version gives support to the assumption that the chorus is of Israel. The chorus turns to God and confesses before Him. The speakers have just now heard the word of God of 52:13-15 and have seen His arm outstretched upon the servant. They say: Who would have believed the report which we have heard; and who is this upon whom the arm of the Lord is revealed? Is it not he who shot up before us[107] as the growth of the desert, wretched and miserable, despised in our eyes, a man of pains and disease? We esteemed him smitten of God because of his iniquities, and now we behold the arm of God upon him! He bore, then, our sins, and was crushed because of our iniquities. Israel, the humble, the crushed, the lowly of spirit, the melancholy, who rolls in the dust, he it is who appears now as the bearer of the weight of the calamity which had afflicted all Israel. The Jewish masses, though the destruction hurt them also, looked on the "crushed ones" with suspicion and scorn. There were in Israel those who hated them and cast them out (66:5). But the "chorus" does not express the sentiments of the haters; rather that of the ordinary folk, everyday people who are always scornful of uncompromising idealists, and especially of the type of the crushed, the lowly, the mourners. The servant is not described, as Duhm imagines, as stricken with leprosy. He is without form or comeliness, ill and in pain, and remote from the society of men ("forsaken of men"). But these are metaphors for contrition and heartbreak and permanent melancholy.[108] The people did not believe in the special righteousness of these mourners of Zion. They thought that these men justified themselves falsely, and that the suffering of the exile was caused also by the sin of these men. They thought that their depressed spirit and their melancholy were a specific smiting of God. Now, however, they know that these afflicted ones are Israel the righteous, who suffers for the sin which is not his. The people strayed like sheep, every man turned to his own way; they were absorbed in everyday affairs, tending to forget what had happened to them and what God had wrought upon them. And the entire weight of God's punishment fell upon these crushed ones.[109]

There is also in 53:5 a hint of the concept that the suffering of the righteous has specific atoning power. Because the humble who were innocent of transgression were smitten along with the rest of the people, God noticed their misery and took pity on the entire nation. The chorus says: the punishment which brought us welfare and salvation, this it is which struck down the servant, and by his stripes we were healed. Thus also in v. 11: the servant did justify the many in that he bore their iniquities. That is to say: because he, though innocent of transgression, suffers along with the nation, the Lord will save all the nation together with him and for his sake. This concept is in accord with the doctrine of association in retribution.

The speech of the prophet

In vv. 1–6 the speakers are a group, and all the propositions of the passage are theirs. In vv. 7–10, it is otherwise; and the content also is different. Vv. 1–6 describe the relationship of the speakers to the servant, how he had formerly appeared to them, and what they now behold in him. Vv. 7–10 are an objective description of what has happened to the servant. The symbolism also is different. Vv. 1–6 speak of the servant's vile aspect, of contempt, disease, pain, and the smiting of God. Disease and contempt are absent from 7–9. The agents are men who oppress the servant; and the sufferings are the evil deeds done him. Only in v. 10 is this suffering related, understandably, to the will of God. Vv. 7–10

are without question the speech of the prophet, not a continuation of the speech of the chorus. This is evident particularly from the end of v. 8. The topic of the verses is not
the relationship of the Jewish masses to the humble ones;
rather, it is the acts of the gentiles against Israel, in particular against Israel the righteous. Only at this point are the
gentiles mentioned, and now in their true role. They oppressed
and afflicted the servant; and he accepted his afflictions in
silence as a lamb and as a sheep.[110] He was taken away from
rulership and authority and imprisoned;[111] and who will recount all that befell him?[112] He was put into the pit—the
captivity of the exile—and cut off out of the land of the
living.[113] It was not for his own sin, the prophet charges, that
the servant was punished; the calamity befell him for the
transgression of my people, Israel (v. 8).[114] And, since he was
in prison with the transgressors, it was to be expected that
his grave would be with the transgressors and the wicked
when he died; and that his burial would be without honor
or lamentation.[115] V. 10 is, it appears, to be read: And the
Lord who takes delight in the contrite caused him disease.
God who loves the contrite (57:15; Ps. 34:19) brought all
this affliction on him. With the word-phrase "caused him
disease," the prophet reverts to the symbolism of the chorus.
The idea which is expressed at this point is that the suffering
of Israel the righteous is, in addition to being punishment for
the sin of Israel as a whole, also a trial: it is suffering which
has formed Israel the humble and contrite, the Israel which is
unconditionally faithful. The purpose of the chastisements was
the contrite one.[116] The close of v. 10 is apparently the
prophet's prayer: if his soul offers itself in restitution, let
him, pray, see his seed, prolong his days, and carry out suc-
cessfully what the Lord had appointed for him.[117] The phrase
"if his soul would offer itself in restitution" is very obscure.
The verb "will make"(תשים, offer) should not be understood
as future, rather as a continuing present: if Thou makest
(or hast made) him a trespass offering. The servant is still

160

engulfed in his humiliation, and his grandeur will be realized only in the future (*cf.* 11–12). The meaning of the phrase is simply: since Thou hast placed punishment upon him. The word אשם ("in restitution") should be pointed: אָשֵׁם (guilty). If Thou dost make his soul guilty ("his soul" in the sense of "him"; *cf.* 1 Kings 19:2: [if] I make [not] thy life as the life of one of them), that is, since Thou has made him to suffer and to be punished (*cf.* Prov. 30:10; Ps. 34: 22, 23) bestow on him a goodly reward.[118]

God's reply

Vv. 11–12 are the answer of the Lord. Because of the suffering which he did bear, the servant shall see (his seed), he shall be full (of days). Because he justifies by his knowledge the many, the masses of the house of Israel (in the visionary court of justice), and because he bears the punishment of their sins, his portion will be among the great ones of the earth. He delivered his soul to death,[119] was imprisoned in the prison with transgressors; and thus did suffer for the sins of others. And he even prayed for the sinful multitude of the house of Israel.

If this chapter is obscure and its sense very difficult to determine, it is because the prophet here presents Israel on the visionary stage in two roles: Israel the humble and suffering; and all Israel, the "sheep." In addition, there is the difficulty of the several speakers. The suffering of Israel the humble is the problem of the chapter. There was an explanation for the suffering of Israel as a whole; it was the result of sin. But what was the reason for the suffering of the faithful, of "the men that sigh and that cry"? To this there are two answers. Israel the humble suffered along with the nation when it was punished according to the principle of association of sin and retribution. Further, in 53:10 (and in 57:15) the prophet suggests a second explanation: God loves the contrite and meek of spirit. The suffering of the humble is a "trial." God is pleased with the righteous man who suffers chastisements for the transgression of others, who accepts His chastisements with love, who intercedes for the sinners with whom he is punished. The "contrite" is the truly righteous man; and the humble, therefore, are the true Israel. By their merit all Israel will be redeemed; and they, in particular, will be glorified when Israel is redeemed.

Redemption and the destruction
of the pagan kingdom

We find, therefore, in the prophecies of Deutero-Isaiah of the period immediately following the conquest of Babylon (chs. 49–54), two metaphors for Israel the righteous: the servant of the Lord, and Zion the mother. The servant is Israel exiled and subjugated, and Zion is the homeland destroyed and subjugated. The fate of Israel, whose subjugation continues after the return in Cyrus' reign, is symbolized in both figures. The servant and Zion alike have enemies who seek to "condemn" them (50:8–9; 54:17). Both look to salvation. Israel is still, even after the return, a nation dispersed and scattered, given over to the power of pagan rulers. Jerusalem is still a widow; her God has not returned to her, and she, also, is subjected to the pagan rule. The subjugation of the nation and the city to the pagan rule is a profanation of the Name, blasphemy. Cyrus does not know the God who delivered Babylon to him. The hope that the nations from the rising of the sun, and from the west, would of their own recognize that the Lord, he is God, was no more. There was no hope that they would build Zion, and restore freedom to Israel. The redemption of Israel would come only with the destruction of the pagan empire, that is, of the Persian monarchy.

For all his disappointment, the prophet still trusts that

salvation will come shortly (51:5; 56:1). He encourages Israel not to fear the taunts (51:7), not to be afraid of "the fury of the oppressor" (*ibid.*, 13). In the symbolical spirit of Isa. 27:1 and the manner of Ps. 89:11, he calls on the Lord to put on the arm of His strength as in the days of old, when He hewed Rahab in pieces and pierced the dragon and divided the sea before the redeemed of Egypt (Isa. 51:9–10). The slaughter of the "dragon," that is, the destruction of the new heathen kingdom, which was greater and more mighty than any of the others, and the heir of all of them, will precede the redemption of Israel. Prior to redemption will come the drowning of "pharoah," the monarch of the subjugation. Then, and only then, "sorrow and sighing shall flee away." To the taunters of Israel the prophet foretells that "the moth shall eat them up like a garment, And the worm shall eat them like wool" (*ibid.*, 7–8). The fury of the oppressor shall be as nothing (*ibid.*, 13). Israel was sold for nought to the nations. First, Egypt enslaved them; later, Assyria oppressed them; "Now therefore, what do I here? saith the Lord" (52:3–5).

This question is an expression of bafflement at the continuance of subjugation after the destruction of Babylon, which, however, is not mentioned explicitly. The word "here" stands for the entire pagan world, Babylon-Persia-Media. Israel is enslaved "for nought"; they that rule over her howl; and the name of the Lord is blasphemed all the day (5). In the manner of Pss. 98:1–4; 77:15–16, Deutero-Isaiah prophesies that the Lord will redeem Israel with "His holy arm," the arm of His strength, "in the eyes of all the nations" (52:9–10). He challenges Israel to depart "from thence," from the midst of all the heathen nations, to separate himself from all their uncleanness: Touch no unclean thing! (v. 11, *cf.* 1, "The uncircumcised and the unclean.") Israel shall go forth as the departure of an armed camp: they will be bearers of "the vessels of the Lord . . . the Lord will go before you" as a vanguard and "will be your rearward" (vv. 11–12).

Thus, the radiance of the earlier good news of the prophet was overcast. The old motif of an eschatological battle with the heathen world reappears in this message. The good news is accompanied by the dark shadow of reproof and warnings of judgment and punishment to Israel, which has not repented with full heart, and to the nations which had trampled on subjugated Israel and on Zion in her affliction and humiliation. The prophet has not changed; he remained faithful to his convictions. But the situation had changed. Persia was the heir of Babylon, and the Persian kingdom also was pagan. Deutero-Isaiah was compelled to return to the stance of Isaiah and Jeremiah and the other earlier prophets.

The joiners. The concept of religious conversion

Nonetheless, Deutero-Isaiah retained his universalistic outlook. This reality had not changed; the fate of Israel was bound up with the fate of the world. The redemption of Israel, dispersed among the peoples, would have to be a world event—a revolution in the lives of the nations. The prophet continued to prophesy the return of the gentiles from idolatry, even though only after the day of judgment. And in addition, in 56:1–8, he expresses a new thought which is the pinnacle of universalism. Here, for the first time, the concept of religious conversion is adumbrated, the institution which was to take form in Jewry only in a later period, and which would make possible the spread of monotheism throughout the world. Chapter 56:1–8 is a turning point, an historical monument.

Among Christian scholars there are some who regard Jewish proselytism as a way of segregation, and not of universalism. The ancient faith of Israel had made no religious demands on the proselyte, and in this sense was "liberal" with respect to the alien. Not so Judaism. Judaism required the proselyte to follow all the commandments, and made his participation in the worship of God dependent on full accept-tance of Judaism. Therein it lagged "far behind most religions."[120] These scholars discover the requirement in 56:1–7, wherein there is none of the breadth of Deutero-Isaiah. Here the proselyte is required to keep the sabbath and hold fast to the covenant. This is "on a low plane of ideas."[121]

The critics assume that there was religious conversion at the time of this prophecy. The fear of these aliens that the Lord would separate them "from His people" was the result of an agitation against the proselytes which appeared, it seems, in the Jewish community. In Jerusalem there was a tendency to religious and ethnic apartheid. The diaspora was more broadminded. This prophet, "a wise, benevolent lawgiver," expresses his opinion in favor of the proselytes.[122] But all these interpretations are incorrect.

It was in the concept of conversion that Jewry came to realize that the essence of Judaism was faith, a system of beliefs and opinions, a world view and way of life, a universal religion for all humanity. Therewith Judaism was detached from the nationalistic context in which it was bound during its historic development, and transformed from a national to a universal religion. The proselyte accepts the religion of Israel, and this acceptance is independent of cultural, social, territorial, or national attachment. The proselyte becomes an "Israelite" immediately, even though remaining an alien in his culture and nationality. The idea of "Israel according to the spirit," in which Christianity gloried, and which is the pride of Christian theologians to this day, was crystallized in religious proselytism. Religious conversion does, in fact, transform the nationalistic basis of the religion of Israel into a religious symbol. The requirement that the proselyte accept the entire complex of Israel's commandments is a direct result of the idea of religious conversion, and in no way narrowness and separatism; rather it is the supreme universalism. It assumes that all the commandments, even those which are distinctly "Israelite," were given for all men, that every man is able to keep them, even he who is not of the nation Israel.

The religion of Israel did not lag in this requirement "behind" pagan faiths. The pagan religions were not thought of as systems of belief which could be "received" at once as complete laws of life; and they knew nothing of religious conversion. Pagan universalism found expression in syncretism and theocracy, but not in religious conversion. Judaism demanded of the alien what is required of the Israelite. Therewith it raised the faith of Israel to a faith which embraced all humanity.

The question of the joiners became actual in the time of Deutero-Isaiah, but not because there was a "movement" against the "proselytes" (*gerim*). The joiners were not (territorial) *gerim*. They were not proselytes by reason of residence; proselytism of that kind ceased with the national catastrophe. Nor were they religious proseyltes. There was as yet no such thing as religious conversion anywhere in the world. They were a completely new phenomenon, judaizers and not *gerim;* and for that reason they caused perplexity, they were a "problem." Deutero-Isaiah was one of the prophets of universalist attitude, and he envisioned the return of the nations to God. But his vision entailed no immediate practical problem. It was "a rule for the messianic future," for the end of days. But the juristic position of the joiners was something else. These were individuals who now, in the present, had departed from idolatry and joined the faith of Israel. In the age of religious conversion the status of such men was clear. But in the time of Deutero-Isaiah and for several generations following, they were a dilemma. What was the nature of these "aliens"? Did they belong to the people of Israel? Did they share in the anticipation of redemption of the people Israel? This question was asked first of all by the joiners themselves. They were concerned and fearful lest the Lord separate them "from His people" (56:3).

Deutero-Isaiah's prophecy concerning the joiners (56:6–8) actually includes two answers. He gives judgment in this prophecy first with respect to all peoples and then with respect to the joiners and judaizers in particular. The future Temple on Mount Zion will be "a house of prayer for all peoples," including those who are still idol worshipers, who contemn God and His people. Obviously, Deutero-Isaiah cannot promise all the nations of the world that God will include them with "His gathered ones" and bring them to the land of Israel. But he promises the individual joiners, who have already at that time embraced the religion of Israel, that they will not be separated from the nation Israel, and that they will go up with the captivity to the holy mount (see also Isa. 14:1). It is evident that there is no contradiction between the generalized vision and the specific promise to the joiners. Only an involved theology could find a "low plane of ideas" in the prophecy to the joiners.

The prophecy to the joiners marks a turning point and an inversion of concepts. Hitherto, settlement in the land of Israel had been the beginning of conversion. The cleaving of the resident alien to the culture of Israel and its religion were consequent upon residence in the land. The land and life within the limits of Israel's domain were the proselyting forces. In the prophecy of Deutero-Isaiah, the settlement in the land is, we may say, the final act of the conversion, the compensation, a promise and an assurance, the reward to the alien for his attachment to the covenant of the Lord. Religion had become the decisive factor. Through the faith of Israel the alien became a member of the nation Israel, and was endowed even with the right of settlement in Israel's land. The whole concept of religious conversion is comprised in this. The territorial element remains, but its character is changed. To be sure, the answer of Deutero-Isaiah is only an eschatological vision, and he does not solve the juristic problem of the new judaizers. Jewry was destined to struggle with this problem for many generations.

The prophecy to the eunuchs in 56:3–5 also is eschatological, and not a juridical determination respecting the subject matter of the ordinance of Deut. 23:2. It is unconnected with that ordinance. The prophet was concerned with those Jewish youths who had been maimed by an oriental despotism in order that they might serve in the royal court. These unfortunates were certainly numerous among the Babylonian captivity. They worried about their fate and asked what would be their portion in the redemption of Israel, since the pagan despot had, as it were, cut them off from their nation. The prophet encouraged them and promised them compensation: "a monument and a memorial" in the future Jerusalem, which would be "Better than sons and daughters."

The great denunciations. The blind watchmen

In 56:9–59:21 are the great rebukes of Deutero-Isaiah. The motif of these denunciations is eschatological. The redemption had been close at hand; it was imminent. But Israel did not repent; Israel was immersed in sin and thus delayed its redemption. Therefore the redemption would come in the day of judgment.

The moral strictures of this group of prophecies contain no distinctive societal note as do the rebukes of the earlier classical prophets. The censure here is directed against the people as a whole. Only in the first rebuke (56:9–57:3), which is directed against the leaders of the nation, is there an element of class conflict: the watchmen-shepherds are blind and do not guard the flock; and the flock is prey to the greedy dogs. It has been argued that a rebuke such as this could have been uttered only in the land of Israel, where the "shepherds" were of their own nation. But in the Jewish "province" of Persia the rulers were not of their own nation. Aristocrats and the higher priests were their spokesmen to the administration; but the pagan monarch and his officers were the actual rulers, those who dealt with the people and their property as they saw fit (Neh. 9:36–37). However, the Jews did have officers and spokesmen in the diaspora. The prophet does not accuse the shepherds themselves of preying on the sheep (*cf.* Ezek. 34). They were blind watchmen and "dumb dogs." They failed as watchmen. They loved slumber, yea, and turned "each one to his gain," their hearts set on wine and strong drink. Thus the flock was given over to greedy dogs, and every beast of the field and forest could come to ravage without hindrance. This is censure of the leaders of the people in the captivity, leaders who did not protect the nation against the oppression of the officials of the government or against their enemies among the populace. Even in the diaspora the princes could have defended the poor. But they failed of their duty, for which failure the prophet threatens them with punishment.[123]

Idolatry in the past. Scoffing and rebellion now

The castigation of 57:3–13 is rebuke for idolatry. The problem is: against whom is it directed? The verbs of the opening sentences are plural: But draw near hither, Ye sons of the sorceress, The seed of the adulteress and the harlot (v. 3).[124] But beginning with v. 6 and following, second person feminine singular replaces the masculine plural: Among the smooth stones of the valley is thy (fem.) portion, etc. It is clear that the adulteress herself replaces the sons of the adulteress; and that this is upbraiding of the whole people in the manner of Ezek. 16 and 23. The prophet mentions the cult among the trees, the service of the high places "under every leafy tree," the slaughter of children in secret rites, drink and meal offerings to "the smooth stones of the valley," harlotry after the gods of remote peoples. This is of the style of the fulminations of the prophets against idol worship in the land of Israel. There is no reason to assume that it is directed against "Samaritans," or against Israelite idol worshipers of the period of the second Temple. We have previously pointed out that there is no mention of any such popular idolatry in Ezra, Nehe-

miah, Haggai, Zechariah, or Malachi. Nor is it to be assumed
that this is a fragment of an ancient prophecy. The prophet
addresses the Babylonian diaspora. His complaint is: Against
whom do ye sport yourselves? Against whom make ye a wide
mouth And draw out the tongue? (v. 4). This is the community which scoffed at him and his prophecy of glorious redemption of the days of Cyrus' victories, which prophecy had
not been fulfilled. Similar derision is mentioned in 66:5. These
are men to whom the vision of redemption is vain; and it is
with them that he contends. Indeed, the redemption has not
yet come. But there is a reason: the heavy sin of the idolatrous
harlotry of the past still besets Israel. The derision itself testifies to the character of this generation: these also are "children of transgression, A seed of falsehood," "sons of the sorceress," sons of a people laden with sin. Are they worthy of
atonement and of the loving kindness of redemption?

Vv. 5–12 are a summary of the past; and it appears
that the idea which is expressed in the appellations: sons . . .
seed . . . children . . . seed (3–4) carries over in v. 4; and
therewith that the prophet moves from the present to the
past: Ye are the seed of the sorceress and the adulteress,
sons of them "that inflame yourselves among the terebinths,
Under every leafy tree," etc. With this, the invective turns
in what follows against the sorceress herself. Vv. 6–12 bear
the obvious mark of historical summarization. All the verbs
are preterites. The figures are borrowed from the historical
surveys of Ezekiel. The prophet reviews the sins of the past,
of the generations, the guilt of the fathers who offered sacrifice
on the mountains (7, cf. 65:7). The sense of the summary
comes at the end of v. 6: "Should I pacify Myself for these
things?" Can God forget all this? Are the sons of that generation worthy of redemption? The people rebelled against God,
went a-whoring after the gods of the nations. When things
went well they did not fear God; God "held his peace" and was
long-suffering. In v. 13 the prophet returns from the historical
to the present. If the people derides and rebels, in what will

it trust? Will the graven images rescue it in the hour of need? Will not the wind carry them all away? Only in God is there refuge, and only for those who take refuge in Him is there assurance of redemption.[125] The castigation of the scoffers ends with a new prophecy of the ingathering of the exiles (13–19). The prophet directs the good news particularly to the "contrite" and humble of spirit, to those who are submissive to God in truth and in faith. God will not contend forever, neither will He be always wroth. God was angry with Israel and smote him; but Israel went frowardly in the way of his heart, even after the smiting. Therefore Israel has not yet been redeemed. But God is sure; He will heal him and will requite with comforts him and his mourners.[126]

Denunciation and judgment

The final prophecies of Deutero-Isaiah (58–66) are a section of rebuke and judgment. More than in his earlier prophecies, the prophet pronounces judgments on his contemporaries. In chapter 57 the sin is of the past, and the rebuke applies to the idolatry of the past. But beginning with chapter 58 and following, the prophet castigates the exiles on account of their own sins; and therewith the moral element comes to the fore. All of chapters 58–59 is moral rebuke. The idolatry for which the prophet chides in this section is not "historical." Neither the cult of high places nor the worship of idols is mentioned. The idolatry of these passages is something new which emerged in the diaspora, under the influence of the heathen environment. The psychological background of the censure is the bafflement due to the delay of the redemption. Here are the Jewish people who beseech God, who pray for and look to redemption. The people think they are righteous and complain that God does not hearken to their prayers. There are also among them those who "forsake the Lord," who forget the holy mountain, who are beguiled by the surrounding idolatry.

171

These latter are scornful of the faithful and their hopes, and deride them. But there are also among the exiles those who tremble at the word of the Lord, the meek, the contrite, the mourners of Zion. The prophet reckons himself among these, and expresses their point of view. The postponement of the redemption grieves him also; and he gives vent to his feelings in dirge and bitter complaint against heaven (63:7–64:11). Yet he remains firm in his faith. He justifies the decrees against Israel. It is the sin which is the cause of the delay. And salvation will certainly come. Israel is laden with sin. Yet this people is the only people in which there is awareness of God; and this unique awareness is of decisive historical significance. The contention of God with the pagan world is the contention of Israel; and pagan dominion will end only with Israel's salvation. Salvation will come on the day of judgment of the wicked. Now, even more than in his earlier prophecies, Deutero-Isaiah gives symbolic expression to his faith in hyperbolic descriptions of the glory of Jerusalem in the time to come.

Morality and the new cult.
Deeds of loving kindness. The sabbath

The rebuke of chapter 58 is one of the high points among the ethical censures of the prophets. In this chapter, Deutero-Isaiah deals with the problem of cult versus morality, with which problem he had not previously been concerned; and to which he will return in 66:1–3. This people, to whom he declares its transgression, is a people which seeks God daily, which delights to know His ways, asking righteous ordinances, delighting to draw near unto God. This people fasts and afflicts its soul, and then complains: "Wherefore have we fasted, and Thou seest not? Wherefore have we afflicted our soul, and Thou takest no knowledge?" (58:3). This people thinks it is deserving of redemption, and ques-

tions God's justice. Such is the people whom the prophet rebukes. There is no mention of idolatry; the rebuke is altogether
moral. Vainly does this people consider itself "As a nation that
did righteousness, And forsook not the ordinance of their
God." (58:2). Their righteousness is not righteousness, their
fast no fast, and in these they will not be saved. Behold in
the day of fast, their thoughts are on their business, they lend
and exact, strive and contend, smite with the fist of wickedness. They assemble to fast, only to make their voices heard
and to appear as those who cry to God in truth.[127] Not by such
a fast will they be reconciled to God. The fast which God demands is this: to loose the bound, to free the oppressed (imprisoned or bound over for their debts), to deal out bread to
the hungry, to bring the poor into the home, to clothe the
naked, to satisfy afflicted souls, not to deride and to speak
wickedness.

In this reproof the prophetic doctrine of the primacy of
ethical conduct is given a new formulation. The prophet does
not mention the sacrificial cult. He passes judgment on the
new cult, that of the synagogue, the creation of the diaspora.
The people assemble to seek "righteous ordinances," to hear
the law, to fast and to pray. The people believe that in this they
express in foreign parts their faithfulness to God, that in this
they come near to God and show themselves worthy of redemption. The prophet gives judgment on this new piety. This, also,
is only external cultic practice, without meaning. Loving
kindness I desire and not fasting—this is a new culmination
of the prophetic teaching of the primacy of the ethical. This
doctrine certainly struck men's ears more harshly than the
doctrine of the earlier prophets. The piety of the period
following the destruction was in essence a confession of belief,
a commitment to God and to the struggle against idolatry; and
this the people regarded as righteousness in the presence of
God. But the prophet rejects this piety also. It, too, if it is without moral goodness, is not righteousness.

There is, in addition, a new note in the moral demands of this chapter. Hitherto the prophets required righteousness and justice, and condemned perversion of justice, exploitation of the poor, oppression, and spoliation. But now Deutero-Isaiah demands more: deeds of loving kindness, the giving of bread and clothing and shelter to the poor. He requires compassion: *And if thou draw out thy soul to the hungry* (58:10). The redemption of Israel depends upon righteousness and loving kindness and compassion.

There is no question but that the reward which the prophet promises for this moral conduct is redemption from the exile, even though most of the metaphors in vv. 8–12 are general. Darkness and light (8, 10) in his prophecies are symbols of exile and redemption. The "healing" (58:8) also is healing of the smiting of exile (*cf.* 53:2, 4, 5; 57:17–18). In 58:8, the prophet says: "And thy righteousness shall go before thee, The glory of the Lord shall be thy rearward." This is a variant on the prophecy of the ingathering of the exiles of 52:12. "And they that shall be of thee shall build the old waste places, Thou shalt raise up the foundations of many generations" (12) corresponds to 61:4, which is placed in the sequence of the prophecies of redemption (see 60:3, 8; 61:1–2; 63:5, 10–11).

The prophet concludes his invective with an observation regarding the sabbath. Sabbath observance also must be an act of piety and not a formal duty. The sabbath must be a day of holiness, of delight to the glory of God; and to man a day of rest from the toil of earning a livelihood; from pursuing "thy business" and "thy wonted ways" (58:13), a day of rising above the seeking after material goods. The sabbath was also a day of rest to the laborer, of the quality of divine compassion for every living creature. The prophecy concerning the sabbath is, therefore, in harmony with the thought of the chapter, and could be deleted only by reason of the inflexibility of a liberal Protestant theology. This prophecy also concludes with the assurance of redemption.

Rebuke, lamentation, confession

Chapter 59 also is ethical admonition. Here again the basic theme is the delay of the redemption. Included in the chapter are rebuke, lamentation, confession, and prediction; and there is evidence of the influence of the idiom of the wisdom literature. "The Lord's hand is not shortened, that it cannot save, Neither His ear heavy," that it cannot hear the prayer of the people which prays for redemption. It is because of the sin that God will not hear the prayers. The list of sins here, unlike in chapter 58, is a patterned formula: blood, lies, violence, and robbery. Once more, there is no mention of idolatry. In vv. 9–13, the prophet identifies himself with the people, and his words are of the nature of lament and confession. Because of moral evil the people grope in darkness. They cry for salvation; but there is none. And because there is no righteousness and no justice, the God of vengeance will appear to do justice. The Lord will requite His enemies of the nations. And in Israel also He will execute justice. He will come as redeemer to Zion, but only to those who turn from transgression (v. 20).

Against the backsliders. Household idolatry

The censure in the prophetic section 65–66 is different. This rebuke is basically religious-cultic, although not without an ethical strain.

The people whom the prophet here reproves are not those of chapters 58–59, rather those of chapter 57. These are not men who seek God and delight to draw near to Him; they do not afflict themselves and pine for the redemption. The prophet now rebukes "a rebellious people" (65:2), men that provoke God (v. 3), those that "forsake the Lord" and that forget His holy mountain (v. 11). These are men who are radically estranged, the opposite of those who seek God (v. 10). Like the people of chapter 57, they are marked by two characteristics: they have dissociated themselves from the yearning for redemption, they hate the meek ones and deride their expectations of redemption (65:11; 66:5); and they lean toward idolatry (65:3–7, 11; 66:3, 17). Here again the prophet reminds them, as in chapter 57, of the iniquities of the fathers, when they were still in their own land, the sacrifices upon the mountains and the hills (65:7). But he castigates them also for their own idolatry. This idolatry is not worship of idols; rather a kind of black-ritual, demonic and magic. It is significant that in this section, also, the prophet mentions no public idol worship. He does not censure the backsliders for worship of idols in temples, for heathen festivals, for priestly rites and public processions, or for participating in the public rituals of their pagan environment. The rites which he cites are within the home, behind closed doors. These men sacrifice in gardens, burn incense on bricks, sit among graves, lodge in vaults (in order to consult with the dead and with ghost-spirits), eat swine's flesh and the detestable thing, and the mouse in ritual meals (65:3–5; 66:17), and break dogs' necks for satyrs (66:3). Gardens are mentioned twice (65:3; 66:17) and the swine-offering three times (65:4; 66:3, 17). This rite and also the breaking of dogs' necks and the ritual eating of detestable things are mentioned only in these prophecies. These are practices which the exiles must have borrowed from the pagan miscellany among whom they were cast in the Assyrian-Babylonian diaspora. In 65:11, the prophet mentions two gods by name: there are those that forsake the Lord, that prepare a table for Gad (Fortune), and offer mingled wine in full measure unto Meni (Destiny). This may have been an ancient Israelite ritual connected with satyrs, or another of the rites adopted in the pagan diaspora.[128]

These backsliders did not separate themselves from the

captivity and did not join themselves to the gentiles. They were part of Israel, the rebellious Israel, laden with the guilt of the fathers. Their idolatry, unlike that of the gentiles, was a sin. The wrath of God against them was "A fire that burneth all the day" (65:5). God would visit upon them their own and their fathers' iniquities together (65:7). Their estrangement, however, was both religious and national. They did not believe in the redemption; neither did they pray for it. They were the people to whom God called, and who did not hear; to whom He spoke, and who did not answer (65:1, 12; 66:4). They were responsible for the delay of the redemption; and between them and the humble, the servants of the Lord, those who quaked at His word, there was bitter antagonism. They hated the meek ones, cast them out (repelled them contemptuously) on account of their zeal for the name of the Lord. Jeeringly they said, "Let the Lord be glorified, That we may gaze upon your joy" (66:5). Deutero-Isaiah prophesied that the joy would surely come; but it would not be joy for them. The servants of the Lord would rejoice, but they would be ashamed (65:13; 66:5). The day of redemption would be a day of judgment for them: they would all be consumed by the sword (65:12). The elect and the faithful would inherit the mountains of Judah (65:9); and for their sake there would be a remnant to Israel (65:8).

Cult and morality. Repentance. The Temple

The attitude of classical prophecy with respect to the cult is strikingly expressed in the rebuke of 66:1–4.

This is the only prophecy wherein we hear reverberations of the popular agitation to return and to build the Temple by permission of Cyrus. What was the attitude of the prophet to this movement of return? Obviously Cyrus had not fulfilled the hopes of the prophet. This return was not the redemption which he had anticipated. Nonetheless, the agitation of the

177

return was in itself an expression of the faithfulness of the people to the Lord, and this fact the prophet certainly recognized. But the very event was of a nature to intensify the urgency of the problem with which the prophet struggled. If the nation was faithful, why was there an aliyah only by favor of the pagan king? Why was the real redemption delayed? The prophet's answer to this question is given in 66:1–2: this faithfulness is not the true repentance, which God requires of His people, that it may be worthy of full redemption. For all the faithfulness, the sin persists and delays the redemption. Cyrus had granted permission to build the Temple, and the prospect of building the house of God in the holy city thrilled the nation. There was now the prospect of restoring the legitimate cult which the destruction had interrupted. The movement of aliyah was cultic and national. The people believed that with the restoration of the correct ritual it would be reconciled to its God, and God would restore His favor. The prophet now fought this mood, even as earlier, in chapter 58, he had opposed a similar point of view. The cult is not the way to the favor of God. The prophet did, indeed, anticipate the building of the Temple, as we have observed from his other prophecies. The Temple was, in his prophecies, the symbol of the glory of Israel and of Israel's God in the time to come. But the Temple as a glorious symbol and the Temple as a human cultic undertaking were different matters. The nation felt that by its great exertion to build the Temple it was fulfilling its principal duty to God. But in the prophet's scheme of values the matter was otherwise. The essential inner repentance, religious-ethical return, was still lacking.

The Temple. Cult and morality. Humility

In 66:1 Deutero-Isaiah forcefully formulates Israel's concept of the cult, within which the classical prophetic doctrine of the primacy of the ethical developed. God is the Creator of all; all the world is His sanctuary, and He is bound to no shrine built by man, wherein—as in pagan thought—His resting-place might be found. This proposition applies to the entire ritual cult, not merely to the Temple. The cult has no supra-divine, magic-mystical power, as in pagan ideology, and no life-giving potency for the gods. Man is not reconciled to God by cultic worship: "But on this man will I look, Even on him that is poor and of a contrite spirit, And trembleth at My word" (v. 2). In chapter 58, Deutero-Isaiah phrases his demand in the spirit of Amos: righteousness! On his own, he adds: righteousness with mercy; and in his conclusion, speaking of the sabbath, he completes the thought: to rise above pursuit of material goods, to attain to holiness as the supreme good. In 66:2 he phrases his demand in the spirit of Hosea: loving kindness, true devotion to God. He formulates this concept with a special symbol: he demands "humility," meekness and submission to God, obedience to His word in the spirit of reverence. This demand comprises the ethical postulate of chapter 58. The prophet conceives the moral law as the revelation of God's will. It enjoins moral holiness in the spirit of trembling at the word of God. The lowly of spirit in the sight of God is the contrary of him who exacts and robs and smites with the fist of wickedness. The only way to divine grace is religious-moral holiness.[129]

In 66:3–4, the prophet proceeds from his polemic against ritualism in general to censure of specific contemporary cultic practices. He cites examples: he that kills an ox in sacrifice, and also smites or kills a man; he that sacrifices a lamb and offers a meal-offering, and also breaks the neck of a dog or offers swine's blood to satyrs; he that makes a memorial offering of frankincense, and also blesses over a sacrifice of violence.[130] Legitimate cultic practice, therefore, could be combined with deeds which were abominations from the religious or moral point of view. Since, according to 66:1–2, the Tem-

179

ple had not yet been built, the prophet in vv. 3–4 was not describing real persons who offered sacrifices in Jerusalem. Rather, he was describing types which he observed among his fellow Jews. There were many types. Among those who sought the Lord in chapters 58–59, there were the violent and the shedders of blood; they also yearned for the Temple. Even among those who broke the necks of dogs and sacrificed swine, there certainly were some who did not forget the holy mountain. They practiced heathen magic rituals in order to ward off perils, which they anticipated. Concerning them, the prophet predicted that God would bring upon them "their fears" (66:4), the calamities which they sought to dispel. However, even among these there were men who yearned for the restoration of the legitimate cult in its proper place. The prophet in his vision beheld all the misdeeds of these men in the Temple. They served him as examples of the practice of the legitimate cult along with abominable deeds. All these were the guilt-laden, who, in his view, delayed the coming of redemption.

Reasoning with God. Lament and complaint

For all his firm faith in an early redemption, and for all his assurance that the redemption was delayed only by reason of sinfulness, Deutero-Isaiah still could not be unmoved by the pathos of Israel's fate, and the severe suffering laid upon it. He reproves Israel; but he also "reasons" with his God. In his censure he gives expression to the divine justice. But in lament and in prayer he cries out for divine mercy and grace. The quality of justice prolongs the captivity and maintains the rule of the gentiles, which is the dominion of idolatry and of wickedness. But the dominion of idolatry and wickedness is profanation of God's name. The purpose of the captivity is the refining of Israel in the "furnace of affliction." But it is also a

terrible trial, hardening the heart, causing despair and disbelief, prolonging the sin. This is the fateful tragedy, concerning
which Deutero-Isaiah "reasons" with God.

The prophet gives expression to this mood in the poignant
lament of 63:7–64:11. The background is the prolongation of
the exile and the destruction. The prophet does not mention
the aliyah by permission of Cyrus. He envisions Jerusalem as
a widow steeped in mourning. The cities of Israel are ruins,
Zion a wilderness, the Temple burnt; and the subjugation to
idolatry persists. The aliyah has not reduced the measure of
captivity and disgrace; it has changed nothing of the fate of
Israel; neither has it hallowed the name of Israel's God;
wherefore the prophet mourns. He begins by recalling the
loving kindness of God to Israel in the past. In his opening
words and through the lament he recounts the acts of grace
and mercy. All the goodness which befell Israel in days gone
by was God's loving kindness. But Israel was rebellious and
sinful, and God became Israel's enemy. Thus Deutero-Isaiah
justifies the decree. But his heart is rent by the memory of
the splendor of the temple worship then and the thought of
God's name now profaned. In Israel's salvation God will make
for Himself "an everlasting name." Now Israel is brought low,
and the idolatrous enemy rejoices; wherefore the prophet appeals to the divine compassion and zealotry. The accuser becomes the defender. Indeed, he redirects his complaint against
God. It is God who has caused His people to stray from His
paths, and God who has hardened their heart from fearing
Him. He sees the sin itself as the punishment decreed of God.
Because God was wroth and hid His countenance from Israel,
Israel sank down in sin and was bound over into the power of
transgression. In this lament the prophet does not distinguish
between the righteous and the wicked. He envisions Israel on
the stage of universal history: Israel versus the pagan world.
God's wrath went forth against the whole nation; from the
whole people the glory was departed. It was altogether un-

clean, altogether mired down in sin. Because of God's anger Israel could not return in penitence; it could not call on the name of God. And withal, this people Israel is a holy nation, the servants of God, the tribes of His inheritance. "Behold, look, we beseech Thee, we are all Thy people!" On the world stage the foes of Israel are the foes of God. The cities of Israel are the holy cities, the ruined Temple is the Temple wherein God was praised. Therefore the prophet cries out to God the redeemer to appear and to make His name known to His foes.[131]

The prophecies of 62:1, 6–7 also are of the class of impassioned complaints with which the prophet storms the gates of heaven. The prophet who had been anointed to bring good tidings unto the humble, sent to proclaim freedom and liberation to the exiles (61:1–2), asserts that he will not hold his peace and will not rest until his cry is heard and Zion's salvation shall come (62:1). He has set "watchmen" on the ruined walls of Jerusalem, and they also will not hold their peace day or night. He turns to these visionary watchmen: Ye that are the Lord's remembrancers, Take ye no rest, And give Him no rest, Till He establish, And till He make Jerusalem A praise in the earth (6–7).[132]

Prophecies of vengeance and judgment

Persia, notwithstanding Cyrus' permission and the return, was the heir of the pagan dominion, of the foes of Israel and of Israel's God, of those who destroyed the holy cities and burnt the Temple. The subjugation persisted, and the contention of Israel with the pagan world was unaltered. The prophet's awareness of all this intensified his longing for judgment, retribution, and vengeance. After the year 539 he never again mentioned Babylon or Persia. The nation Persia had not harmed Israel. The Persian empire was merely the heir of the subjugation, not its agent. But the pagan world was oppressor and foe. The longing for judgment was directed against the entire pagan world, against pagan dominion. The themes of revenge and retribution appear in 59–66. When the day shall come, God will put on garments of vengeance and a cloak of zeal, He will pay recompense to His enemies, "to the islands"; and the nations of the east and of the west shall be in fear before Him (59:18–20). God will judge the wicked of Israel also—the backsliders; they also are become enemies. But the judgment will be worldwide, retribution to the subjugating nations.[133] In 63:1–6, Edom appears instead of the Babylon of the earlier prophets. Edom is now used by various prophets as the symbol of evil and hostility. The psalmist of Ps. 137 refers to Edom and Babylon in one prayer of vengeance; and in Deutero-Isaiah's later prophecies Edom supplants Babylon. In 63:1–6, the prophet envisions God coming from Edom and Bozrah "with crimsoned garments." A voice asks: "Wherefore is Thine apparel red, And Thy garments like his that treadeth in the winevat?" God replies that He has executed judgment of the peoples, He trod them in His anger, and trampled them in His fury. For the "day of vengeance" and the "year of redemption" were come. God alone had executed judgment; of the nations there was no man with Him, none came to help Him (*cf.* Judg. 5:23). This is a direct reference to the prophet's disappointment in Cyrus; he had expected that Cyrus would do battle for the Lord. But Cyrus battled for himself, and his victory was not the victory of God.[134] Now will come the year of the redeemed —"the day of vengeance" (59:17; 61:2; 63:4; 66:6). The Edom of this prophecy is not the nation Edom; it is the symbol of the hostile pagan world. In "Edom" and "Bozrah" God vanquishes the nations. The battleground of the end of days moves from north to south. But the retribution and vengeance are, in fact, worldwide. God will execute judgment against His enemies, with "all flesh" (66:16–17), with breath (59:19), with sword, fire, and fury (63:1–6; 66:15–16). From every city and every temple the voice of God who requites will be heard (66:6). The carcasses of the transgressors will be consumed by a fire that shall not be quenched. They shall be "an abhorring unto all flesh" (66:24).

Chapters 34–35

The prophecy of Isa. 34–35, which cannot be denied to Deutero-Isaiah, certainly belongs among these final vengeance prophecies. This cannot be one of his earlier prophecies because of the presence in these chapters of the vengeance motif, in the characteristic manner of chapters 59–66. In the beginning of his prophetic career Deutero-Isaiah foretold divine mercy. Chapter 34 describes the judgments of "Edom" and "Bozrah," which are here also symbols of "all the nations" which God hath delivered to the slaughter (v. 2). Here, also, the slaughter will be of "a day of vengeance," "a year of recompense for the controversy of Zion." Here, also, there are the slain and the carcasses, the sword and a fire which shall not be quenched (cf. 66:15–16, 24). The description is turgid. The horizon of the slaughter is cosmic: the heavens and their host shall moulder away and be destroyed (34:4). The land of Edom shall be turned into "burning pitch" (v. 9); it shall be waste forever and the dwelling place of the beasts of the wilderness (vv. 10–17).

Chapter 35 is a prophecy of consolation in the style of the early prophecies of Deutero-Isaiah: the good news of redemption, the description of the way of the wilderness, the ingathering of the exiles. But here, again, the theme of retribution is inserted into the good news of the redemption: Behold, your God will come with vengeance, With the recompense of God (v. 4, cf. as against this, 40:10–11). In addition to the generalized "fear not," we find "weak hands," "tottering knees," and "them that are of a fearful heart" (vv. 3–4),

which may be a reference to the weakening of purpose which
followed the disillusionment in Cyrus.[135] The prophetic message of Deutero-Isaiah from beginning to end is reflected in
these two prophecies, but in reversed order: prayer for retribution, vengeance, Edom, Bozrah, slaughter of the nations;
then consolation, the way of the wilderness, the return of
the redeemed. It is possible that this is intended as a kind of
summation; and that this prophecy, with its message of redemption in joy and gladness, was to have been the conclusion
of the book. It was then erroneously displaced, from its position at the end of Deutero-Isaiah, to the end of the book of the
first Isaiah.[136]

Judgments against the nations and the wicked of Israel. The return of the nations

In the final prophecies, the judgment and the retribution
are the central theme of a vision of the end of days. But this
does not alter the universalistic quality of the prophecies.
Deutero-Isaiah remains faithful to himself to the last. The
judgment will be harsh for the nations; but Israel also will
not be free of punishment. The prophet envisions terrible
things for the backsliders. All of them shall bow down to the
slaughter (65:12). They shall be hungry, thirsty; they shall
be ashamed (65:13; 66:5). They shall cry and wail, their
names shall be for a curse (65:14–15). Fire and sword shall
strike them also (66:14–17). Their carcasses shall be consumed by eternal fire, and they, too, shall be an abhorring
(66:24). Although the day of vengeance will be a day of fury
"for all the nations," there is still no prophecy of extinction of all
the nations. On the contrary, the judgment and the redemption
will be accomplished in full view of the nations. The theophany of the glory of the Lord in the sight of the nations is the
climactic event of the end of days. Therein will occur the return of the peoples to God. Jerusalem will be a light unto the

nations; nations shall walk at its light and kings at the brightness of its rising (60:3).

The glory of Jerusalem. The meek-poor

In the descriptions of the glory of Jerusalem and of Israel
in his later prophecies, Deutero-Isaiah develops and broadens
the themes of his earlier prophecies, in particular the motif of
the consolation of Zion the mother-widow of 49:14–26;
54:1–17. Jerusalem is destined to be the glory of the world,
a joy of many generations, a city of gold and silver and brass;
the wealth of the nations will be brought unto it; in it will be
the Temple of the cypress, plane tree, and larch (60:1–17).

Deutero-Isaiah is the prophet of the meek, the contrite.
But these meek-poor are not a social class. Deutero-Isaiah is
not a prophet of the downtrodden, as were Amos, Isaiah,
Micah, and Zephaniah; and those critics are in error who
trace a line from Amos and Isaiah, by way of Deutero-Isaiah,
to the songs of "the poor ones" of the book of Psalms.[137] This
prophet's meek-poor are a religio-national class—the faithful,
the mourners of Zion, contrite of spirit, brokenhearted. Such
men were to be found in every status in Israel. Indeed, Deutero-Isaiah tended to apply this phrase to all Israel in that it
was in exile and suffering. The "poor and needy" of 41:17
are really the whole of Israel. All Israel has been refined in
the "furnace of affliction" (48:10); they are all "His
afflicted" (49:13). Zion is the "afflicted" (51:21), "afflicted,
tossed with tempest" (54:11). Even in chapters 60–66, there
is no definite separation between the solace of the afflicted and
of the people as a whole. Thus the ideal of Deutero-Isaiah is
not the "afflicted and poor people" of Isaiah and Zephaniah.
The people of Zion of the time to come are not a nation of
peasants and shepherds, poor and toilsome. Deutero-Isaiah
goes to the very limit in describing the wealth of Zion and its
people in the future: And strangers shall stand and feed your

flocks, And aliens shall be your plowmen and your vine-dressers. . . . Ye shall eat the wealth of the nations, etc. (61:5–6; 66:10–12). To be sure, in his more sober prophecies he describes the Israel of the future as a nation of peasants and vinedressers who gather grain and wine (62:9), builders of houses and planters of vineyards (65:21), raising sheep and cattle (65:10). But he certainly does not imagine them as a people afflicted and poor.

Apocalyptic overtones

In Deutero-Isaiah's descriptions of the end of days there is something of the visionary of the new universe of apocalyptic prophecy. In the days of retribution all the host of heaven shall moulder away, And the heavens shall be rolled together as a scroll (34:4). Creation shall be renewed (65:17). God will create new heavens and a new earth (*cf.* 66:22). Israel will be the blessed of the Lord, they shall prolong their days "as the days of a tree," infants of days shall not die (65:20–22). Their salvation will be an eternal salvation. No foe shall come unto their land (62:8). There will be an end to moral evil. Violence shall no more be heard in thy land, Desolation nor destruction within thy borders (60:18). In a variation of Isa. 11:6–9 the prophet foretells peace among the beasts in the holy land of the future (65:25). The terror of destructions and exile will be no more, the "former troubles" will be forgotten. Nor come into mind (65:16–17). Sin, the source of evil, will have been rooted out. Deutero-Isaiah now completes the promise of the eschatological forgiveness of transgression of the earlier prophecies by the assurance of the abolition of sin. Like Jeremiah and Ezekiel, he prophesies moral renewal, a new heart. All the children of Zion shall be "taught of the Lord" (54:13). The Lord will enter into a new covenant with Israel, which covenant shall be: the word of the Lord shall not depart from their mouths, henceforth and for ever (59:21). The people of Zion shall be "all righteous," they shall inherit the land for ever (60:21). The redemption itself will be accomplished miraculously. God will appear clothed in righteousness, with helmet of salvation to execute judgment on the enemies in the sight of the nations of east and west (59:17–19). All Israel will return together to Zion from the far reaches of the earth (60:4, 9). Unearthly messengers, visionary figures, will go through the gates, clear the ways, cast up highways, lift up an ensign over the peoples. God will go at the forefront of His people to Zion (62:10–12). "In one day" Zion will bring forth her children (66:7–9). God will send such as escape of them unto the far off nations to declare His glory among the nations; and further, they shall bring the sons of Israel "for an offering unto the Lord" (66:19–21). The everlasting fire, also, which burns in the carcasses of those who rebelled (66:24), is a supernatural, foreboding lineament in the descriptions of Deutero-Isaiah, foreshadowing the "Gehenna" idea of later writings.

No imperium of Israel

Throughout Deutero-Isaiah's dithyrambic descriptions of the splendor and glory of golden Jerusalem the motif of the kingdom is missing. Israel's hope of redemption was, above all, the hope of restoration of the monarchy, and the hope of redemption was always bound to the house of David. It is, therefore, surprising that the kingdom motif is absent in such detailed descriptions of the future as those of Deutero-Isaiah; and it is all the more surprising in that Deutero-Isaiah does not negate the monarchy. In 55:3 he promises Israel that God will make an everlasting covenant with them, Even the sure mercies of David. The plain meaning of this assurance, apart from theological interpretation, is the renewal of the kingdom of the house of David, which was promised David as an ever-lasting covenant and a sure mercy. Every word of this prophecy is taken from Ps. 89 and II Sam. 7; 23:5, which tell of the everlasting covenant made with David and of the sure mercies which are promised him.[138] Deutero-Isaiah thinks that there will be gentile kingdoms in the future. Kings and princes will lead the peoples, and it is they who shall bow down to Jerusalem and lick the dust of her feet (49:23), who shall walk at her light, bring unto her the wealth of the nations or be "in procession" to her (60:3, 10, 11, 16). But he says nothing of a king of Jerusalem of the time to come. There is no monarch who has dominion from sea to sea, to whom the nations offer gifts, whose enemies lick dust (Ps. 72:8–11). There is also no ruler who shall have dominion from sea to sea and shall speak peace unto the nations (Zech. 9:9–10). There is not even the righteous king of Isa. 11:1–5. Deutero-Isaiah weaves into his prophecies (65:25) the vision of peace among the beasts (Isa. 11:6–9); but he leaves out the first part of Isaiah's vision, that is, the vision of the future king.

These facts confirm the character of Deutero-Isaiah's visions of the future. We have already remarked that there is no place in the prophecies of Deutero-Isaiah for the idea of a pagan world empire, such as Jeremiah envisaged, and which apocalyptic prophecy took over from him. Deutero-Isaiah does not regard the Persian monarchy as one more pagan world empire, for which there is a fixed term according to God's plan; and, likewise, he does not consider Israel the heir of the pagan world empire. Deutero-Isaiah rejects empire, in the sense of rule of one nation over another. The image of David also is transfigured in Deutero-Isaiah's speculum of "witness . . . prince and commander." Deutero-Isaiah does not foretell a conqueror and ruler. The world of the future is to be a world of many kingdoms—of free nations, with no world empire, not even of Israel. Israel will not subjugate the nations nor exact tribute from them. There will be no Israelite empire.

189

A light of the nations

The situation of Jerusalem in Deutero-Isaiah's vision of the end of days is to be understood against the background of this concept.

Jerusalem is the eternal city in the vision of the end of days, but not the capital of a universal empire. It possesses no authority and none of the secular accoutrements of empire with which it might subdue nations. It has no mighty king and no powerful army. All the nations flow unto this city, and it consumes the wealth of nations. But the nations do not come to Jerusalem as conquered foes, and they do not carry tribute to a conqueror and ruler. They shall go up to Jerusalem exulting and with praise (42:11–12). They shall bring gold and frankincense, And shall proclaim the praises of the Lord (60:6); the Temple shall be a house of prayer also for them (56:7). They are deeply stirred, excited as they go, drunk with light, rejoicing in light, as the blind whose eyes are suddenly opened. For, behold, darkness shall cover the earth, And gross darkness the peoples; but the glory of the Lord shall be seen upon Zion; and nations shall walk in its light, And kings at the brightness of its rising (60:2–3). The God of Israel will be revealed to all the nations in the redemption of Israel. Then only will man's supreme cognition, the knowledge of God, be given to the nations. Jerusalem symbolizes spiritual redemption. The nations shall go up to the house of God in Jerusalem with song and praise. The gold and silver, the flocks and rams which they shall bring to Jerusalem are not tribute of the conquered. They express gratitude and holy reverence, brought in joy as offerings to God and to the city of God. In this sentiment they exalt Israel, feed their flocks, cultivate their soil, name them "priests of the Lord," "ministers of our God" (61:5–6) and bring the wealth of the nations to them. This is the offering of atonement for the wrongs which they had done to Israel, for the exile and the subjugation, the rejection and the humiliation. What they had received from Israel was not to be valued by all this silver and gold. God had entrusted the treasure of his loving kindness to Israel, and Israel had guarded it even in the furnace of affliction and suffering. And now the gentiles also would be endowed with a share of this great loving kindness.

Deutero-Isaiah does not prophesy of the beating of swords into plowshares or of the king of peace. Nonetheless, there is no warfare in his world of the future. All the peoples are united in their awareness of God; all lift their eyes to the brightness of the rising of Jerusalem. Jerusalem is the city of Israel's holiness and kingdom, but also the heart of all nations. To be sure, there will be rebellious peoples. But there will be no place for them in the world of the future. Either they will come "in processions," or they will perish (60:11–12). Indeed, the nations which afflicted Israel and spurned her will be unable to forget their deeds; they shall come "bending" (60:14). But this, also, will be forgotten in the course of time, and a day will come when the "former things" shall not be remembered (65:16–17). And from one new moon to another, And from one sabbath to another, "all flesh" shall come to worship before the Lord (66:23).

Vision and event

Something of the magnificence of this glorious dream was destined to become the reality of history. The Jerusalem of the days of the second Temple did become the spiritual capital to the Jews of the entire diaspora. They brought silver and gold, the wealth of nations, to Jerusalem, coming up from east and west to bow down in Jerusalem before the Lord. And also to the Christian community in its early days, Jerusalem was the eternal holy city, to which they, too, brought the wealth of nations. Even the gentile Christian community raised its eyes to Jerusalem. But after the destruction its "Jerusalem" was transferred to another location—to Rome, the "eternal city"—and the redeemer and his principal apostle resettled there from Jerusalem. That city, when its political dominion was ended, became, because of them, the holy city of numerous peoples who throughout the generations were to bring to it the "wealth of nations," thanks offerings for the law of grace which had gone forth from Jerusalem. The distance between the vision and the event was vast. Yet the power of the vision of this marvelous prophet is astonishing. The prophet felt and, in vision, saw that in Jerusalem, afflicted and in ruins, delivered into the power of a mighty pagan government, there was yet a spiritual force which was destined to subdue many nations, to cause them to take pity on her dust, and to prostrate themselves before her God. National and universal elements are combined in Deutero-Isaiah's vision. The nations are destined to go up to Israel's Jerusalem, restored and magnificent, and to bring "all the flock of Kedar" as burnt offering and sacrifices of acceptance to the glorious house. In the event the vision was cut in two. The nations destroyed Jerusalem; and then only they began to bow down to its God. But there can be no doubt that even in the particularistic vision of the prophet, Jerusalem ruled over no peoples by force. Jerusalem was beacon only and ideal; and Deutero-Isaiah, with intuitive artistic sensitivity, described Jerusalem in its magnificence as a "royal diadem" in the open hand of its God, and not as a "city of the great King." For Jerusalem as the eternal city is only the city of God.

The Literary Style of Deutero-Isaiah

Continuation words from chapter 40 to 41 (see above, p. 70):

. . . in the wilderness . . . in the desert . . . (to) a plain (valley) (40:3–4); valleys . . . wilderness . . . in the wilderness . . . in the desert (41:18–19); . . . mountain and hill . . . mountains and hills (40:4, 12), mountains . . . hills (41:15).

And (they) shall see . . . together (40:5); That they may see . . . together . . . that we may . . . behold (see) together (41:20, 23).

. . . that tellest good tidings to Zion . . . that tellest good tidings to Jerusalem (40:9); . . . unto Zion will I give . . . And to Jerusalem a messenger of good tidings (41:27).

. . . be not afraid (40:9); Fear (thou) not (41:10, 13, 14).

Who hath measured . . . (40:12 f.); Who hath raised up . . . Who hath wrought . . . Who hath declared (41:2, 4, 26).

Behold, the nations . . . (40:15); Behold . . . they . . . Shall be ashamed . . . (41:11, 24, 29).

. . . nations . . . isles (40:15); . . . islands (isles) And . . . peoples . . . nations . . . isles (41:1, 2, 5).

With whom took He counsel (40:14); but there is no counsellor (41:28).

. . . as nothing . . . as things of nought, and vanity (40:17); . . . as nothing . . . as nothing and as a thing of nought . . . nothing . . . a thing of nought . . . vanity and nought . . . and confusion (41:11, 12, 24, 29).

... craftsman ... goldsmith ... that shall not be moved (40:19–20); ... carpenter (craftsman) ... goldsmith ... should not be moved (41:7).

... hath melted (40:19); Their molten images (41:29).

Know ye ... hear ye ... Hath it ... been told (declared) you from the beginning (40:21). Let them ... declare ... Declare ye, that ... we may ... know ... announce to us (cause us to hear), Declare ... that we may know ... Who hath declared from the beginning that we may know ... there is none that declareth ... there is none that announceth ... there is none that heareth (41:22–23, 26); He that calleth ... from the beginning (41:4).

Scarce are they (אף בל) ... (40:24); yea (אף) I help thee; Yea (אף) I uphold thee ... Yea (אף), do good ... Yea (אף) there is none ... (41:10, 23, 26).

... as stubble (40:24) ... as the driven stubble (41:2).

And the whirlwind taketh (carrieth away) them (40:24), and the wind shall carry them away, And the whirlwind ... (41:16).

... my right (judgment) is passed over (40:27), Let us come near ... to judgment (41:1).

... the ends of the earth (40:28); The ends of the earth ... from the ends of the earth (41:5, 9).

... shall renew their strength (40:31); ... renew their strength (41:1).

Forced transitions and stylistic breaks (*cf.* pp. 71 f.)

In 41:5–7, an exceedingly artificial transition links the descriptions of the peoples coming up for judgment and of the makers of idols. Many critics think that 41:6–7 should follow v. 40:19. But 41:6 would, in fact, be meaningless after 40:19, whereas there is continuity of thought in the whole passage as it is: the nations come up for judgment in fear, and they encourage one another. But the word "courage" (strength) (Be of good courage— חזק) drags in the description of the mutual encouragement of the makers of idols, and the "strengthening" (חזוק) of the idol with nails.[1]

The thought of the context is that along with nations, their gods also come up for judgment (*cf.* 41:21–29; 45:20, 21, *et al.*). The phrase "Thou whom I have taken hold of (from the root חזק) from the ends of the earth" (41:9) is also dragged in by word association (instead of "whom I have brought," or a similar verb).

The transition in 41:17–20 also is awkward. The lack of water and thirst of v. 17 is a metaphor for the spiritual suffering of the exiles. The prophet moves from the metaphorical waters to a description of waters ("rivers") which will be opened in the wilderness to the returnees.

In the second half of v. 25 the two parallel lines do not fit together. The rout of the rulers "as upon mortar" is a completely negative concept, whereas the treading of the clay of the potter is of positive purpose: the making of vessels (*cf.* 45:9; 64:7). We may conjecture that the word "mortar" induced the parallel metaphor, which is completely unsuited to the content.

The figures: A bruised reed shall he not break, And the dimly burning wick shall he not quench (42:3) are metaphors for the extraordinary weakness of the servant of YHWH; of his own strength he cannot accomplish even the least deed. But in the passage "He shall not fail nor be crushed" (v. 4, read (ירוץ.), the servant himself is compared to the wick and the reed: his strength shall not fail until he has fulfilled his destiny. Here again word association is determinant.

In 43:10, the prophet quotes the Lord as saying, "Before Me there was no God formed." This statement is passing strange, for it seems to imply that God was formed, and formed prior to any other god. Obviously the intent of the prophet was to emphasize specifically the eternity of God. Some critics find an echo here of the Babylonian theogony which narrated the evolution of the gods; and that Deutero-Isaiah denies this.[2] But if this were the case, the prophet would certainly have taken care not to use such a "theogonic" expression.

The anomalous expression is to be explained only by reason of the influence of word association. The idea of "formation" (יצירה) dominates chapters 42–46: the root "form" (יצר) recurs sixteen times from 42:6 to 46:11. Thus the word forced itself into 43:10.

Similarly the expression in 44:8: "Yea, there is no Rock; I know not any." The exegetes sensed the ineptness; and some emend the last phrase to "beside Me." But in fact, this, too, is a matter of word association. The verb "to know" (ידע) occurs many times in chapters 40–48. "I know not any" of 44:8 is due to association with ". . . nor know" of the next verse. Similarly, in 43:10: "That ye may know and believe Me," etc., and in 43:19: "shall ye not know it?" And, following this, in 44:18–19, "They know not, neither do they understand . . . Neither is there knowledge," etc.; and, subsequently, in 45:3–6: "That thou mayest know . . . though thou hast not known Me . . . That they may know," etc.

The phrase "The beasts of the field shall honour Me," 43:20, also is strange; the word honour (כבוד) is not used in connection with animals. It is certain that this verb is connected with 43:23: "Neither hast thou honoured Me."

Especially odd is the expression (45:14) "And they shall fall down unto thee, They shall make supplication unto thee," since the word supplication (תפלה, prayer) is used in Scripture only with respect to God. Some critics emend "to thy God," but it is difficult to understand how such a confusion could have occurred. It seems, in fact, that the expression is an association drawn in from 44:17: "He falleth down unto it . . . and prayeth (makes supplication) unto it." The phrase (45:14) is stylistically incongruous, but not a blunder.

In 47:14, there is an artificial transition between the two parts of the verse, which are incompatible. The beginning of the verse tells of the extermination by fire (אש) of the magicians of Babylon. The end of the verse does not correspond to this: "It shall not be a coal to warm at, Nor a fire

(אור) to sit before." The picture of the end of the verse is the conflagration of the city, which, however, had not previously been mentioned. Some critics would delete the end of the verse. But in 44:15–19 these words are again found together: fire (אש), fire (אור), warmeth, burneth, coals. In addition, in 44:20, there is the expression "That he cannot deliver his soul," for which there is a parallel in 47:14. It is clear that word association was the source of the artificial transition from one idea in 47:14 to the other. In 50:11, also, the two words for fire, אש and אור, occur in the same verse.

In 48:2, the statement "For they call themselves of the holy city" refers to Israel. The expression "For they call themselves of the city" is unnatural and without parallel. No doubt the word-phrase "who are called" in v. 1 is the source.

In 48:3–8, we find repeated use of the verbs "to hear," "to know." To v. 7 they are used in their usual meanings: the hearing and knowing the prophecy of things to come in the name of the Lord. This is the sense of these two words as the prophet uses them throughout chapters 40–48. But in 48:8 there is a sudden shift of meaning: "Yea, thou heardest not; Yea, thou knewest not", with the sense: thou hast not hearkened to My voice, and there is in thee no knowledge.

The word "Utter it" (cause it to go forth) in v. 20, with the sense, "proclaim it," follows the "Go ye forth" of the beginning of the verse.

The word "arm" is a metaphor in Scripture for might. It occurs in this sense in 51:5 ("And Mine arms shall judge the peoples"); in 51:9 ("put on strength, O arm of the Lord") and *passim*. But at the end of 51:5, it symbolizes grace and hope: "And on Mine arm shall they trust." This is a stylistic break. Another example of this kind is in 40:10–11. The expression, "And My favour shall not be abolished" (תחת) (51:6) is labored. In antiquity there were apparently other versions of this passage; and on that basis some exegetes emend the passage to "shall not cease" or "shall not be delayed." But it is evident that this is a case of association, influenced by the phrase ". . . Neither be ye dismayed" (תחתו) in the next verse.

The phrase "that hewed Rahab in pieces" (51:9) derives from Job 26:12–13; and on this basis, some critics emend "who smiteth (woundeth) Rahab." But the expressions "that hewed in pieces . . . that pierced" (מחוללת) certainly are drawn in after the verbs: ". . . ye were hewn . . . that bore (תחוללכם) you" of 51:1–2. This obviously is association due solely to the sound of the homonym חלל.

The phrase "These two things are befallen thee" (51:19) is in disaccord with the subject, which is fourfold: "Desolation and destruction, and the famine and the sword." We may assume that this is an association deriving from 47:9: "But these two things shall come to thee . . . The loss of children, and widowhood."

In 55:7–9, there is an artificial transition from one subject to another. In v. 7 ("Let the wicked forsake his way, And the man of iniquity his thoughts"), the way and the thoughts are the evil deeds and thoughts of the sinner. But in the next verses ("My thoughts . . . your thoughts . . . your ways My ways"), it is not the opposition to sinful deeds and sinful thoughts which is meant, but the contrast between man's ways and inadequate thoughts on the one hand, and the ways of God and His supreme thoughts on the other. Some critics delete v. 7. But it is precisely this stylistic incongruity which proves that the text is correct.[3]

Missionary Activity Among the Gentiles

Scripture knows nothing of any prophetic mission to the gentiles. This fact is of particular significance for the understanding of the stance of the biblical period with respect to the problem of the spread of the religion of Israel among the nations (see above, 113 f.). There is a desideratum and longing for the conversion of the gentiles from idolatry, and there is the vision of conversion. But there is no prophetic apostolate to the gentiles to convert them from idolatry. No prophet was ever sent to the gentiles to reprove them for the worship of the gods, or even for moral corruption. The prophets prophesy with respect to the nations, but they are not dispatched to them with religious-moral missions.

Elisha (II Kings 8:7–15) and Jeremiah (Jer. 27:1–11) are charged with political missions only, and concerning matters which relate to Israel. Exceptionally, Jonah is sent to Nineveh with a moral mission; but this story is fiction, and the city is legendary. The arena of the actual apostolic activities of the prophets is Israel only. The opinion that the purpose of the book of Jonah was to arouse Israel to missionary activity among the gentiles[1] is groundless. There is not a single reference to the sin of idolatry in the book of Jonah; and nothing with respect to the struggle against gentile idolatry. The sending of Jonah is unique, an event which occurs only this once. The tale is not intended to initiate any movement, rather to resolve a moral problem.[2] The polemics of Habakkuk (2:18–20) and Jeremiah (10:1–17) against the idolatry of the gentiles are spoken to Israel. Even Jer. 10:11 is not addressed directly to the gentiles. This passage, written in Aramaic, marks the beginning of the warfare against gentile idolatry. But, according to its content, it is only an eschatological warning to the nations of the approaching destruction of idolatry (*cf.* v. 15). Even Jeremiah does not impose on Israel in the name of God the obligation to spread its faith among the gentiles; and certainly he does not say that Israel was chosen to that end from the very beginning. The invectives of Deutero-Isaiah against idolatry were addressed to Israel. Deutero-Isaiah refers to his mission in 48:16 and 61:1; and this mission is to Israel only. He nowhere expressly says that he was sent to the gentiles to preach against idolatry. "Missionary prophecies" are to be discovered in Deutero-Isaiah only by forced exegesis, against the plain meaning and the context.[3] The turning to "the ends of the earth" (45:22) is merely a rhetorical phrase and visionary. It also is addressed directly to Israel.

The fact is that the phenomenon of religious propaganda among the gentiles appears only after the prophetic age, in the postexilic period; and the character of this phenomenon is in any event not prophetic. There are "messengers," but they represent communities or institutions. They are not sent by God. The polemic of the period is theological, of popular or literary quality, and not prophetic. Later, it will make use of the Hellenistic wisdom literature. But there is no statement that prophets worked among the gentiles as messengers of God. John and Jesus, who appear as apostles, do not labor among the gentiles. Jesus states explicitly that he was sent only to Israel and not to the gentiles (Matt. 15:24); and he directs his apostles to go only to the Jews, not to the heathen or to the Samaritans (*ibid.*, 10:5–6, 23). Even Paul, the "apostle to the gentiles," labors first in Israel and begins his apostolic mission among the gentiles only after he despairs of Israel (Acts 13:46–47; 18:5–6; 28:17–28).

Moreover, in addition to the fact that the missionary propaganda among the gentiles was not prophetic, it also did not take on itself the eschatological office of converting the *nations* from idolatry. Christianity succeeded in the course of time in converting whole nations from idolatry; and it is this subsequent success of the Christian mission which is the source of the critics' anachronistic mistake. They confuse the later actuality with the earlier ideology. The Jewry of the second Temple sought to bring individual gentiles to the spirit of Judaism, or to convert them. But it never hoped to overcome idolatry, to convert the whole pagan world or great parts of it by propaganda. The Pharisees encompassed "sea and land to make one proselyte" (Matt. 23:15). This, in some measure, typifies the missionary activity.

Of course there were many converts and half-converts by the time of the end of the second Temple. But among the pagan peoples these were an insignificant minority, individuals. Entire nations did not convert. In all the descriptions of the end of days of the postexilic literature, there are idol worshipers to the end; and they will be judged and destroyed, or else they will forsake idolatry. The visions promised the cessation of idolatry in the end of days. But this was thought of as part of the divine plan of salvation, an act to be wrought only of God. The conversion of individuals was possible by means of a "mission," of "work in time."[4] But to bring "All the ends of the earth," to be "for a light of the nations," "unto the end of the earth" (Isa. 45:22; 49:6), to put an end to the dominion of idolatry—this was not to be achieved by preachment. The end of idolatry would come only with works of eschatological revelation. The early Christian apostles also did not believe that it would be within their power to convert entire nations. They proclaimed the gospel to "the chosen," those who are called, to individuals among the nations. Paul traversed all provinces to preach to the gentiles, and even applied Isa. 49:6 to himself (Acts 13:47). But, in fact, he believed that the end of the world was near, and that the nations would continue to be idolatrous to the last moment, to be judged on the day of judgment. Thus his preaching would rescue individuals only. The later reality was completely different from the earlier ideology.

Israel, it is clear, was charged with no "prophetic mission" to convert the nations. The historical struggle against idolatry was not thought of as a prophetic mission, and its protagonists were not prophets. Its mainspring was the need for apologetics. It influenced individuals only; and the effort was never designed to convert the gentile world. The vision of the end of idolatry is totally unrelated to the actual missionary movement. The hope of conversion of peoples from idolatry was wholly eschatological, to be accomplished not by means of "a mission," but by the divine act of redemption.

BIBLIOGRAPHY

and

NOTES

ANET   Ancient Near Eastern Texts (ed. Pritchard).
AO   Der Alte Orient.
AT   Altes Testament.
ATAO   Das A T im Lichte des Alten Orients.
BJRL   Bulletin of the John Rylands Library.
BRL   Biblische Reallexikon.
BZAW   Beihefte zur Zeitschrift für die alttestamentliche
        Wissenschaft.
BZWANT Beiträge zur Wissenschaft vom Alten und Neuen
        Testament.
DATD   Das A T Deutsch (ed. Herntrich-Weiser).
ET   The Expository Times.
GHAT   Göttinger Handkommentar zum A T (ed. Nowack).
HAT   Handbuch zum A T (ed. Eissfeldt).
HSAT   Die Heilige Schrift des A T, 1922–1923.
HUCA   Hebrew Union College Annual.
ICC   The International Critical Commentary.
JBL   Journal of Biblical Literature.
JNES   Journal of Near Eastern Studies.
KAT   Kommentar zum A T (ed. Sellin).
KHAT   Kurzer Handkommentar zum A T (ed. Marti).
MGWJ   Monatsschrift für Geschichte und Wissenschaft des
        Judentums.
OT   Old Testament.
PEQ   Palestine Exploration Quarterly.
PJB   Palästinajahrbuch.
RGG   Die Religion in Geschichte und Gegenwart.
VT   Vetus Testamentum.
ZAW   Zeitschrift für die alttestamentliche Wissenschaft.
ZDPV   Zeitschrift des Deutschen Palästinavereins.

BIBLIOGRAPHY

Albright, William F. *Archaeology and the Religion of Israel.* Baltimore, 1942.

———. *From the Stone Age to Christianity: Monotheism and the Historical Process.* Baltimore, 1940.

Baeck, Leo. *Die Pharisäer.* 1927.

Baudissin, W. W. Graf. *Einleitung in die Bücher des AT.* Leipzig, 1901.

Begrich, Joachim. *Studien zu Deuterojesaja. BZWANT,* 4. Folge, Heft 25, 1938.

Bentzen, Aage. *Messias, Moses redivivus, Menschensohn.* Zurich, 1948.

Blank, Sheldon H. "Studies in Deutero-Isaiah." *HUCA,* 15, Cincinnati, 1940, pp. 1–46.

Bonkamp, Bernhard. *Die Bibel im Lichte der Keilschriftforschung.* 1939.

Buber, Martin. *The Prophetic Faith.* New York, 1949.

Budde, Karl. *Das Buch Jesaia Kap. 40–66. HSAT,* i, pp. 653–720.

———. *Die sogenannten Ebed-Jahwe-Lieder und die Bedeutung des Knechtes Jahwes in Jes. 40–55: Ein Minoritätsvotum.* Giessen, 1900.

———. *Geschichte der althebräischen Litteratur.* 1909.

Cheyne, Thomas K. *Introduction to the Book of Isaiah.* London, 1895.

Condamin, Albert. *Le Livre d'Isaïe: Traduction critique avec notes et commentaires. Études Bibliques,* 1905.

Cowley, Arthur E. *Aramaic Papyri of the Fifth Century B.C.* Oxford, 1923.

Cross, Frank M., Jr. "The Council of Yahweh in Second Isaiah." *JNES,* 12, 1953, pp. 274–77.

Dalman, Gustaf H. *Jesaja 53, das Prophetenwort vom Sühneleiden des Gottesknechtes.* Leipzig, 1914.

Duhm, Bernard. *Das Buch Jesaia. GHAT.* 1914.

Dürr, Lorenz. *Die Stellung des Propheten Ezechiel in der israelitisch-jüdischen Apokalyptik.* 1923.

———. *Ezechiels Vision von der Erscheinung Gottes (Ez. c. I, v. 10) im Lichte der vorderasiatischen Altertumskunde.* Würzburg, 1917.

———. *Ursprung und Ausbau der israelitisch-jüdischen Heilandserwartung.* Berlin, 1925.

———. *Wollen und Wirken der alttestamentlichen Propheten.* Düsseldorf, 1926.

Eerdmans, Bernardus D. *The Religion of Israel.* Leiden, 1930. Rev. ed., 1948.

Eissfeldt, Otto. *Einleitung in das Altes Testament.* Tübingen, 1934.

———. "The Literature of Israel: Modern Criticism." *Record and Revelation,* pp. 74–109. 1938.

Elliger, Karl. *Deuterojesaja in seinem Verhältnis zu Tritojesaja. BZWANT.* Vierte Folge, Heft 11, 1933.

———. *Die Einheit des Tritojesaja. BZWANT.* 1928.

Engnell, Karl I. A. "The 'Ebed Yahweh Songs and the Suffering Messiah in 'Deutero-Isaiah.'" *BJRL,* 31, 1948, pp. 54–93.

Feilchenfeld, W. *Das stellvertretende Sühneleiden und die Exegese der Jesaianischen Weissagung Kap. 52, 13-15 und Kap. 53.* Dessau, 1883.

Finkelstein, Louis. *The Pharisees.* 2 vols. Philadelphia, 1938.

Friedmann, Meir. *S'rubbabel, Erläuterung der Weiss.* "Siehe, es gelingt meinem Knechte." Wien, 1890.

Gall, August F. von. *Basileia. Eine religionsgeschichtliche Studie zur vorkirchlichen Eschatologie.* Heidelberg, 1926.

Glahn, Ludwig, and Köhler, Ludwig H. *Der Prophet der Heimkehr. (Jesaja 40–66).* Giessen, 1934.

Graetz, Heinrich. *Geschichte der Juden.* Vol. ii, 3d. ed., 2d half. Leipzig, 1873.

Gressmann, Hugo. "Die literarische Analyse Deuterojesajas." *ZAW,* 34, 1914, pp. 254–97.

———. *Der Messias.* Göttingen, 1929.

Gunkel, Hermann. "Der Knecht Jahwes." *RGG,* iv. Tübingen, 1927–31.

Haller, Max. *Das Judentum: Geschichtsschreibung, Prophetie und Gesetzgebung nach dem Exil,* in *Die Schriften des Alten Testaments in Auswahl übersetzt und für die Gegenwart erklärt.* Göttingen, 1914.

———. "Die Kyros-Lieder Deuterojesaja," in *Eucharisterion* Hermann Gunkel. Göttingen, 1923.

Herntrich, Volkmar. "Ezechielprobleme." *BZAW.* Giessen, 1932.

Hilprecht, H. V., and Clay, A. T. The Babylonian Expedition of the University of Pennsylvania. *Business Documents of Murashu Sons of Nippur.* Philadelphia, 1898–1904.

Hölscher, Gustav. *Geschichte der israelitischen und jüdischen Religion.* Giessen, 1922.

Hooke, Samuel H. "The Theory and Practice of Substitution." *VT,* Leiden, 1952, pp. 2–17.

Hyatt, James P. "The Sources of the Suffering Servant Idea." *JNES,* 3, 1944, pp. 79–86.

Jeremias, Alfred. *Das Alte Testament im Lichte des alten Orients.* Leipzig, 1906.

Kaufmann, Yehezkel. *Golah v'Nekar* [Hebrew]. 2 vols. 3d ed., 1962.

Kissane, Edward J. *The Book of Isaiah: Translated from a Critically Revised Hebrew Text with Commentary.* 2 vols. Dublin, 1943.

Kittel, Rudolf. *Geschichte des Volkes Israel.* 3 vols. Stuttgart, 1921–1929.

Klamroth, Erich. *Die jüdischen Exulanten in Babylonien.* Leipzig, 1912.

Klausner, Joseph. *History of the Second Temple* [Hebrew]. Jerusalem, 1949. (Cited: *Historia.*)

———. *The Messianic Idea in Israel* [Hebrew]. Trans. by Stinespring. 1956.

Klostermann, D. A. *Deuterojesaja.* München, 1893.

Köhler, Ludwig H. *Deuterojesaja (Jesaja 40–55). BZAW,* 37. Giessen, 1923.

Lindblom, Christian J. *The Servant Songs in Deutero-Isaiah: A New Attempt to Solve an Old Problem.* Lund, 1951.

Margolioth, Rachel. *The Indivisible Isaiah* [Hebrew]. 1954. Eng. trans., New York, 1964.

Marti, Karl. *Das Buch Jesaja erklärt. KHAT,* x. Tübingen, 1900.

———. *Geschichte der israelitischen Religion.* 4th ed. of August Kayser's *Theologie des Alten Testaments.* Strassburg, 1903.

Meissner, Bruno. *Babylonien und Assyrien.* 2 vols. Heidelberg, 1920–1925.

Menes, Abram. "Tempel und Synagoge." *ZAW,* 50, 1932, pp. 268–76.

Meyer, Eduard. *Die Entstehung des Judenthums,* Halle a. S., 1896.

———. *Ursprung und Anfänge des Christentums.* 3 vols. Stuttgart, 1921.

Morgenstern, Julian. "Two Prophecies from 520–516 B.C." *HUCA,* 22, 1949, pp. 365–431.

Mowinckel, Sigmund. "Die Komposition des deuterojesajanischen Buches." *ZAW,* 49, 1931, pp. 87–112, 242–60.

———. *Der Knecht Jahwäs.* Giessen, 1921.

North, Christopher R. *The Suffering Servant in Deutero-Isaiah.* London, 1948.

Nyberg, Henrik S. *Die Religionen des alten Iran.* 1938.

Peake, Arthur S. *The Problem of Suffering in the Old Testament.* London, 1947.

Pritchard, James B., ed. *Ancient Near East Texts Relating to the Old Testament.* Princeton, N.J., 1950.

———. *The Ancient Near East in Pictures.* 1954.

Robinson, H. Wheeler. *Record and Revelation.* 1938.

Rowley, Harold H. *The Servant of the Lord and Other Essays on the Old Testament.* London, 1952.

207

BIBLIOGRAPHY

Rudolph, Wilhelm. "Der exilische Messias." *ZAW*, 43, 1925, pp. 90–114.

———. "Die Ebed-Jahwe-Lieder als geschichtliche Wirklichkeit." *ZAW*, 46, 1928, pp. 156–66.

Sellin, Ernst. "Die Lösung des deuterojesajanischen Gottesknechtsrätsels." *ZAW*, 55, 1937, pp. 177–217.

Skinner, John. *The Book of the Prophet Isaiah Chapters XL–LXVI*. Cambridge, 1898; revised ed., 1922.

Stade, Bernard. *Geschichte des Volkes Israel*. 2 vols. Berlin, 1887–1888.

Staerk, Willi. "Zum Ebed-Jahwe-Problem." *ZAW*, 44, 1926, pp. 242–60.

Stevenson, William B. "Werden und Wesen des A. T." *BZAW*, 66, 1936, pp. 89–96.

Stummer, Friedrich. "Einige keilinschriftliche Parallelen zu Jes. 40–66." *JBL*, 45, 1926, pp. 171–189.

Torrey, Charles C. *The Second Isaiah: A New Interpretation*. New York, 1928.

———. "Some Important Editorial Operations in the Book of Isaiah." *JBL*, 57, 1938, pp. 109–139.

Volz, Paul. *Jesaia II übersetzt und erklärt*. Leipzig, 1932.

Waterman, Leroy. *Royal Correspondence of the Assyrian Empire*. Ann Arbor, Mich., 1936.

Wellhausen, Julius. *Israelitische und jüdische Geschichte*. Berlin, 1914.

NOTES

Translator's Preface

1 *The Holy Scriptures*, according to the masoretic text. A new translation. The Jewish Publication Society of America. Philadelphia, 5725—1965.

2 Charles, R. H., ed., *Apocrypha and Pseudepigrapha of the Old Testament*. Oxford, 1913.

I. *The Babylonian Captivity*

1 See Cowley, *Papyri*, No. 30, lines 13–14; No. 31, lines 12–13. For the problem of the date of the founding of the colony in Elephantine, see Albright, *Archaeology*, 168.

2 Klamroth, the first to express this opinion, cited most of the proofs. See Klamroth, *Exulanten*, 1–52; Dürr, *Ezechiel*, 145 f.; *id.*, *Wollen und Wirken*, 28 f.; Herntrich, *Ezechielprobleme*, 44 f.; Klausner, *Historia*, [Hebrew] 1, 65–72.

3 Klamroth, *op. cit.*, 24–25.

4 *Ibid.*, 30.

5 *Ibid.*, 36.

6 *Ibid.*, 37.

7 *Ibid.*, 38. In the other passages which Klamroth cites (Isa. 42:7; 43:14; 45:20 *et al.*) the references are not to real prisoners. Rather, they are generalized descriptions of enslavement and captivity.

8 Klausner, *Historia*, 1, 70. Jer. 50:33 (Klausner, *ibid.*) is a generalized expression for national-political subjugation.

9 Klamroth, *op. cit.*, 42. Klamroth's remarks, 41–43, are strange and confused. Immediately following the evidence, 41–42, of the wealth of the diaspora, he assumes, 42–43, that there was "pauperism" in the diaspora; and the evidence therefor is that from Isa. 55:2, it appears that they purchased foodstuffs with money!

10 Klamroth, *op. cit.*, 1–8; Klausner, *Historia*, 1, 66–69.

11 Meissner, *Babylonien*, 1, 123–24, 127, 143 (cited by Klausner, *Historia*, 1) refers to obligations of the provinces and inhabitants generally, and not specifically to the transplantees.

12 Klamroth, *op. cit.*, 6, 7, admits this, and he also explains the

reasons for it. But he does not realize that he thereby invalidates his hypothesis. Klausner's argument, *Historia*, I, 69, 81, that the situation of the exiles from the legal point of view was that of the "*qatinnu*" (see Meissner, *op. cit.*, 375) is invalid. The "*qatinnu*" were subjects of foreign states, resident aliens, whereas the exiles were subjects of the king.

13 Klamroth, *op. cit.*, 5–7.

14 Klausner, *Historia*, I, 75, with reference to the letters published in Waterman, *Royal Correspondence*.

15 Hilprecht-Clay published documents of the house of Murashu in 1898. See Bonkamp, *Bibel*, 540 f.

16 Klamroth, *op. cit.*, 43; Klausner, *Historia*, I, 128.

17 *Cf.* Volz, *Jesaia II*, xvi; Baeck, *Pharisäer*, 49 f.

18 Dürr, *Ezechiel*, 142 f., 146 f., 154–58; *id.*, *Ezechiels Vision*, 6 f., 70; *id.*, *Wollen und Wirken*, 28; Haller, *Judentum*, 32; Kittel, *Geschichte*, III, 85–86, 120–23; Klamroth, *op. cit.*, 58, 61, 80–81; Baeck, *op. cit.*, 49; Klausner, *Historia*, I, 67, 84, 91.

19 See Wellhausen, *Geschichte*, 144; Stade, *Geschichte*, I, 702; Klamroth, *op. cit.*, 62 f., 80–81, 97; Klausner, *Historia*, I, 91–92, 99. See above, I, 659, for references, note 1.

20 Pritchard, *ANET*, 315–16.

21 Meissner, *op. cit.*, II, 126–30; Jeremias, *ATAO*, 284.

22 Virgil, *Aeneid*, I, 6; II, 717.

23 Pritchard, *op. cit.*, 291.

24 *Ibid.*, 351–53.

25 Klamroth, *op. cit.*, 81, cites II Kings 17:24–28 to the effect that it was possible to worship YHWH only in His own land. But Klamroth reads only to v. 28 and does not take into account what follows.

26 See Josephus, *War* 6:5:3; Yoma, 39b: For forty years prior to the destruction of the Temple the lot did not fall on the right, etc.; and the doors of the Temple opened of themselves, etc.

27 Tacitus, *Historiae*, 5:13. Josephus relates: In the night of the Feast of Weeks the priests as they entered the inner court heard a noise and voices calling, "Let us depart from here!" It is to be pointed out that the Talmud vilifies Titus as a blasphemer—"Titus who blasphemed and insulted Heaven—He then took a sword and slashed the curtain. And a miracle occurred. Miraculously blood spurted out, and he thought that he had slain himself." And further, "A gale sprang up at sea which threatened to wreck him. He said: Apparently the power of the God of these people is only over water—If He is really mighty, let Him come up on dry land and fight with me." (Gittin, 56b). As in Scripture, the heathen monarch here elevates himself above God; but he does not attribute the victory to his god. But the pagan historian relates things in a completely different manner.

28 Kittel, *op. cit.*, III, 85–86, says that the queen of heaven is the Babylonian Astarte, and that the women think that this goddess

of the mighty nation is better able to defend her worshipers than is YHWH, and that the Lord cannot defend them. But why is it specifically the women who express this view? And why specifically Astarte, and not Marduk and Nebo? In fact, there is in Jer. 44 no reference to Babylon and its gods; and Kittel's exegesis is pointless. Jeremiah does not argue against the opinion that YHWH cannot defend! And did not the envoys of Hezekiah, and Hezekiah himself, rend their garments when they heard words of this import spoken by the pagan Rab-shakeh? Could Jeremiah possibly have passed over in silence words of this import if spoken by Jews? Could he have failed to rend his garments? Could he have failed to mention this opinion even with a single word?

29 Klamroth, *op. cit.*, 80; also the whole bizarre statement, *ibid.*, 80–81.

30 Klausner, *Historia*, I, 84.

31 The conjecture (Menes, *ZAW*, 1932, pp. 272–73) that the Babylonian captivity attempted to renew the sacrificial cult in the exile and that Ezekiel in chapter 20 reproved them on this account is without basis. Ezek. 20 is concerned specifically with idol worship.

32 R. Akiba interpreted these passages in this sense. See Rosh Hashonah, 18b.

33 *Cf.* Sifre Ekeb (to Deut. 11:13) referring to the passages in Daniel: "Just as the altar service is called service, so is prayer called service."

34 Concerning the book of Kings, see also above, I, 25 f.; II, 293–98, 355 f.

35 See Volz, *op. cit.*, pp. xx–xxiv, 140–43, 149 f., 163 f., 167, *et al.*; Lindblom, *Songs*, 70 f., 99, *et al.*; also Buber, *Prophetic Faith*, 215–30.

36 Concerning Ruth, see above, II, 214.

37 See *ibid.*, 191–93, 213–14, 457–61.

38 See above, I, 42, 209, 619.

39 According to the talmudic sages, the ceremony of the "woman of goodly form" is not a conversion ceremony at all; and a Jew can marry the woman only after she is legally converted. See Yebamoth, 47–48; Maimonides, *Mishnah Torah*, Hilkoth Melakim 8:1–9; and Maimonides' exegesis to Deut. 21.

40 *Re* Jethro, the Canaanites, the sailors of Jonah's ship, and others, see above, II, 442–43.

II. *Deutero-Isaiah*

1 We do not know how these prophecies came to be included in the book of the earlier Isaiah. It is possible that Deutero-Isaiah was a latter-day disciple of Isaiah 1 and bound his scroll with that of his

master. These two writings would then have been copied together and, in the course of time, thought to be one book. There are, in any event, other similar instances, namely, the book of Zechariah and, surely, the book of Hosea. Biblical criticism is agreed that Isa. 40–66 is not the work of the earlier Isaiah. The arguments which have been raised against this hypothesis in recent years do not bear criticism. Concerning this, see Margolioth, *The Indivisible Isaiah* [Hebrew]. The arguments in the introduction are unconvincing and not exhaustive. The exposition in the text of the linguistic similarities is in itself of interest. But more signficant than the similarity is the disparity in the entire manner of presentation, and in the material and linguistic content. In any event, such a question as this is not to be decided on the basis of stylistic evidence.

2 Pritchard, *op. cit.*, 305–7, 312–16.

3 Begrich, *Studien*, 63 f., contests this evidence. If chapters 49 f. are later than 539, why does the prophet not express clearly a negative judgment of Cyrus? Begrich thinks that these prophecies belong to the first period of the prophesying of Deutero-Isaiah before Cyrus became a central figure. According to Begrich, Deutero-Isaiah began to prophesy in the year 553–52, the year when Cyrus began the war against Astyages. This war rocked the world and aroused messianic anticipations in Israel. Deutero-Isaiah appeared at the time and delivered his "eschatological" prophecies of miraculous redemption by the hand of the Lord and of the end of the kingdom of the gentiles. Cyrus does not appear in these prophecies. Evidence of prophecies concerning Babylon without mention of Cyrus are 46:1–2; 47:1–15; 48:20–21; 52:11–12. These early prophecies were not fulfilled, and the prophet experienced a severe crisis at the end of the Median war. The Lydian campaign began in the year 547–46. Cyrus appeared as a war hero, treading down nations. At that time Deutero-Isaiah composed the prophecies relating to Cyrus, which, according to Begrich, are non-eschatological (pp. 72 f.). According to these prophecies, it is Cyrus who is to effect the return of the exiles, the rebuilding of Jerusalem, etc. The period of non-eschatological prophecy ended sometime after 546 (pp. 75 f.). Deutero-Isaiah died a martyr's death at the hand of his people, who, it appears, rejected his prophecies (pp. 146 f.). But this entire hypothesis is contrived, intended merely to support the absurd story of the murder of the prophet. Deutero-Isaiah might have been put to death by the Babylonian government because of his prophecies against Babylon, or by Cyrus, or by fellow-exiles who considered him a false prophet or feared the reaction of the Babylonian government. This, however, could have occurred only prior to the conquest of Babylon and the proclamation of Cyrus' permission to return. Thus it is difficult to harmonize the hypothesis with the fact that Deutero-Isaiah prophesied after 539; and it would have to be shown that all his prophecies are earlier than the fall of Babylon. But how is it possible in this event

to explain the fact that from chapter 49 on there is not only no prophecy concerning Cyrus, but also none concerning the conquest of Babylon or its fall? Why do these two matters disappear at the same time? And does not Babylon necessarily occupy a central position in the "eschatological" prophecies? Further, there is no basis to consider the prophecies concerning Cyrus as non-eschatological. In fact, they are placed in an eschatological setting, which Begrich acknowledges in an aside on p. 119. In all this there is, therefore, no basis for distinguishing periods. Also inconclusive is the argument that there are prophecies in Deutero-Isaiah concerning Babylon wherein Cyrus is not mentioned. Begrich's argument depends on the fragmentizing of the prophecies. In fact, however, 46:1–2 is attached to 46:11 and 48:20–21 to 48:14. In 52:11–12 Babylon is not explicitly mentioned, and the reference may be to the diaspora generally. In any event, this is not a prophecy of conquest or ruin. With respect to the dirge of chapter 47, there are here no concrete details and also no traces of an eschatological point of view. Would the prophet have had to mention Cyrus here by name after all that he had previously said about him? Could anyone have failed to understand? Moreover, it is a strange assumption that the events of the years 553–50 impressed the prophet so greatly that he was stirred to eschatological pronouncement, and yet the hero of the period, Cyrus, was insignificant in his opinion and not noticed by him at all. Was not Cyrus heir of half of the world-empire even in 550! Even more unconvincing is the opinion that after the year 550 the prophet suffered a severe crisis because that was a period of "general pacification" and his prophecies had been disproven (pp. 112 f.). Was there, in fact, a general pacification? War broke out anew as early as 547, and an alliance was concluded by Lydia, Babylon, Egypt, and Sparta. The pact, concluded in the interwar period, is evidence that the nations were preparing for new events. The shock was felt even as far as Sparta, which does not indicate general lessening of tension. The conclusion of the Median war was not, therefore, calculated to belie the "eschatological" prophecies, which were phrased in general terms, without mention of Media or Persia or Cyrus or Astyages. And, on the other hand, there certainly are obvious reasons for a "crisis" after 539. If Deutero-Isaiah did not express a negative attitude toward Cyrus after 539, this is to be explained by his ambivalent attitude toward Cyrus: Cyrus disappointed, but he was no enemy; he had even given permission to rebuild the Temple. This ambivalent attitude characterizes the prophecies subsequent to 539, with which subject we shall be concerned in the following.

4 Cf. Glahn, *Prophet*, 51–53, 73 f. Some scholars discover in chapters 56–66 allusions to a temple which had been rebuilt. See Skinner, *Isaiah*, xxix, citing 56:7; 60:7; 62:9; 65:11; 66:6. Skinner admits that the first three of these passages may be interpreted as referring to a temple to be built in the future, but not the last two. But the facts

are otherwise. Those who "forget My holy mountain" in 65:11 are those who do not yearn to return to Zion. The Temple is not mentioned. Glahn interprets 66:6 as a vision of the future: the voice of the Lord will shortly be heard from His Temple which will be built (*op. cit.*, 103–104). In fact, however, the generally accepted interpretation, that the "city" and the "Temple" of this verse are Jerusalem and its Temple, is to be rejected. The voice is the voice of the Lord who is requiting His foes, and the foes are not in Jerusalem and the Temple, but in their cities and their temples. The passage is, therefore, to be understood: from every city and from every temple the voice of God who requites will be heard. *Cf.* Amos 8:3: "and the songs of the palace shall be wailings." *Cf.* the cosmic description of the tumult of retribution (Jer. 25:30–31).

5 *Op. cit.*, 53 *et passim.*

6 Morgenstern, *HUCA*, 1949, pp. 368 f., finds allusions in Isa. 55:1–5 to the drought and the lack of food which are recorded in Hag. 1:6–11; 2:15–19; and also to Zerubbabel and to the preparation for the building of the Temple in the year 520. But the thirst, money, food, wine, and milk of Isa. 55:1–2 are generalized and symbolical; and the verses are wholly unrelated to the actual drought which is described in Haggai. Also, there is no reference to the building of the Temple or to Zerubbabel in 55:3–5. Morgenstern, *ibid.*, 383 f., finds in Isa. 60:1–3, 5–7 a prophecy for which he is able to fix a precise date, Rosh Hashonah, 516, October 6. But his interpretation depends on very strange imaginings. Friedmann, *S'rubbabel*, 8 *et passim*, discovers allusions to the period of Darius, to "the Samaritans," to the period of Nehemiah, and to astounding events of the time of Zerubbabel in Isa. 40–46, which he thinks is a collection of epistles. But all this is mystical exegesis, without explicit basis.

7 Glahn, *op. cit.*, 71–72, cites 60:7 as proof that the altar was built and sacrificial worship performed. Also he argues very forcefully (73–74) that 60:13 ("to beautify the place of My sanctuary") refers to the Temple which is to be built in the future. But in 60:7 the altar and the Temple are mentioned together, and thus the sense is that the altar also is a vision of the future. Glahn separates them only because this is required by his hypothesis.

8 For the strange ideas and casuistries of Duhm, Marti, and others, see Elliger, *Tritojesaja*, 94 f. Elliger is inclined to fix the date of the dirge later than 538 (p. 98). But in 64:8b–9a (Behold, look we beseech Thee, we are all Thy people, Thy holy cities are become a wilderness), he discovers an indication that there is already a "people" dwelling in the holy cities and in Jerusalem alongside the Temple. But this also is only exegesis. Since Zion and its cities are a "wilderness" there is already a "people" dwelling there! He thinks that the poet himself may have been one of those who have recently immigrated (*ibid.*). But where is there in this passage anything characteristic of

an immigrant? Glahn, *op. cit.*, 90, believes that this dirge is of the year 536; the interruption of the construction was the occasion of this sorrow and grief for the destruction, and gave birth to this bitter complaint. But where is there in this passage any allusion to the construction of the Temple, to disappointed hopes, to the machinations of the adversaries, etc.? No event of the year 536 is reflected here. The subject is the destruction of 586 only. Comparison with 51:17–23 proves (against Elliger, 98) that this dirge could have been composed only in the diaspora.

9 Thus Rashi and Redak explain this verse.

10 Duhm, *Jesaia*, in his exegesis to 57:14 and 62:10–12, examines meticulously the linguistic variations in comparison with chapters 40–55, and tries to show that in chapters 57 and 62 the subject is not the return of the exiles but spiritual repentance. The "stumbling block" and the "stone" are sins or something similar (in the spirit of the midrash of Targum Jonathan). Because, forsooth, "wilderness" is not mentioned in these verses and the phrase "for our God" is not used, as in 40:3, God is already in Zion and has no need to come from Babylon by way of the wilderness, etc. There are scholars (Skinner and others) who repeat similar arguments. The wilderness is also not mentioned in 49:22 and 52:7–10. Moreover, even if God was already in Zion, there was still anticipation of the ingathering of the exiles in the days of Ezra and Nehemiah, and there was still the necessity to traverse the wilderness. In 62:10 there is no "for our God." But in 62:11 the Lord appears, and the people go before Him as in 40:10; God leads the people from afar to Zion. Even the critics who disagree with Duhm follow his dating of chapters 56–66. Elliger, *Tritojesaja*, 85, observes with respect to 57:14–19 that here there is promise only of "peace" and not of a return. Concerning v. 14, he says, *ibid.*, note 1, that this is a "command" which the prophet casts before the people "like lightning out of a clear sky." But all this "lightning" does not alter the fact that this verse is a prophecy of the return of the whole nation, and not a "command." Glahn, *op. cit.*, 58–59, following Duhm, discovers in the linguistic discrepancy between 57:14 ("the way of My people") and 40:3 ("the way of the Lord") an indication that there is already a people in Zion, which interpretation is very weak. He also finds "allusions" in 62:10–12 by minute linguistic analysis (p. 82). He interprets "go through the gates" in the sense: go out through the gates of Jerusalem to meet the returnees. This also is merely speculative exegesis. Comparison with 40:3, 10; 48:20; 49:22 shows that clearing the way and setting up of an ensign are visionary figures which prepare for and foretell the appearance of the Lord who will lead His people. The gates are the gates of the cities through which the exiles will go forth. The explanation of Voltz, *op. cit.*, to 62:10, that this is a call to the returnees to enter the gates of Jerusalem, is not compatible with what follows.

11 According to Glahn, *op. cit.*, 56, the people who are ridiculed by the "sons of the sorceress" of 57:3–4 are the returned exiles. The scoffers are those who were able to prevent the building of the Temple (*ibid.*, 58). In fact, however, there is no mention in the passage either of the exiles who return or of the building of the Temple. The mourners of Zion of 57:18; 61:1–3; 66:10 are the returnees who mourned on account of the interruption of the work of rebuilding the Temple in 536 (*ibid.*, 53, 58). But in these passages, also, there is neither immigration nor the building of the Temple. Also, were there not mourners of Zion between the years 586 and 536? Everything which is described in chapters 58–59, *e.g.*, the exaction of debts (*ibid.*, 71), takes place in Jerusalem. But Glahn does not reveal how he knows that those who exact are doing so in Jerusalem. According to Budde, *Litteratur*, 178; Eissfeldt, *Einleitung*, 385, the invective of 57:3–13 is directed against "idolatrous Jerusalem." But Jerusalem is not mentioned in this passage. The rebuke is directed against Israel. Throughout, the critics bring the returnees and Jerusalem of the returnees into the prophecies by transparent devices.

12 See Duhm, *op. cit.*, 389, 397, *et al.;* Budde, *Litteratur*, 178; Kittel, *op. cit.*, III, 84–104; Elliger, *Tritojesaja*, 77 f., 80–85, *et al.;* Glahn, *op. cit.*, 56–58, 94–96, 101, 103, *et al.* This is one of the most generally accepted theses of biblical criticism.

13 Budde, *Jesaia*, 697, seeks a suitable date for the rebuke of idolatry in 57:1–6. He says that if this is of date following the destruction, it is addressed to the corruption of the Jewish inhabitants who had remained in the land throughout the exile period. Otherwise it is to be dated in the third or fourth century inasmuch as events may have occurred at that time which are unknown to us. Elliger, *Tritojesaja*, 78–79, argues that such a reprimand could have been uttered also in the period between Haggai-Zechariah and Malachi. The similarity of these periods is that we know nothing of them. In this observation, judgment is, in fact, implied on the entire exegesis: of necessity it takes flight into the darkness of the unknown.

14 Eerdmans, *Religion*, 210–17, finds in the whole of Isa. 40–66 a preachment of aliyah by grace of Cyrus, and even a description of the caravan of Sheshbazzar and its entrance into Jerusalem. Agents proclaimed these prophecies and were able to arouse many of the exiles to join the caravan which proceeded from Babylon to Jerusalem by the southern route, the desert and the oases (pp. 212–13). We ask only, how could people be induced to travel this route by prophecies which promised fountains in valleys of the desert and a level highway lined with cedar, acacia, cypress and oil trees, etc.? Would they not have turned back when they saw that there was a real desert to traverse? In 54:1–4 Eerdmans finds an expression of joy because the number of immigrants is greater than the number of inhabitants of Jerusalem (p. 213). This he can do by interpreting "the children of

the desolate" as the immigrants and "the children of the married wife" as the residents of Jerusalem. Several prophecies in chapters 56–66 describe the arrival of the caravan (pp. 215 f.); 60:4 tells of its arrival in Jerusalem (p. 215), which implies that the verse: "They are all gathered together, and come to thee; Thy sons come from far, And thy daughters are borne on the side" refers to the caravan of Sheshbazzar! And so on! By this manner of exegesis it is obviously possible to produce miracles. But Eerdmans does not solve the essential problem: why does Cyrus disappear after chapter 48? Duhm interprets the expression: "Ye that bear the vessels of the Lord" (52:11), in his exegesis of this verse, to mean the priests, who, carrying the sacred vessels, will lead the immigrants. Torrey, *Second Isaiah*, 409, accepts this exegesis. See also Rashi on this verse. Volz and some other scholars interpret it to refer to the vessels of the Temple which Nebuchadnezzar had removed: the prophet believed that the vessels would be returned to them. See also Skinner on this verse. However, the sacred vessels are nowhere called "vessels of the Lord" in Scripture. The bearers of the vessels of the Lord are Israel which is pictured as going into battle behind God, as bearers of the instruments of His warfare. The interpretation, therefore, of Budde and others, and the shallow ridicule of Duhm are out of place. The exit of the emigrants in 52:11–12 is the setting forth an encampment with bearers of vessels, and advance and rear guards. *Cf.* Isa. 13:5.

15 Torrey, *Second Isaiah*, 1 f., 7 f.; Glahn, *op. cit.*, 118 f.

16 Elliger, *Deuterojesaja*. Elliger thinks that Trito-Isaiah was the author of 52:13–53:12, 47, etc. He expanded and reworked the other servant songs and many other sections. Elliger, both in his *Deutero-* and his *Tritojesaja*, using vocabulary evidence in a very faulty manner, seeks to determine literary adherence by word statistics. He finds words which are peculiar to 56–66 or occur in these chapters more frequently; ergo, these chapters are a separate unit, distinct from 40–55. Certain words of a chapter occur more often in Trito-Isaiah than in Deutero-Isaiah; ergo, the chapter belongs to Trito-Isaiah. The calculation is schematic, pedantic, and, as North, *Servant*, 177, says, "with a complete lack of any sense of humor." Each word is a unit of statistical calculation, and when Elliger does distinguish, the distinctions are formal, without any feeling for the significance or lack thereof, and without consideration of the fact that an author may use words in different ways. Transgression (פשע) occurs three times in the singular and once in the plural in Trito-Isaiah, but five times in the plural in Deutero-Isaiah (*Tritojesaja*, 45. However, the statistic is inaccurate!). Sheep (צאן) is used four times in Trito-Isaiah, and once in Deutero-Isaiah (p. 52). Vineyard (כרם) is used only twice in Trito-Isaiah. Yet (עוד) occurs seven times in Trito-Isaiah in the temporal sense with negative implication, and only twice in Deutero-Isaiah (*ibid.*). Look upon (נבט) in the hiphil is used in

both, but in Trito-Isaiah the subject is YHWH! (p. 55). Evidence that 52:13–53:12 belongs to Trito-Isaiah: believe (אמן) in the hiphil occurs in Deutero-Isaiah only once (*Deuterojesaja*, 9) and, similarly, dry ground (אריץ ציה) (*ibid.*). Grave (קבר) occurs only once, outside of 53:9, in Trito-Isaiah and, similarly, violence (חמס) (p. 12). With respect to chapter 47: virgin (בתולה) occurs only one other time in Trito-Isaiah and, similarly, throne (כסא) (p. 107).

This entire system of proof is invalid. Proof is to be had from word use only where different terms with similar meaning are used consistently, as in the Priestly Code and Deuteronomy, or where there is something characteristic in the author's vocabulary. But what is proven by words such as sheep, throne, grave, etc.? Moreover, the statistics of Elliger in his *Deuterojesaja* are based on the assumption that a number of chapters and fragments in 40–55 belong to Trito-Isaiah, which assumption is without basis except by reason of hair-splitting casuistry. It is particularly unfortunate that Elliger ignores material which might discredit his statistics; *e.g.*, in analyzing chapter 60 (*Tritojesaja*, 51 f.), he neglects the expressions: Arise (52:2); the glory of the Lord (40:5); darkness . . . light (50:10); Lift up your eyes on high, And see (40:26); Lift up thine eyes . . . and behold: All these gather themselves together, and come to thee (49:18); Bring My sons from far, And My daughters . . . (43:6), and others. This statistical compilation is, therefore, without value. Indeed, the very effort to discover Trito-Isaiah also in chapters 40–55 demonstrates the extent to which chapters 40–66 are interconnected and unified.

17 Mowinckel, *ZAW*, 1931, explicitly emphasizes this, and it is also the assumption of other critics. Budde, *Lieder*, 38, contests the confining of the prophet to a single idea, to which he is required always to return. But he himself divides chapters 56–66 into twelve fragments on the basis of the self-same assumption.

18 *Cf.* Begrich, *op. cit.*, 60–61.

19 See above, III, 50.

20 See Gressmann, *ZAW*, 1914; Köhler, *Deuterojesaja* (Köhler deletes 44:9–20 and various other verses); Volz, *op. cit.;* Mowinckel, *ZAW*, 1931. Begrich, *op. cit.*, also deletes a number of prophecies. He deletes 42:18–25, and he does not count 45:8 because he cannot understand its meaning, see p. 5. See also: Elliger, *Deuterojesaja*, 222; Eissfeldt in Robinson, *Record*, 94 f.

21 Mowinckel, *ZAW*, 1931, p. 90, says that the editor could have placed 52:7–10 after 40:8, but he decided according to key words. But, in fact, there are many words connecting 52:7–10 with the other prophecies of return, whereas the connection between 52 and 53 is very tenuous.

22 Torrey, *Second Isaiah*, 199–202. Examples: 56:1, צדקה, in the sense of good deeds and of salvation; 50:4, למודים, in the sense of teaching, wisdom, and in the sense of pupils; 63:3, 6, נצח,

blood, strength; 54:9, כִּימֵי נֹחַ, as in the days of Noah (according to some writers), and then מֵי נֹחַ, the waters of Noah; 54:15 גּוּר, (the foe) who attacks, and (the stranger) who sojourns; and others.

23 Köhler, *op. cit.*, 93–95. Examples of variation: But My salvation shall be for ever, and My favor shall not be abolished . . . and My favor shall be for ever, and My salvation unto all generations (51:6, 8). He shall make the right to go forth to nations. . . . He shall make the right to go forth according to the truth (42:1, 3). Recurring sounds: The grass (חָצִיר) withereth, the flower (צִיץ) fadeth . . . the grass withereth, etc. (40:7, 8). To set up an image that shall not be moved . . . And he fasteneth it with nails that it shall not be moved (40:20; 41:7); And Israel whom I have chosen . . . Jeshurun whom I have chosen (44:1, 2); And openeth not his mouth . . . and openeth not his mouth (53:7). But not all of Köhler's examples are apt.

24 *Ibid.*, 94, 96–97.

25 See above, III, 109–12.

26 The accepted emendation (of Duhm) of this verse: from the foundations, or from the foundation, of the earth (in place of: the foundations of the earth) is not convincing, inasmuch as, according to this emendation, the sentence is still not completed. Apparently this should read: who laid the foundation of the earth. *Cf.* vv. 26, 28.

27 Duhm, *op. cit.*, proposes: "Let them await my argument" (יַחֲלוּ נֹכְחִי) an emendation which other scholars accept.

28 Condamin points this out in his exegesis of this verse. See Skinner, *op. cit.*, 17.

29 Elliger, *Tritojesaja*, 69 f., discusses this. He attributes the repetition of words to the paucity of Trito-Isaiah's vocabulary (64 f.), and thinks that word poverty is characteristic specifically of Trito-Isaiah (see his *Deuterojesaja*, 18). Köhler, *op. cit.*, however, had earlier determined this quality as characteristic of Deutero-Isaiah (see above, p. 69). But there is without question a common quality to the whole of 40–66, even though chapters 56–66 are not marked by poverty of vocabulary. *Cf.* North, *op. cit.*, 175.

30 See Volz, *op. cit.*, 243.

31 See Duhm, *op. cit.*, 390 f. Duhm also includes the command of circumcision, which, in fact, is not mentioned here, in his exegesis of the conditions of Isa. 56:6. Torrey, who argues for the unity of chapters 40–66, is forced to regard 56:1–7 as a later insertion. See *Second Isaiah*, 426–28. So great is the stumbling block!

32 *Cf.* Gunkel, *RGG*, IV, 1548.

33 42:13–14. See below, 102.

34 *Cf.* North, *op. cit.*, 84 (opposing Begrich).

35 Biblical scholarship has struggled with 48:16. It is the prophet who speaks at the end of the verse; but modern critics inter-

pret the beginning as a continuation of God's words. This is, to use Rashi's word, a mixing of matters; and the critics tend to delete the end of the verse. Rashi and Redak take the entire verse as the speech of the prophet, which is certainly correct. Nonetheless, the verse requires emendation. V. 16 introduces the passage 16–19, which continues 12–15. Following 45:19, it would be preferable to read, "I have spoken, not in secret, from the beginning." "From the time that it was" refers to the wars of Cyrus, which are the topic of 12–15; thus, from the beginning of the occurrence of these events. The words "there am I" (שם אני) are inappropriate. It appears that these words, together with the letter ה, which precedes them (appended in the masoretic text to the preceding word) and the ועתה (and now) which follows, are displaced and garbled. The original probably was: from the time that it was I have proclaimed it, and now the Lord, etc. . . . Words are missing at the end of the verse. On the basis of Isa. 34:16, the completion of the verse should be: "and His spirit ordered me to say" (the words were absorbed into the "Thus saith" of v. 17). It follows that the critics who refer the "Oh that thou wouldest hearken" (v. 18) to the future and not to the past (cf. Isa. 63:19, Ps. 81:12, Gen. 23:13) are right. This is confirmed also by the end of v. 19. Thus the sequence of the verses is: "I prophesied concerning the victories of Cyrus from the beginning and not in secret. From the beginning I declared what would come. And now, when the prophecies of victory are being realized, I have been sent to say: If ye will hearken to My commandments, the goodness is assured to you and to your seed forever. For the prophecy of redemption also will be fulfilled: Go ye forth from Babylon." Vv. 12–21, chapter 48, are therefore a prophecy specifically of the time of the fall of Babylon.

36 See Budde, *Litteratur*, 159–60; Hölscher, *Geschichte*, 122.

37 Budde, *Litteratur*, 160.

38 See Volz, *op. cit.*, xvii. But the statement that Deutero-Isaiah was "the founder of the synagogue" (*ibid.*) is an exaggeration.

39 See Budde, *Litteratur*, 160; Kittel, *op. cit.*, 111, 239 f.; Volz, *op. cit.*, xxi; Buber, *op. cit.*, 208 f.

40 If the prophetic garb is abstracted from Isa. 1:10–17; 5:11–23; 9:7–10:4; 25:7–13; Jer. 2:4–3:17; 5:20–31; 7:21–28; 17:20–27; Amos 4:6–10; Mic. 6:1–8 *et al.*, there remain "theological" propositions and religious-ethical sermons.

41 The verse is to be divided in this manner, even though contrary to the masoretic punctuation (one calleth: Clear ye in the wilderness the way . . .). The passage is divided in this way also in the Septuagint, the Vulgate, and apparently the Targum of Jonathan, and so quoted in Matt. 3:3 and the parallel passages. Rashi's exegesis is unclear. Redak attaches "in the wilderness" to "Clear ye the way"; also Duhm, Köhler, Volz, *et al.* Opposing this, see Torrey, *Second Isaiah*, 305. The argument on the basis of parallelism to "Make plain

in the desert" is valueless. Since the voice calls in the wilderness, the idea of the wilderness is implied in the words "Clear ye the way."

42 According to the version "And I said," of the Septuagint and the Vulgate; and in the Dead Sea scrolls: ואמרה. Against this, see Cross, "The Council of Yahweh in Second Isaiah," *JNES*, 1953, pp. 274–77. Cross thinks that those who rendered thus did not understand that 40:1–8 is a dialogue between God and the angels (p. 276). In any case, the voice which calls is not "merely a poetical device," as Torrey says, *Second Isaiah*, 305. But the referent is also not the voice of (real) angels (Duhm, Volz, Cross, *et al.*). God appears in this and all subsequent theophanies of Deutero-Isaiah without any divine retinue. The voices are ephemeral visionary figures. The herald of good tidings also is thus naturally explained.

43 Some critics interpret the herald as "Zion which tells." Zion is summoned to proclaim the good tidings to the "cities of Judah." But in 40:2, Zion is the recipient of the good tidings. Similarly, in 41:27; 52:7, the herald proclaims the good news to Zion. In other prophecies, also, the prophet comforts and encourages Zion. Female heralds are mentioned in Ps. 68:12. Skinner and other critics vainly press matters in order to interpret the "herald" in collective sense, as a group of heralds. The teller of good news remains a visionary figure.

44 Meyer, *Ursprung*, II, 19; Kittel, *op. cit.*, III, 200; Volz, *op. cit.*, 75–76.

45 Buber, *op. cit.*, 209.

46 See Meyer, *Ursprung*, II, 17 f.; Kittel, *op. cit.*, III, 21 f. (*re* the international intellectual climate prevailing in Greece, Babylon, Media, and Persia); Volz, *op. cit.*, xix; Klausner, *Historia*, I, 135. Also the fanciful arguments of v. Gall, *Βασιλεία*, 185 f. (that Deutero-Isaiah obtained his eschatological ideas from the religion of Zarathustra). Against the superficialities of v. Gall, see Kittel, *op. cit.*, III, 211, note 4. Eerdmans, *op. cit.*, 214–15, 325, also discovers Persian influence in Deutero-Isaiah. From 66:3, Eerdmans learns that Deutero-Isaiah accepted the Persian belief in the sanctity of dogs and the prohibition of killing dogs. Nothing need be said concerning such exegesis.

47 Concerning literary points of contact, see Stummer, *JBL*, 1926, pp. 171–89; Kittel, *op. cit.*, III, 210 f.; Dürr, *Ursprung*, 146 f. Engnell, *BJRL*, 1948, pp. 57 f., 68 f., finds "countless" proofs. See also Hyatt, *JNES*, 1944, pp. 84 f.; Jeremias, *op. cit.*, 605–11; Köhler, *op. cit.*, 119–20.

48 Dürr, *Ursprung*, 146, and Stummer, *loc. cit.*, 172–73, find parallels to the description of the way (Isa. 40:3–5) in a hymn to Marduk. But these descriptions are grounded in observation of royal progressions everywhere. Deutero-Isaiah describes in particular the straightening of the way of the wilderness, and this is certainly reminiscent, both linguistically and substantively, of Israel's journey in the wilderness following the exodus from Egypt (Deut. 8:2, 15; 32:10–12;

Jer. 2:6, *et al.*). We find the expression: Fear thou not (Stummer, 177) also in Gen. 15:1; Jer. 30:10; Joel 2:21–22; Lam. 3:57, *et al.* Stummer himself remarks (*ibid.*) that the expression, "(I) hold thy right hand" (41:13; 42:7; 51:18) occurs with reference to a Hittite seer. This, therefore, is a current figure in the near-eastern culture circle. There are parallels to the divine enthronement metaphor (Isa. 52:17, Stummer, *loc. cit.*, 184–85); also in the Ugaritic literature; and it is a standard figure in the coronation hymns of the book of Psalms, which are certainly very old. Hyatt (*op. cit.*, 84 f.) tries to demonstrate connections between Deutero-Isaiah and the Ugaritic writings. He thinks that Deutero-Isaiah, even if he wrote while in the land of Israel, might have been acquainted with the myth of the god who dies and is resurrected. Of course he might have known the myth, but there is no evidence at all that he did, indeed, know it. With respect to Deutero-Isaiah's knowledge of theogony, see Appendix I.

49 Dürr, *Ursprung*, 147; Hyatt, *op. cit.*, 84.

50 See above, III, 546–47.

51 Stummer, *loc. cit.*, 178–79; Kittel, *op. cit.*, III, 210.

52 Formerly the opinion was widespread that Isa. 45:7 was directed against the belief in Ahura (the god of light and the good) and Ahriman (god of darkness and evil). However, Nyberg, *Religionen*, 101–9, tries to prove that in the early Persian religion Ahurmiz (Ahura Mazda) was considered the god both of light and darkness. On this basis, Buber, *op. cit.*, 212, surmises that the prophet was protesting specifically against this early Persian faith. *Cf.* also Nyberg, *op. cit.*, note 1 to p. 374 (478–79).

53 Nyberg, *op. cit.*, 343 f.

54 See the attempt of Stevenson in "Werden und Wesen des A. T.," *BZAW*, 1936, pp. 89–96.

55 According to the traditional pointing (Isa. 42:22): snared in (הֻפַּח) from פַּחַת, to place in snares, in chains. Some critics point the word בַּחוּרִים (young men) as בַּחוֹרִים (in holes) in parallelism to "in prison houses." Perhaps the phrasing should be: הֻנַּח בַּחוֹרִים (put in holes). *Cf.* Lev. 24:12; Num. 15:34 (they put him in ward).

56 The exegetes understand the word מִשְׁפָּט (right) in the sense of the world order, the law of nature and history, or in the sense of providence (see Redak, also Skinner, Volz, *et al.*). But Deutero-Isaiah is fond of word-play, and included in the expression both "the path of right," the world order generally, and the particular right (justice) of Israel at that moment.

57 A variant reading is "their worshipers" in place of "their witnesses."

58 *Cf.* Ps. 35:27: "Let them shout for joy . . . that delight in my righteousness; Yea, let them say . . . 'Magnified be the Lord.'" Accordingly, Isa. 42:21 might better be read: "The Lord delights in

his righteousness in order that he might make the teaching great and glorious." It is to be observed that this verse follows the desideratum: "They shall be turned back, greatly ashamed" (v. 17). Similarly, also, in Ps. 35, see v. 26 (and v. 4). See also Pss. 40:15–16; 70:3–5. Ps. 35 also speaks of the aid of the Lord in the cause and the judgment (11, 23–24). Cf. also the parallel expressions: "that rejoice at my hurt" (35:26), "that delight in my hurt" (40:15; 70:3); also Isa. 53:10: "Yet it pleased the Lord to crush him."

59 According to widespread interpretation, the sense of the passage is that God will give the ransom to Cyrus: He will allow Cyrus to conquer Egypt, Ethiopia, and Seba; and for this payment, he will liberate Israel. See the commentaries of Duhm, Skinner, Volz. Cheyne and Duhm arraign Deutero-Isaiah for this chauvinism; and Volz (op. cit., 37) concludes from this passage that, according to the thought of Deutero-Isaiah, Cyrus will continue to be the ruler of the world, God's viceroy on earth; but he will liberate Israel. See also Mowinckel, Knecht, 24, and, opposing this political interpretation, Torrey, Second Isaiah, 334. The sense of the passage, according to Torrey, is only that Israel is dearer to God than the other peoples. This, in fact, is the meaning. However, the prophet is here again using the metaphor of the lawsuit and the judgment. "Ransom" is, in the Bible, a legal concept. See Köhler, op. cit., 118. Indeed, the prophet assures Cyrus victory over nations and kings, and promises him treasures of darkness and hidden riches of secret places, etc., all for the sake of Israel (45:4). Also, even if we assume that the meaning of this promise is the assurance to Cyrus of world dominion (see below, 99–100), what is the reason for the addition of a specific "ransom" for Israel?

60 Many emendations have been proposed for 45:9–11, not all of which are necessary. But the (imperative) "ask me" is unsuitable, and it seems desirable to emend: "do ye ask Me," interpreting the phrase as a question: "Will ye search Me out and require an accounting from Me of the things that are impending?" The sense of "concerning My sons" is: "Will ye command Me concerning what I do for the sake of Israel?" Torrey, Second Isaiah, 71, 360, in accordance with all his artificial and imaginative exegesis of Deutero-Isaiah, interprets the "My sons" as "the Gentiles." Vv. 17, 19, 25 prove that the reference is to the salvation of Israel. See also 43:6: "My sons . . . And My daughters"; also 50:1.

61 There are difficulties in 45:24–25 which cannot be resolved on the basis of the masoretic punctuation. But v. 25 proves that the justified are the seed of Israel; and this is certainly the subject matter of v. 24. The sense of the verse is: Only in the Lord, of Me, shall one (the seed of Israel) say, is victory (righteousness) and strength; Even to Him shall he come (Israel will come to the Lord seeking refuge); but all that are incensed against him (against Israel) shall be in confusion. The Targum of v. 24 reads they shall come (plural);

thus also the Dead Sea scrolls (the subject being the nations), and according to the Masorah, "the plural is understood." The Septuagint phrased (the final word): "against them"; and it might be preferable to read: "Only in the Lord, of Me shall they say, is righteousness and strength; Even to Him shall they come, but all that are incensed against them, shall be in confusion."

62 Some critics read in 51:14 צֹרֵר (bound) in place of צֹעֶה (bent down). Perhaps it should be עָצוּר (imprisoned). Preferable to: "into the pit," is: "in the pit," with the sense: "in the dungeon," which is an expression meaning prison house. The phrase "Neither shall his bread fail" refers to the bread of affliction of the prison house: Neither shall his food fail, as in the past. V. 16 is similar to 49:2, and it appears that here, also, the meaning is that God will teach the prisoner to speak before his judges and will protect him in the shadow of His hand. Accordingly, there is continuity in the whole passage 12–15, and the despair of the exegetes is not justified.

63 See Jer. 36:26.

64 Cf. Lam. 3:53–54: "They have cast my life in the dungeon. . . . I said, I am cut off." And, ibid., 5–7: "He hath made me to dwell in dark places, as those that have been long dead. . . . He hath hedged me about. . . . He hath made my chain heavy." Cf. also Ps. 143:3, 7.

65 Köhler, op. cit., 110–20, considers in detail Deutero-Isaiah's use of the figure of the lawsuit or judicial argumentation, and explicates the various expressions. He also points out (112–13) the use of this figure in other biblical passages (Isa. 1:10; 8:3; 32:9; Mic. 1:2; 3:1, 9; 6:2, et al. However, not all of Köhler's examples are apt). Likewise, Köhler shows that Deutero-Isaiah's use of the words צדק, צדקה (righteousness) in the sense of redemption is explained by the lawsuit motif: acquittal in the trial is the redemption (115–16). However, in the summation of the ideas of Deutero-Isaiah which are expressed in the lawsuit passages, Köhler distinguishes only two basic motifs: the case of God against the gods and their worshipers; and the case of God against Israel on account of its transgressions (116–19). In fact, Deutero-Isaiah does use the figure of the lawsuit also in his reproofs of Israel. Thus there are three law cases in the prophecies of Deutero-Isaiah; the third is the case in favor of Israel. Prophets prior to Isaiah had also used the figure of the case against Israel. But Köhler does not realize the particular motif of Deutero-Isaiah, that is, the interweaving of God's case against the gods with His action in favor of Israel against the nations. The argument against idolatry is combined in the prophecies of Deutero-Isaiah with the assurance of redemption to Israel and of Israel's vindication in its contention with the nations. The inner connection is expressed by the office which the prophet assigns to Israel: to be God's witness and His servant. In the real world the action of God is also the suit of Israel. Israel is the witness and the servant who contends in the cause of God against the gods; and the prophet himself contends for Israel against the gods. In this

NOTES

Deutero-Isaiah creates a symbol and expression for the new historical reality: for the struggle of Israel with gentile paganism, and also for the new hostility which will thereby be engendered.

66 Proof by appeal to prophecy can in no event be viewed as "monotheistic proof." See Volz, *op. cit.*, 23; also Peake, *Suffering*, 31, 53. Blank, *HUCA*, 1940, pp. 1 f., goes to extremes. According to Blank, Deutero-Isaiah considers the ability to foretell future events the test of divinity (pp. 3, 19). Blank even reads into the words of Deutero-Isaiah a theological proof of the validity of monotheism against polytheism; only a God who is sole ruler of the world can have certain knowledge of the future. Accordingly, the God who knows the future is the sole God. However, there is no trace of such an argument in Deutero-Isaiah's prophecies. Deutero-Isaiah contrasts God with the idols, not the One with the many. There is no theoretical argument against the idea of polytheism in Deutero-Isaiah, and indeed in all of Scripture.

67 "For they call themselves of the holy city" in v. 2 is to be taken as the reason for the prophet's summons to "the house of Jacob" to hear his words, and as the continuation of the phrase, "Who are called by the name of Israel, And are come forth out of the fountain of Judah."

68 48:6 may be emended: "Thou hast heard a vision . . . I have announced unto thee new things in their time." Some critics emend v. 10: "I have refined thee to Me as silver." But this word may be a play on words, which is typical of Deutero-Isaiah. "Silver" is parallel to "affliction," and its meaning here is wealth and affluence in general. The word "silver" depends on: "I have refined thee," but the meaning of the expression as here used is: "I have not tested thee by riches but by affliction." Riches also are considered a test and a cause of men's turning from God. See Deut. 8:12–14; Prov. 30:8–9, *et al.*

69 See Mowinckel, *Knecht*, 23–24, 33; Begrich, *op. cit.*, 68–69, 117–18. Volz, *op. cit.*, 37, 142–43, says Cyrus was to be "the vicar of the Lord on earth"; and, following Volz, Buber, *op. cit.*, 221: Cyrus is the "counselor of the valiant God" concerning whom Isaiah prophesied (9:5). No man will again sit on the throne of David, etc. Buber does not explain how the prophet arrived at the notion that Cyrus would be preferable to a king of the dynasty of David.

70 Volz, *ibid.*, 37.

71 See above, III, 458.

72 Volz, *op. cit.*, 37, cites Isa. 43:3 to prove that Deutero-Isaiah imagined Cyrus as world ruler also in the future. Cyrus would receive dominion in Egypt, etc., from the hand of God as "ransom" for the freeing of Israel. But this is a vain exegesis. See above, 93–94.

73 Volz, *op. cit.*, lays stress on this.

74 See Wellhausen, *op. cit.*, 150; Meyer, *Entstehung*, 78, 234; *id.*, *Ursprung*, 19; Gressmann, *Messias*, 1, note 2; Haller, *Judentum*, 39, 43; Mowinckel, *Knecht*, 33; Skinner, *op. cit.*, xlvii (but see p. 64,

limitation); Volz, *op. cit.*, 37, 142; Buber, *op. cit.*, 221; **Eerdmans**, *op. cit.*, 212, 214, 325; Lindblom, *op. cit.*, 97–98. North, *op. cit.*, 85, repeats the opinion of Sidney Smith that the exiles killed the prophet because he made Cyrus the "messiah." Against the opinion that Deutero-Isaiah considered Cyrus the "messiah," see Kittel, *op. cit.*, III, 218. See also Duhm, *op. cit.*, 313.

75 See above, II, 716–18, 723–25.

76 Structurally, Isa. 42:10 is very close to Ps. 149:1; but in the psalm the verse is the opening of a song of the "saints" who "execute vengeance upon the nations," whereas the verse in Deutero-Isaiah is an introduction to the song which the nations themselves will sing.

77 Volz, *op. cit.*, pp. xviii, 166–67.

78 Haller, Festschrift to Gunkel, 1923, pp. 261 f.

79 Mowinckel, *Knecht*, 24.

80 In place of "(that) gird yourselves" (מעזרי) some critics, following the Peshitta, read "lighters of" מאירי and this, apparently, is the correct version. "Firebrands" (זיקות) are sparks, and not fiery arrows. It is widely held that the kindlers of fire and the lighters of firebrands are the wicked who persecute the righteous and the faithful. But in this passage the prophet is not speaking of persecutions. The kindlers of fire are the opposite of those who walk in darkness of the preceding verse (50:10). For "who is among you," *cf.* 42:23. The sense of the passage is: those among you who fear the Lord and obey the voice of the prophet, who walk in darkness and have no light (who suffer the grief of the exile), let them trust in the Lord and have faith in His salvation. The prophet turns in v. 11 to the renegades: these kindle fire for themselves. They seek their salvation in the diaspora, in assimilation among the gentiles. He threatens them: they will go up in the flames which they kindle.

81 See above, III, 592–93, 601; also below, 147–48.

82 Similarly, in 42:7 and 49:8–9. We shall consider these verses below.

83 Gressmann, *Messias*, 287–329 (concerning the figure of Josiah, 327–29); Kittel, *op. cit.*, III, 222–39; Mowinckel, *Knecht;* Rudolph, *ZAW*, 1925, pp. 90–114; *ibid.*, 1928, pp. 156–66 (opposing him, Staerk, *ZAW*, 1926, pp. 242 f.); Elliger, *Deuterojesaja*; Sellin, *ZAW*, 1937, pp. 177–217; Dürr, *Ursprung*, 76–77, 111, 132, 142–45; Begrich, *op. cit.;* Engnell, *loc. cit.;* Bentzen, *Messias*, 42–71; Wellhausen, *op. cit.*, 152; Budde, *Lieder;* Eissfeldt, *Einleitung*, 372–89. For the synthetic concept (the servant is both prophet and nation), see Klausner, *Messianic Idea* [Hebrew], 94–98; Albright, *From the Stone Age*, 254–55; Buber, *op. cit.*, 217–30; Kissane, *Book of Isaiah*, II, p. lxviii. See also North, *op. cit.*, excellent historical and topical survey; for the most recent interpretations, Rowley, *Servant*, 3–88.

84 See Finkelstein, *Pharisees*, II, 485–87.

85 See above, III, 648–49.

86 Kaufmann, *Golah v'Nekar* (*Exile and Alienation*) [Hebrew], I, 283 f.

87 See Dalman, *Jesaja 53*, 16–18, 58; Peake, *op. cit.*, 33, 56.

88 See above, III, 462–63.

89 Budde, *Lieder*, p. 10, note 1, attempts to anticipate the argument that in 53:6 the reference is not to the sin of idolatry, because the Lord had revealed Himself only to Israel. Budde argues that the universalism of Deutero-Isaiah does not, in fact, completely accord with the particularism of the ancient religion of Israel. But in the stories of Genesis it is implied that the first theophany was to all mankind. Idolatry is a sin in that it is a going astray from this revelation. But Budde's argument fails of the point. The decisive consideration is not that the religion of the Lord was not revealed to the gentiles according to the "old" religion, but that idolatry is not explicitly reckoned a sin for the gentiles in any passage in Scripture; and that no prophet threatens the gentiles with punishment on account of the sin of idolatry. Deutero-Isaiah also does not specifically mention idolatry as a sin to the gentiles. Neither Deutero-Isaiah nor any other prophet says that the gentiles are in need of expiation for this sin. The prophets envision the abrogation of idolatry in the time to come as a gracious revelation; and they do not make it dependent on the purging of the sin of the idolatry of the gentiles. Also in the creation stories there is no evaluation of the sin of gentile idolatry since idolatry is neither mentioned nor alluded to in these stories.

90 Feilchenfeld, *Sühneleiden*, 5 f., finds an acknowledgment of this kind in vv. 4–6, 8: "our diseases . . . and our pains," the diseases and pains, which we, the gentiles, caused him; and "he was wounded because of our transgressions"—he was pierced through by our hands, of us, the transgressors (also: "crushed because of our iniquities"); "And the Lord hath made to light on him the iniquity of all of us—his wounds are the fruit of our iniquities" (p. 6), all of us caused him sufferings (p. 18). See also Friedmann, *op. cit.*, 17. But all this exegesis is erroneous. Nowhere in Scripture are the deeds of the wicked referred to the righteous in inverted language of this sort. In particular, the exegesis of "the Lord hath made to light on him," etc. (v. 6), is absurd. It is obvious here that it is God, and not the wicked, who caused the "lighting upon" and the hurt is the iniquity-punishment. Likewise v. 3 ("a man of pains, and acquainted with disease") makes it clear that the servant is imagined as "smitten of God," and that it is not those who are speaking who had harmed him.

91 See above, II, 595 f. The doctrine of retribution.

92 *Ibid.*, 598 f. Collective retribution.

93 Hooke, *VT*, 1952, pp. 2–17, tries to find in Scripture the roots of the idea of subrogation; but until he comes to the servant of the Lord he is unable to bring proof that the concept of substitution is

implied in the biblical ideas of retribution. The concept is not contained in Exod. 32:30–33 (Hooke, *ibid.*, 11–12). Moses does not offer himself as substitute atonement for the nation, but wants to be punished with the people if God will not forgive their sin and will punish them. The rabbinic exegetes did indeed interpret that Moses offered himself to die in place of Israel; and based their exegesis on Isa. 53:12 (Sotah 14a, midrash of Rabbi Simlai); and, somewhat similarly, Maimonides in his exegesis of Exod. 32:33. But, according to this interpretation also, God rejects this kind of retribution and says: Whosoever hath sinned against Me, him will I blot out of My book (Exod. 32:33). The concept is also absent from Job 33:22–24 (Hooke, *op. cit.*, 14). The "ransom" there is the "uprightness" of him who is about to die, and for whom there is an angel-intercessor to vouch for him before God.

94 Moreover, even in the Christian Scriptures, the idea of the Messiah who is killed for "the pardoning of sins" is recognized as strange, without organic connection with the system of Jewish apocalyptic imagery, into which it can be fitted only with difficulty. The blood of the Messiah is shed, as it were, to redeem the world from "sin." And yet sin still besets the world as before. Nothing is forgiven, terrible troubles impend, and only a remnant will be saved—everything as in the apocalyptic literature which preceded the "sacrifice." Indeed, the "sacrifice" itself not only did not blot out sin; rather it increased it. The crucifixion was itself a sin; and the non-belief in it and its purpose was held to be an added transgression. The concept of death for the sake of forgiveness of sin contradicts the entire eschatology of the "New Testament." Nonetheless, the idea is explicit in the books of the New Testament. On the other hand, it is not explicitly stated anywhere in the Jewish Scriptures, and even in Isa. 53 can be found only by means of allusion. And, since there is no natural place for it among the scriptural eschatological ideas, it should not be read into the passages by forced exegesis.

95 The expression "and set thee for a covenant of the people" (which occurs again in 49:8) is a peculiar and difficult phrase. There is no basis for the exegesis of many Christian scholars that the sense of "for a covenant" is to "mediate a covenant." There is no indication of the concept of a mediator. The servant himself will be the covenant of the people, and the sense of the expression is a covenant-people.

96 51:16: "And I have put My words in thy mouth, And have covered thee in the shadow of My hand, That I may plant the heavens, And lay the foundations of the earth," etc. This sentence structure is peculiar, but precisely on that account it is not "suspect." The arguments of Volz, *op. cit.*, 126–27, against vv. 16–17 are irrelevant. The prophet here, as in many other prophecies, associates his nationalistic assurances with descriptions of God's cosmic deeds. V. 15 is the continuation both logically and linguistically of v. 13. Israel is fearful

of men and forgets that its God is the Creator of the world and all-powerful. There follows: "For I am the Lord . . . Who stirreth up the sea . . . (Who) put My words in thy mouth," Who protects thee, the God Who plants the heavens, Who lays the foundations of the earth, and Who says to Zion "Thou art My people." The prefix "to" (lamed = *l*) of the verbs (plant, lay, say) of the preceding statement (v. 16) obviously does not indicate the task of the nation which is addressed in 16a. Rather these are the deeds of God, as is the case with the deeds of 42:7 and 49:8–9. We observe that the lamed ("to") refers back to the beginning of v. 15: "For I am the Lord thy God . . . That I may (to) plant the heavens" etc. We find similar motifs and similar syntax in 42:5–7: "Thus saith God the Lord, He that created the heavens, and stretched them forth, He that spread forth the earth, etc. . . . I (am) the Lord . . . To open the blind eyes," etc. We observe that the prefixed lameds ("to") of "to open . . . to bring out" refer to "I (am) the Lord." (See below with reference to the sequence after 49:8–9.) The heavens and the earth of 51:16 are not the new heavens and the new earth of the time to come, as Redak and many modern exegetes interpret them.

97 Compare "The tongue of them that are taught" (50:4) "And every tongue that shall rise against thee in judgment" (54:17).

98 The words "To bring back to Him" in v. 5 refer to "saith the Lord," and describe the act of the Lord, not of the servant.

99 The change of tenses in v. 5 "For I am honourable" (imperfect) . . . "is become" (perfect) is surprising. Some critics would point the waw prefixed to the verb כבד (I am honourable) with the vowel qamesh (waw-consecutive) in place of the (masoretic) shewa (waw-conjunctive).

100 The words "that thou shouldest be My servant" (מהיותך) in v. 6 are parenthetic. The sense is: because thou art, the prefix (mem) having the sense of causation. *Cf.* 48:4 (Because I knew), 40:26 (By the greatness of His might), 43:4 (Since thou art precious), 53:5 (because of our transgressions . . . because of our iniquities). The verbs: "to raise up . . . to restore" follow: "It is too light." See Duhm, *op. cit.*, 342.

101 In vv. 8–9 the verbs "to raise up . . . to cause to inherit . . . saying" follow "I have answered thee and I have helped thee"; "I have answered thee and I have helped thee to raise up the land," etc. It is God, not the servant, who acts.

102 The motifs, counsellor, response, word, appear together also in Isa. 41:28: "but there is no counsellor, that . . . can give an answer (word)." *Cf.* also 44:26 ("the word . . . and the counsel"); also 45:21; 46:11.

103 V. 4: "that are taught" . . . wisdom, "as they that are taught" . . . as pupils. Torrey points out this play on words. *Cf.* above, note 22.

104 The text of 52:14–15 presents difficulties. For "at thee," read "at him." For כן משחת read אבן משחת (indeed marred). Some critics read: כי משחת (because marred). The verb יזה is derived from the root נזה and interpreted: he shall startle, (or) cause to jump. Some critics read: ישתעו, ירכזו were agitated, (or) afraid, etc. Possibly: יזועו (were made) to tremble.

105 See Budde, *Lieder*, 7; Dalman, *op. cit.*, 26–27.

106 The passage is quoted in this way also in John 12:38 and Romans 10:16.

107 In v. 2: before us, in place of, before him ("right forth").

108 The words "crushed" (v.5), "to crush him" (v.10) refer explicitly to the afflictions of "the contrite (crushed) ones" (57:15) in that the humble are "broken-hearted." They are diseased and in need of binding up and healing (61:1). Likewise, the consolation of the mourners is called healing (57:18). *Cf.* Ps. 147:3: "Who healeth the broken in heart, And bindeth up their wounds." The speakers of Isa. 53, themselves, also require healing (v. 5).

109 It is not to be assumed that the words "All we like sheep did go astray, We turned every one to his own way," refer to the sin of idolatry of the peoples. Budde's translation, *Lieder*, 10 (*wir gingen alle in die Irre . . .*) is misleading. The simile of going astray "like sheep" is too weak to represent the denial of God in favor of the gods of wood and stone of all the peoples. By comparison with the parallel passages (47:15; 56:11) we see that the reference is to frivolousness, to the pursuit of commonplace pleasures.

110 The servant himself was "oppressed" and "humbled," and suffered silently (*cf.* Lam. 3:28–30); but he was not led forth to execution. The expressions "As a lamb . . . to the slaughter" and "as a sheep before her shearers" are merely similes for the muteness and the submission. The verse does not mean that the servant was brought forth to slaughter, or that his beard was plucked, as some critics opine. (See the following.)

111 עצר (oppression) is dominion, rulership (see 1 Sam. 9:17. *Cf.* Judg. 18:7). משפט (judgment) is the authority of the judge or king. See Torrey, *Second Isaiah*, 419; Klausner, *The Messianic Idea*, 97. For the word לקח (taken away) *cf.* 52:5: "taken captive," "taken into servitude." This meaning also is implied here: from rulership he was taken away to servitude and imprisonment. That the servant is imagined as a prisoner in jail is to be understood from the statement that he was numbered with the transgressors (53:12). Further, Deutero-Isaiah in other passages compares the exile to a "dungeon" (42:7; 49:9). The redemption is a bringing forth (43:8), redeeming (50:2). Zion was taken captive, held in bands (52:2).

112 דור (generation), from דּוּר (move in a circle) is, in Hebrew, the time-period of men living at the same time or age; in this passage apparently referring to the individual: the period of life,

the chapter of his life, the biography of the servant. (*Cf.* Isa. 38:12.) The word ישׂוחח (did reason), a synonym for: tell, recount with the sense: who can recount his very many afflictions?

113 The meaning of "For he was cut off out of the land of the living" is not actual death. The prisoner sits in dark places, "as those that have been long dead" (Ps. 143:3, Lam. 3:6), "in darkness and in the shadow of death" (Ps. 107:10, 14). He feels himself "cut off" (Lam. 3:54). He is in the "lowest dungeon" (*ibid.*, 55). He is become "like them that go down into the pit" (Ps. 143:7). The Lord only is his portion "in the land of the living" (*ibid.*, 142:6).

114 "To whom" (למו) is here in the singular with the sense of "to him" (לו) as in Isa. 44:15. For if the meaning in 53:8 were "to them," the prophet would have breached his allegory, and the reference would have been to specific misfortunes. This form is found frequently in allegorical language. The Septuagint reads: "stricken unto death." Even if this version were correct, it would not prove that the servant was here imagined as put to death. Rather it would be a figure for: so afflicted that he came very near to death. (See the following.)

115 "And they made his grave with the wicked" etc. Since, as all agree, there is in the entire chapter no reference to the rebirth of the servant and his rising from the dead, it cannot be assumed that he is imagined as put to death and buried. According to the collectivist interpretation also, the prophet could not possibly have failed to mention specifically the resurrection, since that would be a decisive turning point, and since, in any case, the whole description is individualistic. The ancients possessed family graves, but they were wont also to specify sepulchres for themselves (Isa. 22:16). The present passage does not say that the servant was buried with the wicked, but that "they made" his grave with the wicked (see the following).

The phrase "and with the rich" (ואת עשיר) (singular) is difficult. It is sometimes read "and with evil doers" (ואת עשי רע). The Septuagint and the Targum read "and with the rich" (plural). Accordingly, we may surmise: And when he should die (במותו, in place of במותיו his tomb, literally, in his deaths) they made his grave with the transgressors, and with those who were wicked.

116 The talmudic sages quite rightly related the "chastisements of love" (Berakot, 5a) to this passage.

117 From this verse in particular we learn that the servant is not thought of as dead and buried. It is unimaginable that the prophet would begin the description of the reward of the servant who was dead with the words "let him see his seed and prolong his days" without mentioning his resurrection. Moreover, his sufferings are summarized here by the words "to crush him by disease." There is crushing and disease, but not death.

118 Even if we retain the masoretic אָשָׁם (restitution) and

interpret the word in the sense of guilt-offering, there is still in this metaphor only a hint of the idea that the suffering of the righteous who are punished along with the community atones for the community. This thought does not exceed the idea of association of retribution, and is far removed from the idea that someone might be destined to a special "messianic" suffering on account of the sins of others.

119 The figure: he bared his soul unto death, implies no more than the other metaphors of imprisonment in the pit, or the simile of the prisoner as "long dead," etc. The talmudic sages interpreted the passage as referring to Moses (Sotah, 14a).

120 Duhm, op. cit., 394.

121 Torrey, Second Isaiah, 427.

122 Volz, op. cit., 202–6.

123 The meaning of the phrase "That the righteous is taken away from the evil to come" (57:1) is apparently that the righteous is taken away from the tribulations which are on the way; and wherein the leaders of the people will receive their due. 57:2 would be, following the accepted exegesis, quite surprising. Is it mercy that the righteous man who is taken away in the guilt of the wicked rests in his grave? Duhm thinks the passage is a bitter complaint. But the wording does not support this exegesis. Rather, we observe that "peace" is mentioned here in summary fashion, the peace which will come after the evil. Afterward, "He entereth into peace" (a phrase meaning salvation: see 57:19; 54:10, 13; 60:17; 66:12); and then those who walk in uprightness will rest in their beds. Resting in beds occurs many times in Scripture as a metaphor for security and peace (Lev. 26:6; Hos. 2:20; Pss. 3:6; 4:5, 9; 149:5).

124 Following the emendation of Klostermann, in place of "adulterer and the harlot." The Septuagint version is: adulterers and (an) harlot.

125 There are obscurities in the details of the censure and defects in the text. The "smooth (stones) of the valley" (6) are apparently heaps of stones, a species of monument (cf. Gen. 31:45–52), which were set up in streams, and before which services were performed. "Thy symbol" (v. 8) refers, it appears, to a sign of some kind on a harlot's house. "For thou hast uncovered . . . from Me" is meaningless. Perhaps it should be: "Thou hast removed thy veil" (cf. 47:2: "Remove thy veil"), which would mean: Thou hast bared thyself for the bed. "And (thou hast) chosen (cut)" (ותכרת) has been read as: "And thou didst buy" (ותכרי) ("bought" Hos. 3:2) "their couch"—cohabitation with them, love-making with them. In place of "thou sawest," possibly "thou didst make free"—thou didst make place for them in thy bed. In place of "And thou wentest to the king" (9), perhaps: Thou didst anoint thy foot (cf. Deut. 33:24; Amos 6:6; see also Luke 7:38; John 12:3). "And didst send . . . down to the nether-world" does not refer to worship of the gods of Sheol,

which idea is completely absent from Scripture. The expression completes the phrase "(to) far off." In thy seekings thou hast gone even to Sheol, which is a hyperbole in the manner of Ps. 139:8; Amos 9:2. It is difficult to appraise the expression "a renewal of thy strength" (the life of thine hand) (v. 10). Apparently the meaning is: Thou didst find everything which was lacking to thee; "Therefore thou wast not affected" (Thou hast not been anxious [sorry]; *cf.* 1 Sam. 22:8). V. 11: And of whom hast thou been (so) afraid and in fear, that thou didst deceive and didst conceal thy deeds? That is to say: Thou hast acted openly, for Me thou didst not fear. V. 12: "thy righteousness" is ironical. The emendation "thy idols" has been proposed in place of "them that thou hast gathered" (v. 13).

126 "I have seen his ways" (18) is surprising after "in the way of his heart." Perhaps "his ways" should be "his crushed ones" (plural substantive of the adjective דך, see Prov. 26:28), or "his melancholy" (from דכי— דכאון, depression, melancholy). This accords well with v. 15 concerning the "contrite" (דכא).

127 58:4 ought perhaps to be read: Ye do not fast *except* (כי אם) to make your voice to be heard on high. The masoretic text is interpreted: Ye fast not this day (כיום) a fast wherein your voice will be heard in heaven.

128 *Cf.* the custom of the Babylonian Jews of preparing a couch for Gad, for the good fortune of the home (Sanhedrin 2a, also Rashi to same). *Cf.* Genesis Rabba, parasha 71 ("Gad of the house").

129 Duhm's interpretation of this prophecy is the climax of tortuous and senseless exegesis. In this prophecy, Duhm discovers expression of opposition to the "Samaritans" and their wish to build their own temple, and a defense of the chosen Temple in Jerusalem. He refers: "For all these things hath My hand made" (66:2) etc. to the structure of the Temple in Jerusalem! A number of critics follow this interpretation, among them Skinner, even though he rejects Duhm's exegesis of v. 2. The exegesis of Volz, following other critics, that the building of the Temple and the sacrificial cult is definitely negated in 66:1–2 is contrived. He thinks that the prophetic, as opposed to the priestly, point of view is expressed, that is, the negation of ritual sacrifice, the evaluation of the destruction of the Temple as evidence of God's will to put an end to the temple cult, and the absolute requirement that the old forms of worship be replaced by the synagogue worship (pp. 288–89). Volz, however, is able to produce only one bit of evidence for this prophetic intent, namely, the Gospel of John (4:21). The proof from Jer. 29:5 f. is one of Volz's pious distortions, as can be seen from 29:14; 27:21–22, and other prophecies of Jeremiah. The effort to find a negation in principle of the temple sacrifices in the prophets' words derives from the Christian tendency to present Christianity (which does not have rites of sacrifice) as the realization of the prophetic demands. But the effort is vain. It is possible to find a negation in

principle of the Temple in Isa. 66:1–2 only if these verses are detached from all the other prophecies of Isa. 40–66. By this manner of exegesis any result can be had. But in these verses, also, there is no hint of any opposition between the two forms of ritual, the old and the "progressive" (Volz, *ibid.*). The prophetic contrast is: ritualism and religiosity vs. moral probity. The argument of the prophets is directed against the evaluation of any cultic practice as of supreme value. Thus it applies also to rituals of the kind practiced in synagogue worship (see Amos 5:23; Isa. 1:15; Jer. 14:12; Zech. 7:5–6). The censure of Isa. 58 is directed wholly against the synagogue worship. Obviously, the prophetic polemic is valid also with respect to the "progressive" cult of Christianity, in particular with respect to everything associated with the divine sacrifice. *Cf.* above, II, 70–74, 471, note 65.

130 Smiting and bloodshed are mentioned also in chapters 58–59. "That slays (smites) a man" has been interpreted to mean human sacrifice. But the term smite (מכה) is not used with respect to sacrifice. The phrase "that blesses wickedness" has been interpreted: that blesses an idol. But the term blessing (ברכה) is not used with respect to idols. The word און (wickedness), as used in Isa. 55:7; 58:9; 59:4, 6, 7, implies moral iniquity. Also in 41:29 (vanity) it is descriptive of idols, and is not a conventional epithet. The Targum certainly is correct in using the term nought (למא.) The practice of blessing the sacrifice is mentioned in 1 Sam. 9:13. *Cf.* Prov. 15:8; 21:27; Ecclus. 34:18 f.

131 There are difficulties and defects in the particulars of this lament. In 63:7, in place of כעל, according to, possibly פעל, reward, with the sense: all the recompense which he has bestowed on us, etc. *Cf.* below, note 133. In v. 11, "I remember" is preferable to "Then He (His people) remembered." *Cf.* Ps. 77:4, 7, 12: When I think (remember) thereon; I will call to remembrance, I will remember. The word עמו (his people) following "Moses" should be עבדו (his servant). For "with the shepherds of His flock," following the Targum: where is the shepherd of His flock? The singular "shepherd" is preferable to the plural. In 63:18–64:2, there are words which must await the prophet Elijah. In v. 18, for the word-phrase למצער ("well nigh"), perhaps במצור (in straits). The subject is: "Our adversaries"; they have driven out (ירשו) in the sense: they have dispossessed, hiphil, (הורישו). The sense of vv. 19 f. is: Oh that Thou wouldest rend the heavens, and come down, and oh that the mountains might quake at Thy presence as the brushwood burnt in the fire, and as the waters which the fire causeth to boil, To make Thy name known to Thy adversaries —Nations would tremble at Thy presence, when Thou wouldest do tremendous things, which we had not hoped, whereof from of old men had not heard, nor ear perceived, nor eye seen, that a god beside Thee worketh thus for him that waiteth for him.

The conclusion of 64:2 is certainly a dittograph of 63:19. In 64:4

possibly: Oh that Thou wouldest meet him that exulted . . . or: Oh that Thou wouldest appear to him that exulted (or: "him that is poor. . ."). "Upon them have we stayed of old, that we might be saved" might be: "as the wrath of old and we were unfaithful." *Cf.* 57:17; 64:6.

132 This passage also in influenced by the book of Lamentations. See Lam. 2:18.

133 Jer. 28:14; 50:29; 51:6, 56 (and I will recompense them according to their deeds . . . He will render . . . a recompense. . . . For the Lord is a God of recompenses, He will surely requite) are parallel to Isa. 59:18. (According to their deeds, accordingly He will repay. . . . He will repay recompense.) Thus 59:18 should read: "For (He is) a God (כי אל for כעל, according to) of recompenses, He will pay reward" (פעל for the second כעל), etc. *Cf.* above, note 130.

134 Duhm, *op. cit.*, 434, finds in this passage indication of praise of Cyrus. Trito-Isaiah complains that there is, in his time, no such man among the gentiles as Cyrus, whom Deutero-Isaiah knew to be battling for God, etc. But such a Cyrus is the product of Duhm's imagination. The historical Cyrus presented himself as the champion of Marduk and other gods. The exegesis of Volz, *op. cit.*, 264, also is faulty. Volz thinks that this passage is merely a poetic figure for the expression of God's unity and the fact that He alone is ruler. But stressing the fact that the nations did not come to help does not express a concept of unity. This is not praise of God, rather it is complaint: "And I looked, and there was none to help," etc. (63:5).

135 There are many difficulties in the text of chapters 34–35. In place of "hath drunk its fill in heaven" (34:5), perhaps: "hath drunk its fill in blood (the bloods)." (*Cf.* v. 7: shall be drunken [hath drunk its fill] with blood.) V. 12 is notoriously difficult. Perhaps vv. 11–12 should read: But the pelican and the bittern shall possess it, And the owl and the raven shall dwell therein, proclaiming a kingdom therein, And He shall stretch over it The line of confusion, and the plummet of emptiness. As for her nobles, nothingness, And all her princes shall be nothing. They shall "be called"—they shall proclaim. In 35:7, the emendation בצה (mire) in place of רבצה (her lying down) has been made. *Cf.* Job 8:11–12: rushes, mire, herb. In v. 8, in place of: it shall be for those; The wayfaring men (the walker in the way): and it shall be for him a walk and a way. (In place of הלך, מהלך, with the sense, a way. *Cf.* Ezek. 42:4.)

136 Torrey, *Second Isaiah*, argues that chapters 34–35 belong with 40–66, but thinks that they are the opening chapters of Deutero-Isaiah. The separation of chapters 34–35 from chapter 40 by the narratives concerning (the first) Isaiah (36–39) was intentional, not an accident. The editor inserted 36–39 between 35 and 40 in order to attach the two portions together by a kind of peg. Chapters 36–39 are a "locking device." At the time when the two sections of the book of

Isaiah were combined, there were men living who knew the prophecies of Deutero-Isaiah as a distinct unit. If this section had not been inserted into chapters 1–39 by means of a "locking device," the tradition that this was "an unauthentic increment" would have been preserved (p. 103). See also Torrey, *JBL*, 1938, pp. 138–139. But the hypothesis that this is a "device" is not plausible. The "device" is decidedly naïve and could have misled no one. If the editor had wanted to supply a basis for the opinion that the prophecies of Deutero-Isaiah belonged to Isaiah I, he would have placed chapters 36–39 at the end of the book. The examples (of locking devices) cited by Torrey, *Second Isaiah*, note, p. 103, are not similar to the matter at hand. This (separation of chapters 34–35) is merely an accident.

137 See above, II, 677–80, 688.

138 The interpretation that the mercies have been withdrawn from the dynasty of David and given to Israel (with hairsplitting of the phrase "with you," 55:3) is pointless. The mercies of the house of David are mercies also of Israel. This is evident of itself and, further, is explicitly stated in II Sam. 7. Isa. 55:4 (Behold, I have given him for a witness to the peoples, A prince and commander to the peoples) proves the intent of 55:3. The meaning of the word "witness" in this verse is "judge." *Cf.* Mal. 3:5; Mic. 1:2.

NOTES TO APPENDIX I

1 *Cf.* Skinner, *op. cit.*, 19. But Skinner thinks 41:7 is a later prosaic gloss of a scribe who expounded and erroneously expanded the meaning of the word (חזק). However, this stylistic leap is characteristic of Deutero-Isaiah.

2 See Stummer, *loc. cit.*, 180–81; Skinner, *op. cit.*, 43; Volz, *op. cit.*, 41.

3 For the influence of the psalm literature on the style of Deutero-Isaiah, see above II, 717–18, 723–25.

NOTES TO APPENDIX II

1 See Peake, *op. cit.*, 56.

2 See above, II, 279–87.

3 See Lindblom, *op. cit.*, 54 f. According to Lindblom, the "missionary revelations" are 45:20–25; 48:1–11, 17–19; 51:4–6, 7–8; 55:1–5, 6–7. But in none of these prophecies is anyone actually charged with spreading the knowledge of the Lord among the gentiles.

4 See Volz, *op. cit.*, 74.